T0330172

Money, Distribution and Economic Policy

NEW DIRECTIONS IN MODERN ECONOMICS
Series Editor: Malcolm C. Sawyer,
Professor of Economics, University of Leeds, UK

New Directions in Modern Economics presents a challenge to orthodox economic thinking. It focuses on new ideas emanating from radical traditions including post-Keynesian, Kaleckian, neo-Ricardian and Marxian. The books in the series do not adhere rigidly to any single school of thought but attempt to present a positive alternative to the conventional wisdom.

A list of published titles in this series is printed at the end of this volume.

Money, Distribution and Economic Policy

Alternatives to Orthodox Macroeconomics

Edited by

Eckhard Hein and Achim Truger

Macroeconomic Policy Institute (IMK),
Hans Boeckler Foundation, Germany

NEW DIRECTIONS IN MODERN ECONOMICS

Edward Elgar
Cheltenham, UK • Northampton, MA, USA

Published by
Edward Elgar Publishing Limited
The Lypiatts
15 Lansdown Road
Cheltenham
Glos GL50 2JA
UK

Edward Elgar Publishing, Inc.
William Pratt House
9 Dewey Court
Northampton
Massachusetts 01060
USA

Cased edition reprinted 2009, 2015

A catalogue record for this book
is available from the British Library

Library of Congress Control Number: 2006937965

ISBN 978 1 84720 063 1

Printed and bound in Great Britain by the CPI Group (UK) Ltd

Contents

List of contributors   vii

Introduction   1
Eckhard Hein and Achim Truger

PART I   HETERODOX ECONOMIC THEORY AND MONEY IN MACROECONOMICS

1   What is the Cambridge approach to economics?   11
    G.C. Harcourt
2   Heterodox economics: a common challenge to mainstream
    economics?   31
    Sheila Dow
3   Elements of a monetary theory of production   47
    Trevor Evans, Michael Heine and Hansjörg Herr
4   The monetary circuit approach: a stock-flow consistent model   66
    Jean-Vincent Accoce and Tarik Mouakil

PART II   DISTRIBUTION AND AGGREGATE DEMAND

5   What drives profits? An income-spending model   97
    Olivier Giovannoni and Alain Parguez
6   Wages and aggregate demand: an empirical investigation for
    France   119
    Stefan Ederer and Engelbert Stockhammer

PART III   ECONOMIC POLICIES

7   New institutions for a new economic policy   141
    Jesús Ferreiro and Felipe Serrano
8   Structural reforms and macroeconomic policy – the example
    of Germany   158
    Gustav A. Horn
9   Theories of fiscal policies and fiscal policies in the EMU   169
    Anthony J. Laramie and Douglas Mair

10 The link between fiscal and monetary policy – lessons for
    Germany from Japan   186
    Richard A. Werner
11 Monetary policy, macroeconomic policy mix and economic
    performance in the Euro area   216
    Eckhard Hein and Achim Truger

Index   245

Contributors

Jean-Vincent Accoce: PhD, Université Montesquieu-Bordeaux 4, Centre d'Economie du Développement, France.

Sheila Dow: Professor at the Department of Economics, University of Stirling, UK.

Stefan Ederer: Research Assistant at the Vienna University of Economics and Business Administration, Department of Economics, Institute for Monetary and Fiscal Policy, Austria.

Trevor Evans: Professor of Economics at the Berlin School of Economics, Germany.

Jesús Ferreiro: Associate Professor of Applied Economics at the University of the Basque Country, Bilbao, Spain.

Olivier Giovannoni: PhD, University of Nice Sophia-Antipolis, CEMAFI, France, and Post-doctorate at the LBJ School of Public Affairs, University of Texas at Austin, USA.

G.C. Harcourt: Emeritus Reader in the History of Economic Theory at the University of Cambridge, UK, Emeritus Fellow, Jesus College, Cambridge, UK, and Professor Emeritus, University of Adelaide, Australia.

Eckhard Hein: Senior Researcher at the Macroeconomic Policy Institute (IMK) at Hans Boeckler Foundation, Duesseldorf, Visiting Professor at Carl von Ossietzky University, Oldenburg, Germany and at Vienna University of Economics and Business Administration, Austria.

Michael Heine: Professor of Economics at the University of Applied Sciences, Berlin, Germany.

Hansjörg Herr: Professor for 'Supranational Integration' at the Berlin School of Ecomomics, Germany.

Gustav A. Horn: Director of the Macroeconomic Policy Institute (IMK) at Hans Boeckler Foundation, Duesseldorf, Germany, and Adviser to the European Parliament.

Anthony J. Laramie: Professor of Economics at Merrimack College, Massachusetts, USA.

Douglas Mair: Professor Emeritus of Economics at Heriot-Watt University, Edinburgh, UK.

Tarik Mouakil: PhD, Université Montesquieu-Bordeaux 4, Centre d'Economie du Développement, France.

Alain Parguez: Professor of Economics at the University of Franche-Compté at Besançon, France.

Felipe Serrano: Professor of Economics at the Department of Applied Economics V, University of the Basque Country, Bilbao, Spain.

Engelbert Stockhammer: Assistant Professor at the Department of Economics, Vienna University of Economics and Business Administration, Austria.

Achim Truger: Senior Researcher at the Macroeconomic Policy Institute (IMK) at Hans Boeckler Foundation, Duesseldorf, Germany.

Richard A. Werner: Professor and Chair in International Banking at the University of Southampton, School of Management, UK.

Introduction

Eckhard Hein and Achim Truger

After a period of New Classical dominance in the 1980s, nowadays ortho-dox macroeconomics is dominated by the New Consensus view, in particu-lar when it comes to economic policy analysis.[1] This view has New Keynesian features: similar to the old Neoclassical Synthesis and to Mon-etarism, there is a short-run impact of aggregate demand on output and employment. Due to nominal and real rigidities, for which 'micro founda-tion' is provided, the short-run Phillips curve is downward sloping. In the long run, however, there is no effect of aggregate demand on the 'Non Accelerating Inflation Rate of Unemployment' (NAIRU), which is deter-mined by structural characteristics of the labor market, the wage bargain-ing institutions and the social benefit system. Therefore, the long-run Phillips curve remains vertical. Monetary policy applying the interest rate tool is able to stabilize output and employment in the short run, but in the long run it is neutral and only affects inflation (Fontana and Palacio-Vera 2005). The economic policy implications of modern orthodoxy are quite straightforward: prevent unemployment in the short run by means of applying appropriate monetary policies and reduce the existing NAIRU by means of structural reforms in the labor market and the social benefit system, which reduce laborers' nominal wage demands and hence inflation pressure and allow for more expansive monetary policies.

Allowing for short-run real effects of monetary variables, the New Consensus model can be considered as some progress compared to New Classical economics and the Real Business Cycle school with their short-and long-run neutrality of money, and economic policy inefficiency hypothesis. In the New Consensus models it is also conceded that it is the short-term interest rate which is the central bank's instrument variable and which is applied in order to target inflation. Modern theory has thus accepted what inflation targeting central banks have done in reality for a considerable period of time – and what Post-Keynesian authors have been arguing for a few decades now.[2]

But the New Consensus view still suffers from an inappropriate treat-ment of money and effective demand. And it has nothing to say on the relationship between functional income distribution, aggregate demand

and employment. Taking into account the features of a modern monetary production economy with distribution conflict, it is by no means clear how the short-run rate of unemployment affected by monetary policy should adjust to a stable long-run equilibrium rate, the NAIRU. There have also been advanced convincing arguments that the NAIRU, instead of being a strong attractor, rather follows the path of actual unemployment determined by effective demand and monetary policies.[3] The economic policy implications of the New Consensus model may therefore be seriously misleading.[4]

The present volume covers contributions which are critical of modern orthodoxy. They explore alternative approaches to macroeconomics and economic policy analysis. The volume is divided into three sections. Section 1 presents contributions dealing with the development of heterodox economic theory and the role of money in macroeconomics. Section 2 addresses the relationship between distribution and aggregate demand. Section 3 provides contributions on macroeconomic policy issues from a broader heterodox perspective.

I.   HETERODOX ECONOMIC THEORY AND MONEY IN MACROECONOMICS

In the introductory chapter, G.C. Harcourt, who was brought up in the Cambridge tradition himself and who significantly contributed to it, reflects on 'What is the Cambridge approach to economics?'. He concentrates on the approaches and methods which are characteristic of economists steeped in the Cambridge tradition. Harcourt takes the Cambridge approach to economics to mean the approaches of the great days of the Faculty of Economics and Politics in Cambridge. Those days were principally associated with the development of Economics as a separate Tripos from 1903 on and ending with the retirement, then deaths of the first generation of Keynes's 'pupils' and/or close colleagues – Piero Sraffa, Joan Robinson, Austin Robinson, Richard Kahn, James Meade, Nicholas Kaldor, David Champernowne and Brian Reddaway – in the 1980s and 1990s.

'Heterodox economics: a common challenge to mainstream economics?': this question is addressed by Sheila Dow. According to her view, both orthodox and heterodox economics have been going through a process of change, which some have suggested spells the end of schools of thought as a useful construct. This chapter puts forward the argument that thinking of heterodox economics in terms of schools of thought can still play a constructive role in the development and communication of ideas. It need not detract from the challenge posed by heterodox economics to orthodox economics, but rather, as a way of organizing knowledge, contribute to that challenge. The discussion of schools of thought illustrates why it is useful to classify thinking in this way: different schools of thought attach different meanings to terms. Thus different understandings of the term 'schools of thought' have created some confusion. Sheila Dow uses a new diagrammatic framework to provide an account of how schools of thought have been understood in different ways in the past, and how they are understood differently now.

In the chapter 'Elements of a monetary theory of production', Trevor Evans, Michael Heine and Hansjörg Herr attempt to suggest a minimum consensus for an alternative to Neoclassical economics. This consensus first stresses the importance of money and the fact that the central dynamic of a capitalist economy involves advancing money with the aim of making more money. It argues that a modern banking system provides an extremely flexible supply of money that can be expanded as required by the rhythm of investment and growth. The authors hold that it is the decision by firms to advance money for investment that is decisive in determining the level of employment, and that attempts to increase employment by reducing the wage rate are misguided. Rather, since prices in a developed economy are largely based on costs plus a mark-up, this is more likely to carry the risk of deflation. The chapter rejects the idea that there is some pre-given long-term economic growth path, and argues that it is the pattern of the business cycle which determines the way the economy grows in the long term. Evans, Heine and Herr conclude with some comments on the limits of economic policy in a system where workers, but not employers have an interest in full employment, and where employers can refrain from investing if they do not consider economic conditions sufficiently favorable.

The chapter by Jean-Vincent Accoce and Tarik Mouakil presents 'The monetary circuit approach: a stock-flow consistent model'. In opposition to the Neoclassicals or the Neo-Keynesians, the Monetary Circuit approach rejects the idea of an economy based on exchange. The economy is rather analyzed as a monetary economy of production. Therefore, Accoce and Mouakil claim that the Monetary Circuitists can be seen as true heirs of the Keynesian theory. However, there are some problems with this approach: lack of formalism, omission of stocks and only basic analysis of the banking system. Applying a stock-flow consistent accounting framework developed by Wynne Godley and Marc Lavoie, which links stocks and flows together and integrates money in the best Cambridge Post-Keynesian tradition, Accoce and Mouakil tackle these problems and attempt to contribute to their solution.

II. DISTRIBUTION AND AGGREGATE DEMAND

In 'What drives profits? An income-spending model', Olivier Giovannoni
and Alain Parguez investigate the relationship between the different types
of income and their expenditure. As a case study they use the United States
from 1954 to 2004. The authors employ an a-theoretical approach and
estimate a large-scale error-correction system with particular attention to
profits. The dynamics of the system are studied using the four different
concepts of 'temporal causality', 'feedback causality', 'variance causality'
and 'impact causality'. Special attention is paid to definitions and methodology. The main finding is that profits turn out as an adjusting variable,
both in the short and in the long run. Giovannoni and Parguez obtain the
result that profits are primarily driven by consumption-related and policy
variables.

   Stefan Ederer and Engelbert Stockhammer deal with 'Wages and aggregate demand: an empirical investigation for France'. They observe that in
recent policy debates the suggestion of a reduction of wage costs as a means
to increase employment and growth has figured prominently. However,
other things being equal, an increase in wage incomes will have a positive
effect on consumption and a negative one on investment and net exports.
Therefore, the effect of a redistribution of income between capital and
labor will depend on the relative size of these effects. The chapter applies a
neo-Kaleckian growth model to France and estimates consumption,
investment, export and import functions. The results indicate that the effect
of a wage cut on consumption is larger than that on investment. Thus the
domestic sector of the French economy is wage-led. However, the sensitivity of net exports to labor costs turns the open economy profit-led. This
raises challenging policy issues. Wage coordination is proposed to avoid
prisoners' dilemma situations.

III. ECONOMIC POLICY

Jesus Ferreiro and Felipe Serrano discuss 'New institutions for a new economic policy'. They argue that the inclusion of asymmetric information
problems in the traditional models of economic equilibrium has enriched
economic theory. Further on, it has put the analysis of the institutional
framework surrounding markets in the focus of empirical and theoretical
studies. However, one of the main problems faced by economic agents,
the problem of fundamental uncertainty as defined by post-Keynesian
thought, has not received the same attention in orthodox economic theory.
Ferreiro and Serrano argue that the problems created by Post-Keynesian

uncertainty cannot be ignored, but have to be at the centre of any theory that tries to understand the real working of market economies. The chapter focuses on the institutional implications of taking fundamental uncertainty seriously and argues that economic policy has to be closely related to the design of institutions.

Gustav A. Horn outlines the connection between 'Structural reforms and macroeconomic policies'. He starts with the observation that when growth declines, most orthodox economists tend to demand structural reforms to ensure a return to a stable growth pattern. Labor market reforms designed to increase the flexibility of labor supply are regarded as particularly appropriate for fostering growth. The basic hypothesis underlying all these efforts is that the growth path of an economy can be improved by structural reforms alone. By way of example, he presents an econometric simulation for Germany, a country particularly affected by this line of thought. He argues that structural reforms should be embedded in a favorable macroeconomic policy framework in order to avoid negative side effects. Otherwise these reforms may actually prove self-destructive in growth terms. In the light of these findings the reform process in Germany is seen as having been severely marred by neglect of the macroeconomic context. And the present dismal situation in that country, and by extension in a number of other European countries, is found to be at least partly attributable to this neglect, which, moreover, places in jeopardy all further attempts at reform.

The chapter by Douglas Mair and Anthony J. Laramie is on 'Theories of fiscal policies and fiscal policies in the EMU'. They argue that leading public finance economists have expressed reservations against the adequacy of the theoretical foundations of mainstream public finance, but continue to use the competitive general equilibrium model as their preferred medium. Rather than proposing a return to the Keynesian approach to public finance, the chapter advocates a new approach inspired by Kalecki. The basic framework of a dynamic Kaleckian model which identifies the macroeconomic effects and incidences of a balanced change in the structure of taxation is presented. This underlines the importance of tax-induced changes in the distribution of income as a factor in determining macroeconomic effects. The necessary conditions for a change in the structure of taxation to have a positive effect on an economy's long-term growth rate are identified. The chapter then explores the macroeconomic implications for the European Monetary Union (EMU) if one of its member states were to pursue the fiscal strategy proposed in this chapter. A positive fiscal stimulus to the growth performance of one member state could have beneficial effects in the rest of the EMU. The chapter concludes by arguing for a reappraisal of fiscal policy from a Kaleckian perspective.

'The link between fiscal and monetary policy lessons for Germany from Japan' is explored by Richard A. Werner. Monetary policy decision makers, such as the European Central Bank (ECB), often argue that responsibility for fiscal policy and other growth policies lies entirely with the government. This contribution examines these arguments. It is found that there is no evidence to support the argument that weak economic performance in Germany is due to problems with the economic structure. Instead, monetary policy carries a far larger responsibility for economic growth and the effectiveness of fiscal policy than is generally recognized. A macroeconomic model centered on credit quantities is employed, which clarifies the link between fiscal and monetary policy and the determinants of nominal GDP growth. Empirical evidence from Japan is used to test the model. Implications for other countries, especially Germany and the EU, are pointed out. These include the recommendation for the German government to implement monetization of fiscal policy via credit-based policies, which can be achieved even within the institutional setting of an independent and uncooperative central bank.

The final chapter by Eckhard Hein and Achim Truger is on 'Monetary policy, macroeconomic policy mix and economic performance in the Euro area'. In order to explain slow growth and high unemployment in the Euro area, in particular if compared to the USA, Hein and Truger suggest a macroeconomic policy view focusing on the more restrictive stance of monetary, fiscal and wage policies in the Euro area. In the present chapter they focus on the particular role of monetary policy, because the ECB seems to be the major obstacle to higher growth and employment. Wage policies and fiscal policies are taken into account at the outset, but then the determinants of ECB policies are assessed in more detail. The analysis confirms that it is the ECB's overemphasis on a too low inflation target which is a major problem for macroeconomic performance in the Euro area. And the ECB is too exclusively occupied with inflation and wage developments and puts insufficient emphasis on the development of real variables. It is finally argued that, in order to improve growth and employment, the ECB should raise its inflation target and pay more attention to real economic activity.

ACKNOWLEDGEMENTS

This book has emerged from the 9th conference of the German Research Network 'Alternative Conceptions of Macroeconomic Policies under the Conditions of Unemployment, Globalisation and High Public Debt'. The conference was on 'Macroeconomics and Macroeconomic Policies – Alternatives to the Orthodoxy'. It was organized in cooperation with the Post Keynesian Economic Study Group, UK, and the Association pour le Développement des Etudes Keynésiennes, France, and took place in Berlin, 28–29 October 2005. Further papers from the conference are published in two books (Hein *et al.* 2006, Arestis *et al.* 2007), and in a special issue of *Intervention. Journal of Economics*. We would like to thank the contributors to this volume for their cooperation and the participants in the conference for the stimulating discussions. Special thanks go to Barbara Schnieders for assistance in the editing process and to the Hans Boeckler Foundation for organizational and financial support for both the conference and the publications.

NOTES

1. See for example Clarida *et al.* (1999), Romer (2000) and the textbook by Carlin and Soskice (2006).
2. See Fontana (2003) for a recent review of post-Keynesian monetary theory.
3. See Sawyer (2002), Arestis and Sawyer (2005) and Hein (2006) for a discussion of the NAIRU in a post-Keynesian/Kaleckian framework.
4. For a more extensive discussion of the New Consensus model from a post-Keynesian perspective see Arestis and Sawyer (2004), Lavoie (2004), Setterfield (2004), Fontana and Palacio-Vera (2005) and Palacio-Vera (2005).

REFERENCES

Arestis, P., Hein, E. and E. Le Heron (eds) (2007), *Aspects of Modern Monetary Policy*, Basingstoke: Palgrave Macmillan.

Arestis, P. and M. Sawyer (2004), *Re-examining Monetary and Fiscal Policy for the 21st Century*, Cheltenham, UK and Northampton, MA, USA: Edward Elgar.

Arestis, P. and M. Sawyer (2005), 'Aggregate demand, conflict and capacity in the inflationary process', *Cambridge Journal of Economics*, 29, 959–74.

Carlin, W. and D. Soskice (2006), *Macroeconomics: Imperfections, Institutions and Policies*, Oxford: Oxford University Press.

Clarida, R., Gali, J. and M. Gertler (1999), 'The science of monetary policy: A New Keynesian perspective', *Journal of Economic Literature*, 37, 1661–707.

Fontana, G. (2003), 'Post Keynesian approaches to endogenous money: A time framework explanation', *Review of Political Economy*, 15, 291–314.

Fontana, G. and A. Palacio-Vera (2005), *Are long-run price stability and short-run output stabilization all that monetary policy can aim for?*, Working Paper No. 430, Annandale-on-Hudson, NY: The Levy Economic Institute of Bard College.

Hein, E. (2006), 'Wage bargaining and monetary policy in a Kaleckian monetary distribution and growth model: Trying to make sense of the NAIRU', *Intervention. Journal of Economics*, 3, 305–29.

Hein, E., Heise, A. and A. Truger (eds) (2006), *European Economic Policies – Alternatives to Orthodox Analysis and Policy Concepts*, Marburg: Metropolis.

Lavoie, M. (2004), 'The New Consensus on monetary policy seen from a Post-Keynesian perspective', in Lavoie, M. and M. Seccareccia (eds), *Central Banking in the Modern World: Alternative Perspectives*, Cheltenham, UK and Northampton, MA, USA: Edward Elgar, pp. 15–34.

Palacio-Vera, A. (2005), 'The 'modern' view of macroeconomics: Some critical reflections', *Cambridge Journal of Economics*, 29, 747–67.

Romer, D. (2000), 'Keynesian macroeconomics without the LM curve', *Journal of Economic Perspectives*, 14 (2), 149–69.

Sawyer, M. (2002), 'The NAIRU, aggregate demand and investment', *Metroeconomica*, 53, 66–94.

Setterfield, M. (2004), 'Central banking, stability and macroeconomic outcomes: A comparison of New Consensus and Post-Keynesian monetary macroeconomics', in Lavoie, M. and M. Seccareccia (eds), *Central Banking in the Modern World: Alternative Perspectives*, Cheltenham, UK and Northampton, MA, USA: Edward Elgar, pp. 35–56.

PART I

Heterodox economic theory and money
in macroeconomics

1. What is the Cambridge approach to economics?

G.C. Harcourt

1.1. INTRODUCTION

I take the Cambridge approach to economics to mean the approaches of the great days of the Faculty of Economics and Politics in Cambridge (it is now, significantly, the Faculty of Economics – period). Those days were principally associated with the development of Economics as a separate Tripos[1] from 1903 on and ending with the retirement, then deaths of the first generation of Keynes's 'pupils' and/or close colleagues – Piero Sraffa, Joan Robinson, Austin Robinson, Richard Kahn, James Meade, Nicky Kaldor, David Champernowne and Brian Reddaway – in the 1980s and 1990s.[2]

The dominant group in the Faculty at present seems to wish the Faculty to be a clone of the leading United States departments, especially Harvard, MIT, Stanford and Yale, for example, but certainly not Chicago. In doing so it seems to have forgotten two important principles of good economics: comparative advantage and a role for differentiated products. As a liberal educator I strongly support teaching students what is going on at the frontiers of mainstream research in a discipline, even if it is done in a critical manner (after all, we are talking about *university* education); but I also think it sensible, indeed necessary, to preserve what elsewhere I have called the Cambridge tradition, in which I was brought up in Australia in the early 1950s and to which I have tried to contribute over my working life (still going on) at Adelaide, Cambridge and elsewhere; see Harcourt (2001a, 2001b, 2003, 2006), Harcourt and Kerr (2003), for example. In this chapter I concentrate on the approaches and methods which are characteristic of economists steeped in the Cambridge tradition.

1.2. MALTHUS

I start with Thomas Robert Malthus, a Fellow of my college, Jesus, the person called by Keynes 'The first of the Cambridge economists', (Keynes

[1933] 1972, p. 71) – by which he meant the first person to think like Keynes (Keynes never considered modesty a virtue). Keynes admired the first edition of the *Essay* on population (Malthus 1798) more than the second edition (1803) because, though it was mostly deductive in form, it was so all-of-a-piece that its message came through loud and clear, at times in an extremely witty fashion. In the second edition, this clarity was rather over-laid by copious empirical evidence and qualifications of ifs and buts – see Keynes ([1933]1972, pp. 34–5).[3]

1.3.   MARSHALL AND HIS LEGACY

This last was also an outstanding characteristic of Keynes's other mentor in economics, Alfred Marshall, whose capacity for putting up fog-like smoke screens when weak points in an argument, or unpalatable conclu-sions were present, was second to none. I thoroughly agree with Joan Robinson. She wrote: 'The more I learn about economics the more I admire Marshall's intellect and the less I like his character' (Joan Robinson [1953b] 1973, p. 259). Her judgment is amply confirmed with detailed evidence, evi-dence which does *not* detract from the essential message, by my former PhD student and distinguished Marshall scholar, Rita McWilliams Tullberg. Rita coupled her evaluation of Marshall with her admiration (universally shared in the profession, I would guess) of Mary Paley Marshall, whose treatment by Marshall after they married is a major scandal of our trade, see, for example, McWilliams Tullberg 1990, 1991, 1992, 1995.

   Be that as it may, Marshall *was* a really great economist. He bequeathed to us his development of demand and supply analysis as a means of han-dling that elusive but fundamental concept, time, by his partial equilibrium approach incorporating three different analytical periods – market, short and long. Not that this allowed him ever fully to overcome the basic incon-sistency in his 'vision'. On the one hand, there is his understandable pride in his development of static, partial equilibrium analysis with its judicious use of the *ceteris paribus* pound in order to illuminate complex real-life sit-uations. On the other hand, there is his 'vision' of economies as evolving organic systems so that biology and its method, rather than (classical) physics and its method were the appropriate analogy and framework.

   In one sense it has been the endeavor to break out of the first approach and form ways of working within the second that has been the greatest challenge and organizer of the contributions of the people I have placed in the Cambridge tradition. Naturally enough, no one has been completely successful but all saw the problem clearly and worked away at providing solutions. To my mind, the two who have come closest, and so bequeathed to us the most promising ways forward, are Richard Goodwin and Kalecki. They developed their ideas pretty much independently of each other but had in common some of the same mentors – Smith, Marx and Keynes, for example.[4]

Marshall also worked with a dichotomy between the real and the monetary. Breaking out of this in order to analyze the nature of a monetary production economy was the greatest challenge that Marshall's most illustrious pupil, Keynes, was to face. Marshall also provided the ingredients but was very timid about using them himself for the other major strand that came out of his work – the rise of the economics of welfare through his successor in the Chair of Political Economy, A.C. Pigou, and continued to this day by, for example, Tony Atkinson and, of course, Amartya Sen. Atkinson acknowledges James Meade's influence and example – part of Meade's great range of contributions was his deep concern with equity and equality in economic policy and political life generally. Sen is an obvious successor to Pigou in this strand of Marshall's influence.[5] But I shall leave this strand for others to write on as I want to concentrate on Keynes and his contributions and on those of his followers, not only because macroeconomics is the subject of the conference[6] but also because it is the developments associated with it that I am most familiar with from teaching and research.

Both strands reflect Marshall's desire that even more than light-bearing, economics should be fruit-bearing, that is to say, have sensible applications to the making of policy. Pigou's *Economics of Welfare* (1920) was one of the first major examples of this philosophy; and, of course, Keynes's approach is the example *par excellence*, the inspiration and example for many of the people whose contributions I discuss below.

1.4.   KEYNES

Keynes was Marshall's pupil after he graduated in 1905 and was preparing for the Civil Service examinations. As an undergraduate, though, he read mathematics and spent much time on philosophy, including moral and political philosophy. G.E. Moore and Edmund Burke were major influences on him at that time and subsequently. He always regarded economics as a branch of moral philosophy, even though Marshall, after a long battle, had created a separate Economics Tripos by the time Keynes became his pupil. Incidentally, the first major book in political economy that Keynes read was William Stanley Jevons's *The Theory of Political Economy* (1871). He remained an admirer of Jevons, who 'chiselled in stone', as opposed to Marshall (whose *Principles* he also admired) who 'knitt[ed] in wool' (Keynes [1933] 1972, p. 131). Until after the publication of *A Treatise on Money* in 1930, Keynes claimed to be working within the Cambridge and especially the Marshallian approach to economics, using supply and demand analysis, distinguishing between market, short and long periods, accepting at least for the long period, a dichotomy between the real and the monetary so that in monetary matters the quantity theory of money explained the general price level, and viewing markets and systems as equilibrating mechanisms.

The role of the economic analyst was to explain the conditions of equilibrium, the forces that would return the system to equilibrium if it had been shocked away from it, and the mode of transition between one equilibrium position and another new one when the values of the fundamentals determining the equilibrium position changed. In what was intended to be his masterpiece, a definitive treatise on money, Keynes wrote:

> My object has been to find a method which is useful in describing, not merely the characteristics of static equilibrium, but also those of disequilibrium, and to discover the dynamical laws governing the passage of a monetary system from one position of equilibrium to another. (Keynes [1930] 1971, p. *xvii*)

It is true that early on after the end of World War I Keynes was putting more emphasis on short-term malfunctions and the need for theory and policy to cope with them than did Marshall – hence Keynes's best known remark about the long run and mortality, which was included in the passage in *A Tract on Monetary Reform* [1923] (1971) where he was cheeking his old teacher.[7] But in *A Treatise on Money* he still felt inhibited about tackling in too great detail, the intricate analysis of short-period output in aggregate because it was out of place in a treatise on money; see, for example, Keynes (1973a, pp. 145–6).

Yet events and the increasing realization of the significance of what he had learnt from his philosophical musings, together with the influence of Richard Kahn in particular[8] and the members of the 'circus' in general, his close association with Dennis Robertson in the 1920s and arguments with Ralph Hawtrey, led Keynes increasingly to change his approach. He brought into play three main philosophical tenets for a subject such as economics. Their source is *A Treatise on Probability* (Keynes [1921] 1973), the published version of his fellowship dissertation for King's College, Cambridge, in 1908–1909. He argued that, in certain disciplines, of which economics is a leading example, the whole need not be only the sum of the parts. Keynes's realization of this, that overall systems could have separate lives of their own, that the behavior of parts could itself be constrained by overall relationships, and that profound implications follow from this, played an increasingly important influence in his subsequent work in economics. His full and mature realization of all this came to fruition in *The General Theory* (Keynes [1936] 1973), especially in one of the meanings that he gave to the term 'general', and his repeated stress on the need to avoid the fallacy of composition when the workings of the economy as a whole are analyzed. In the preface to the French edition (20 February 1939) he wrote:

> I mean [by a *general* theory] that I am chiefly concerned with the behaviour of the economic system as a whole . . . I argue that important mistakes have been made through extending to the system as a whole conclusions which have been correctly arrived at in respect of a part of it taken in isolation. (Keynes 1973, p. xxxii)

Another issue which preoccupied Keynes in *A Treatise on Probability* was his systematic pondering on the principles of reasonable behavior in an uncertain environment. This fitted with Marshall's stress, which runs through the *Principles* (Marshall [1890] 1961), on the nature of reasonable behavior of businesspeople, particularly in their own uncertain environments. Of course, Keynes also discussed not too sensible or reasonable behavior by decision makers of all kinds in a similar environment and their implications for systemic behavior. Ted Winslow (2005) puts far more stress on economic decision making being *not* sensible and on Keynes arguing this than I have. After reading his closely argued and documented paper I am more inclined to agree with his emphasis.

Keynes's philosophical reasoning also discerned many different appropriate languages for different situations, issues and aspects or dimensions of both of them. In effect he believed there was a spectrum of such languages running all the way from poetry and intuition through lawyer-like arguments to mathematics and formal logic. All these were consistent in their appropriate settings with arguments being possible and knowledge being acquired (see Harcourt 1987, Sardoni 1992).

The major outcome of these endeavors was the publication of *The General Theory* in 1936. It contains Keynes's analysis of a monetary production economy in which the dichotomy between the real and the monetary has been scrapped, money being integrated in the analysis right from its start. The equilibrium method was retained, but the equilibrium of the system – perhaps rest state is a better phrase – need not be the special case of full employment; investment leads and saving responds, mostly through changes in income associated with the working of the Kahn-Meade multiplier, with the rate of interest being determined principally in the money market by reconciling the demand for and supply of money; and the expected rates of profit on investments having to match up to the nominal rate of interest (rather than as in 'classical' thought, the nominal rate being consistent with the natural rate in order to avoid cumulative inflations or deflations, a Wicksellian as well as Keynesian insight). The general price level was principally determined in the short term by the productivity of variable factors, primarily labor and the level of the money wage. In 1937, Keynes added the finance motive as an important determinant of the demand for money, drawing attention to the availability of finance as the ultimate constraint on investment expenditure rather than the willingness to save; see Keynes (1973b, pp. 201–26). Meade put it very well when he wrote that 'Keynes's intellectual revolution was to shift economists from thinking normally in terms of a model of reality in which a dog called *savings* wagged his tail labeled *investment* to thinking in terms of a model in which a dog called *investment* wagged his tail labeled *savings'* (Meade 1975, p. 82, emphasis as original).

Though Keynes remained essentially a Marshallian equilibrator in method, he did take us a considerable way towards tackling dynamic processes and tendencies with his method and theory of shifting equilibrium (Keynes [1936] 1973, pp. 293–4). By it he allowed feedbacks from one set of determinants of rest states to other sets if, initially, the rest states, in particular the point of effective demand, were not achieved; see Kregel (1976). This constituted a bridge which partly allowed the profession to move from static analysis to more evolutionary, dynamic analysis of the second part of Marshall's 'vision' and provided the base on which the postwar developments by Keynes's colleagues principally were to build. Keynes also adapted the apparatus of *The General Theory*, the use of aggregate demand and supply relationships, to analyze inflationary situations such as were expected to arise in wartime; see 'How to pay for the War' (Keynes 1978, ch. 2). This illustrates that, theoretically and subsequently through wartime policies, he had indeed created a *general* theory of employment, interest and money, and now prices as Omar Hamouda (1997) pointed out. Finally, David Vines makes crystal clear in his splendid review article (2003) of Robert Skidelsky's third volume of his majestic biography of Keynes (Skidelsky 2000), that, in his wartime writings for the Treasury and for Bretton Woods, Keynes laid the conceptual foundations for postwar international macroeconomic analysis and policy.

1.5.   JOAN ROBINSON AND COLLEAGUES

During the 1920s and 1930s both Kahn and Joan Robinson used Marshall's approach and method in their pioneering contributions to the theory of imperfect competition – Kahn in *The Economics of the Short Period* ([1929] 1989),[9] Joan Robinson in *The Economics of Imperfect Competition* (1933a). They were both tackling a real question: why did firms survive in prolonged slump conditions, albeit with excess capacity, when the implications of Marshallian/Pigouvian analysis of competitive conditions was either full capacity working or complete shut down. But, as we shall see, Joan Robinson subsequently repudiated the method of her book, saying it was 'a shameless fudge', to wit, that the equilibrium price and quantity for each mini-monopoly in a competitive environment waited patiently 'out there' to be found by trial and error, the groping process of businesspeople's price setting and production and employment decisions. That is to say, there is a denial of path-dependence processes so that where the firm ended up was independent of the path that it took to get there; see, for example, Joan Robinson ([1953a], 1960, p. 234) for a succinct statement of her argument. In the first ever issue of what Dennis Robertson called 'the Green Horror', the *Review of Economic Studies*, Kaldor clearly outlined the nature of path dependence in what must have been one of his earliest published papers (1934).[10] Kahn, Meade, Austin and Joan Robinson and Piero Sraffa were continuously criticizing and helping Keynes as he moved from *A Treatise on Money* to the making of *The General Theory* (see Keynes, 1973a, Harcourt 1994, 1995). Kahn provided an essential ingredient with his (and Meades's) concept of the multiplier; Joan Robinson provided two preliminary reports (Joan Robinson 1933b, 1933c).[11] After the publication of *The General Theory*, she published her 'told to the children' version of the new theory, (Joan Robinson [1937a] 1969), and a selection of essays (Joan Robinson [1937b] 1947), which extended the theory to the open economy, foreign exchange markets and the Marshallian long period at the level of the economy as a whole. She still used Marshall's method and orthodox concepts, for example, the then fashionable concept of the elasticity of substitution between capital and labor in an explanation of the distribution of income between profits and wages in the Keynesian consumption function. Austin Robinson wrote an illuminating review of *The General Theory* in *The Economist* in 1936; his own work after that was very much the application in a common but deep sense of what he found in Marshall's *Principles* and *The General Theory* (see Harcourt 1997, 2001a).[12]

1.6.   JOAN ROBINSON AND SRAFFA

Sraffa was rather intellectually aloof from these contributions. He, of course, provided criticism – he was already renowned for his remorseless logic and critical skills – but he was preoccupied with the edition of

Ricardo's works and correspondence (which finally emerged in 1951!) and his conceptual critique of the foundations of the neoclassical theory of value and distribution combined with the rehabilitation of Classical economics, especially its organizing concept of the surplus and its long-period method (Sraffa 1960). He had mounted a devastating attack on Marshall's partial equilibrium method and its limited application to the real world in his 1925, 1926 and 1930 articles and his lectures at Cambridge at the end of the 1920s. His 1926 article served as an impetus to Joan Robinson to write her 1933 book. He also, at this time, developed at least one basic aspect of the critique of Neoclassical capital theory in the 1950s–1970s (see Bradford and Harcourt 1997, p. 131). Sraffa did ruthlessly and enthusiastically support Keynes in the fight back against Hayek's criticisms of *A Treatise on Money* (see Sraffa 1932).

Joan Robinson first met Kalecki in 1936 and quickly recognized that he had independently discovered the principal propositions of *The General Theory*; furthermore, his discoveries were placed in a more appropriate setting, a Marxian analysis of capitalism using the departmental schema of production and reproduction. This became even more clear to her after she read Marx at the beginning of the war and wrote her 1942 *Essay on Marxian Economics*. By the time she wrote *The Accumulation of Capital* (Joan Robinson [1956] 1969) she was mainly working within a Kaleckian framework.

1.7.   POSTWAR DEVELOPMENTS

In the postwar period there were two, possibly three major developments in Cambridge concerning approaches and topics.[13] The first is what Joan Robinson called 'the generalization of *The General Theory* to the long period'. This had two major stimuli: the seminal writings on dynamic theory by Roy Harrod in his 1939 article and 1948 book; and the awakened interest in the postwar era in development problems in both war-torn Europe and in the developing countries themselves. The major contributors to this in Cambridge were Joan Robinson, Kaldor, Kahn, Goodwin, Allan Brown and Richard Stone, and in my generation, Luigi Pasinetti.[14] Kalecki independently tackled similar problems.

The developments were a new look at the old Classical and Marxian preoccupations with distribution, accumulation and growth, tackled afresh in the light of the 'Keynesian' revolution. For Kahn and Joan Robinson, two steps were involved: first, working within a 'Golden Age' framework – the analysis of mythical situations – in order to set out precise definitions of core concepts, and of the relationships between them, in order to get a 'feel' on the nature of development and its accompanying interrelationships within a mostly competitive capitalist structure, (though the economics of planned economies, usually of a democratic socialist variety, were not completely neglected).

The analysis that was most difficult technically yet said by Joan Robinson to be of secondary importance in an analysis of the growth process was the analysis of the choice of techniques in the investment decision at the level of the economy as a whole. It was, though, linked on to the second preoccupation, the critique of the conceptual foundations of the neoclassical theory of value and distribution, in Cambridge associated with Joan Robinson and, most fundamentally, with Piero Sraffa in what became known as the Cambridge – Cambridge controversies in the theory of capital (see Harcourt 1969, 1972, Cohen and Harcourt 2003, Bliss *et al.* 2005). There were again two strands to this: a doctrinal critique of concepts within the framework of either stationary states or steadily growing Golden Ages; and a methodological critique associated with using 'differences' to analyze 'changes'. This procedure, it was argued, was common to the method associated with the revival of Classical political economy by, for example, Sraffa, and to Neoclassical procedures associated with comparative statics analysis.[15]

Returning to the first theme, Golden Age analysis was a preliminary to the more satisfyingly fruitful task of analyzing situations in historical as opposed to logical time. In logical time we try to answer questions framed as 'what would be different if . . .'. In historical time we ask 'what would follow if . . .'.[16] Here Kahn and Joan Robinson, on the one hand and Kaldor, on the other, diverge.

From the very start Kaldor intended his analysis to relate exclusively to the second theme. He started from his famous concept of 'stylized facts' – observed empirical regularities on development and distribution that needed to be explained by the then emerging models of growth, many of them his. He had in common with Sraffa, Joan Robinson and Kahn dissatisfaction with mainstream theories of value, distribution and growth, as witnessed to in probably his best known paper, 'Alternative theories of distribution' (Kaldor 1955–56). In it, having set out and dismissed all that had gone before, he set out his version of a 'Keynesian' macroeconomic theory of distribution, albeit set in the long period and assuming full employment. Kalecki had already in the 1930s provided such a theory for the short period and without assuming full employment while explicitly including microeconomic pricing behavior; see especially Kalecki (1936). Also, in common with Joan Robinson and Kahn, Kaldor provided a solution to one of Harrod's problems, whereby if there was a divergence between the warranted rate of growth, g_w, and the natural rate of growth, g_n, a change in distribution would so change the value of the overall saving ratio (because of the different saving behavior at the margin of wage-earners and profit-receivers) as to make g_w approach g_n in value.

Joan Robinson set out the methodological critique very clearly but never solved the problem of analysis in historical time itself. She wrote:

> The short period is here and now, with concrete means of production in existence. Incompatibilities in the situation . . . will determine what will happen next. Long-period equilibrium is not at some date in the future; it is an imaginary state of affairs in which there are no incompatibilities in the existing situation, here and now. (Joan Robinson 1962b, p. 690; 1965, p. 101 in the 1965 reprint)

By the late 1960s Kaldor decided that he had failed to solve the same problem. He changed direction for the rest of his life, incorporating an insight from his teacher at the London School of Economics (LSE), Allyn Young, the concept of cumulative causation,[17] about which I say more below.

1.8.   CAPITAL THEORY CRITIQUE

As I noted, there were two aspects to the capital theory critique. The first was in effect a doctrinal critique in which it was legitimate to use highly abstract constructions in order to express in an ideal setting the fundamental stance of an approach, for example, that in neoclassical economics price is an index of scarcity. The object is to see whether in these settings, the insight rigorously goes through, that the theory meets Sraffa's stringent conditions for a theory to be logically robust. He stated the conditions in his intervention in the discussion at the Corfu Conference on capital theory.

> [O]ne should emphasise the distinction between two types of measurement. First, there was one in which the statisticians were mainly interested. Second, there was measurement in theory. The statisticians' measures were only approximate and provided a suitable field for work in solving index number problems. The theoretical measures required absolute precision. Any imperfections in these theoretical measures were not merely upsetting, but knocked down the whole theoretical basis . . . The work of J.B. Clark, Böhm-Bawerk and others was intended to produce pure definitions . . ., as required by their theories . . . If we found contradictions, . . . these pointed to defects in the theory. (Sraffa 1961, pp. 305–6)

The capital-reversing and reswitching results were taken to undermine the conceptual foundations of the Neoclassical theory of distribution, especially in its aggregate production function and marginal productivity forms, but also, Sraffa, Krishna Bharadwaj, Garegnani and Pasinetti would argue, in all its forms. Bliss, Hahn, Samuelson and Solow, for example, while accepting the results, deny that they constitute a fundamental critique of the highest form of Neoclassical theory (see Dixit 1977). As Cohen and Harcourt (2003, 2005) point out, the disagreement rumbles on.

Joan Robinson, though, increasingly concentrated on the second strand of history versus equilibrium, a strand not acceptable to the Sraffians (neo-Ricardians). (We shall probably never know what Sraffa himself thought.) Her stance is, ironically, increasingly accepted now by the most sophisticated mainstreamers, for example, by Franklin Fisher, at least as far as the application of aggregate production functions to real-world data is concerned and by Bliss, at least as far as high theory is concerned; see Bliss's introduction to Bliss *et al.* (2005).[18]

Of course, the debates were not confined to capital theory because Neoclassical growth models associated with Solow and Swan (eminent Keynesians, I should add) were developed alongside the Cambridge capital theory controversies. As we know they stressed Marshall's 'dynamical principle of "Substitution" . . . seen ever at work' (Marshall [1890] 1961, p. xv) as a possible solution to Harrod's problems of instability if the economy was not on g_w and how it would approach g_n if initially, they were not equal to one another. 'New' endogenous growth theory is still Neoclassical in inspiration and analysis but also draws on Schumpeter explicitly and later Kaldor (sometimes without knowing it); see Kurz (1997).

To my mind the most promising solution so far to the conundrum in Marshall's approach and the issues raised by Joan Robinson in particular are to be found in Kalecki's later writings and, independently, in Goodwin's writings, especially those which come out of his classic 1967 paper, 'A growth cycle', in the Dobb *Festschrift* volume (Feinstein 1967). In Kalecki's last paper on these issues, published in the *Economic Journal* in 1968, he wrote 'the long-run trend [is] but a slowly changing component of a chain of short-period situations . . . [not an] independent entity' (Kalecki 1968, 1971, p. 165). This viewpoint on method embraces Goodwin's approach of cyclical growth, with trend and cycle indissolubly mixed as well and does, it seems to me, tackle directly Marshall's conundrum. It is, moreover, consistent with the later Kaldor's stress on cumulative causation processes.

As many of you may know, I illustrate these processes and their contrast with the mainstream approach, at least before some convergence between the two started, with the modern writings on path-dependent equilibrium and hysteresis processes, by the analogy of a wolf pack. There are two major views on the workings of markets and economies. The dominant one is akin to a wolf pack running along. If one or more wolves get ahead or fall behind, powerful forces come into play which return them to the pack. (The parallels with the existence of an equilibrium position that is unique and stable, and that the forces responsible for existence are independent of those responsible for stability are, I hope, obvious.) The other view has the forces acting on the wolves who get ahead or fall behind making them get further and further ahead or fall further and further behind, at least for long periods of time. This captures the notions of virtuous or vile processes of cumulative causation.

I submit that theories incorporating these views, plus Kaldor's analysis of markets where stocks dominate flows, and expectations by transactors on both sides of markets dominate the more usual factors determining supply and demand and price setting, as set out in Kaldor (1939), help us to make much more sense of the recent behavior of foreign exchange, stock and property markets and indeed of whole systems than do the currently fashionable macroeconomic theories. The latter include the use of Frank Ramsey's benevolent dictator model (in a completely inappropriate setting for which it was never intended), representative agent models, real business cycle theory and New Keynesian analysis.[19]

1.9.   ECONOMIC HISTORY

Cambridge also has a long and distinguished history associated with contributions to economic history, history of economic theory, and applied and policy work. As to economic history, there is the pioneering work of John Clapham, Maurice Dobb (from a Marxist standpoint), Phyllis Deane, Charles Feinstein, Robin Matthews and Brian Mitchell, principally in a Keynesian setting. Dobb, of course, was the leading Marxist economist in the United Kingdom for many decades; he bequeathed to us a rich legacy of careful scholarship in economic history and history of economic theory with at least two classics, *Political Economy and Capitalism* (Dobb [1937] 1940) and his last book, *Theories of Value and Distribution since Adam Smith* (Dobb 1973), as well as insightful, beautifully written articles on the economic history of Russia and on the problems of developing economies. In addition to her pioneering work on the history of the industrial revolution, Phyllis Deane took over Dobb's lecture slot on the history of theory when he retired and wrote her wonderful little volume, *The Evolution of Economic Ideas* (Deane 1978), which was set in the framework of Kuhn's paradigm explanation of the nature of scientific development. Both Dobb and Deane thought it impossible to make sense of a subject such as economics without analysis of theories, applications, policies and people within their historical context, a point of view which I heartily endorse and try to follow in my teaching and research; see, for example, Harcourt (2006).

1.10. THE DIRECTORS

The Department of Applied Economics (DAE) at Cambridge, alas now no more, has had four outstanding but very different directors – Richard Stone, Brian Reddaway, Wynne Godley and David Newbery. As my colleague, Michael Kitson, wrote in our joint article reviewing the achievements of 50 years of the National Bureau of Economic Research, (Harcourt and Kitson 1993, Harcourt 2001a), all of their approaches could be placed under the following rubric (with, of course, different emphases).

> The Cambridge approach to applied economics . . . stresses the limitations of much of orthodox neoclassical theory, however elegant, in explaining economic phenomena in the real world. Instead, it emphasises the importance of relevance in economics, incorporating the lessons of history, the institutional context and prevailing social and political conditions. Theory and measurement are thus mutually interdependent as robust empirical analysis is dependent on relevant theory, which in turn depends on reliable observations. Cambridge advances in theoretical and applied economics have, therefore, gone hand in hand. Furthermore, techniques have never been allowed to obscure the analysis – the medium is not the message. (Harcourt and Kitson 1993, Harcourt 2001a, p. 221.)

When Stone ceased to be Director in 1955 he directed and developed with Allan Brown the Cambridge growth project. It combined in an integrated whole previous work on demand analysis, input-output analysis and the national accounts, all of which featured in the research of the DAE under Stone's directorship. Reddaway and Godley shared an affinity in that Marshall and Keynes were their principal mentors. Reddaway presided over down-to-earth, common sense applied projects, usually with implications for policy. Respect for what data actually means and what it could and could not tell us, and a healthy skepticism about techniques divorced from what the basic data could take predominated. Godley drew on Marshall's concept of the long period and Keynes's analysis of the processes at work in modern capitalism to provide a logical framework of relationships incorporating the profit and loss account, the balance sheet and funds statement, macroeconomic constraints that must always bind in empirical work on explanation and policy. Newbery is very much a sophisticated Marshallian interested in applied microeconomic problems and also in developing economies and, now, the problems of transition economies.

In his later years Meade returned to his Keynesian roots and combined his humane civilized outlook with the use of the techniques of control engineers. (He first came across these in the work of his great friend and protégé at the LSE, Bill Phillips.) Meade worked with Andrew Blake, David Vines and Martin Weale as well as with control engineers (see Meade 1982, Vines *et al.* 1983, Weale *et al.* 1989).

1.11.   THE CAMBRIDGE TRADITION TODAY

There are still some colleagues in the Faculty at Cambridge working within the Cambridge tradition as I have defined it – Gabriel Palma, Bob Rowthorn, Ajit Singh, Frank Wilkinson, for example – and on method, principally through Tony Lawson's influential contributions to critical realism; see, for example, Lawson (1997, 2003). As I often tell Lawson, the central core of truth in critical realism is to be found in Marx's method and Keynes's methodological critique of Tinbergen's early econometric work on investment – but I would say that, wouldn't I.

Frank Hahn is not within this tradition, at least not consciously. But his courageous attacks on the Monetarists and New Classical macroeconomics seem to suggest that he recognizes aspects of Keynes's method when he writes that he finds himself at times able only to provide 'arguments that are merely plausible rather than clinching' (Hahn 1982, p. xi).

Here I must close if only for reasons of space and exhaustion. I hope I have written enough to encourage readers to chase up at least some of the readings in the references at the end of the chapter.

NOTES

1.   Previously Economics was part of the Moral Sciences Tripos.
2.   Though sadly Michal Kalecki never had a permanent post in the Faculty, his influence on Joan Robinson in particular, and his remarkable contributions were so great that he must play a major role in the narrative. Personally, I regard him as the greatest all-round political economist of the twentieth century.
3.   Let me quote what Keynes said of Malthus's approach, for the latter is still a role model for economists to follow, and Keynes's beautifully written paragraph is a succinct, lucid description of the Cambridge approach to economics: Malthus was

> above all, a great pioneer of the application of a frame of formal thinking to the complex confusion of the world of daily events. Malthus approached the central problems of economic theory by the best of all routes. He began . . . as a philosopher and moral scientist, . . . brought up in the Cambridge of Paley, applying the à *priori* method of the political philosopher. He then immersed himself . . . in the facts of economic history and of the contemporary world, applying the methods of historical induction and filling his mind with a mass of the material of experience. . . . finally he returned to à *priori* thought, . . . to the pure theory of the economist proper, and sought . . . to impose the methods of formal thought on the material presented by events, . . . to penetrate these events with understanding by a mixture of intuitive selection and formal principle and thus to interpret the problem and propose the remedy. In short, from being a caterpillar of a moral scientist and a chrysalis of an

historian, he could at last spread the wings of his thought and survey the world as an economist! (Keynes [1933] 1972, p. 107)

4.   In Goodwin's case we should add Knut Wicksell, Roy Harrod, Wassily Leontief and Joseph Schumpeter.
5.   Sen was my exact contemporary as a PhD student at Cambridge in the 1950s. I always thought he would be the first person among my contemporaries at Cambridge who would get the Nobel Prize. Another contemporary who should have but I fear will not, is Luigi Pasinetti, probably the last of the great system builders in our profession and, today, the senior living heir to the Cambridge tradition discussed here.
6.   I should say that, as with my mentor Joan Robinson, I regard the dichotomy between micro and macro a major error, a distinction which cannot be defended logically. There is always a macroeconomic background to microeconomic behaviour and vice versa. I think the Marxist view that the macroeconomic foundations of microeconomics are of fundamental importance is a vital insight, 'see Crotty (1980), and, though not coming from Marx but from Marshall and Keynes, the work of Wynne Godley.
7.   'But this *long run* is a misleading guide to current affairs. *In the long run* we are all dead. Economists set themselves too easy, too useless a task if in tempestuous seasons they can only tell us that when the storm is long past the ocean is flat again.' (Keynes [1923] (1971), p. 65)
8.   Kahn wrote a fellowship dissertation for King's in 1928–29 on the economics of the short period and was always skeptical of the quantity theory of money as a causal explanation of the general price level; see footnote 9 below.
9.   Kahn's dissertation was not published in English until 1989 just after his death. (An Italian translation was published in 1983 due to the efforts of Marco Dardi.) Had it been published in the 1930s, it and his 1931 *Economic Journal* article (Kahn 1931) on the multiplier would surely have seen him receive the Nobel Prize.
10.   Kaldor was at the LSE in the 1930s but joined the Cambridge Faculty after the Second World War when he was already well known as an enthusiastic and original Keynesian who had broken with Robbins's and Hayek's approach at the LSE.
11.   One was written in 1931 but only published in 1933.
12.   He wrote two classics on industrial organisation in the 1930s and 1940s, both using Marshall's methods and incorporating detailed observations on and knowledge about production methods and market structures (Austin Robinson [1931] 1953 and [1941] 1956).
13.   I abstract from the influence of Frank Hahn who came to Cambridge in the early 1960s and who, according to Bob Solow, single-handedly pulled the Faculty, kicking and screaming, reluctantly into the 20th century.
14.   Maurice Dobb and Amartya Sen also made important contributions, which, however, were on the whole separate from those of the people in the text. Frank Hahn's and Robin Matthews's 1964 survey of growth theory provided the definitive model for survey articles ever afterwards.
15.   This is not an uncontroversial view. The most sophisticated neoclassicals have a neoclassical (Irving) Fisherian 'vision' of the accumulation process but are often and increasingly suspicious of comparative statics results. Franklin Fisher is an outstanding proponent of this view as is Christopher Bliss. Joan Robinson and the neo-Ricardians shared a classical–Marxian–Keynesian 'vision' of the accumulation process but differed radically on method. The latter argue that the long-period method is the only legitimate way of doing precise rigoros theory, which Joan Robinson rejects as far as descriptive analysis in historical time is concerned.
16.   For a further discussion of the differences, see Joan Robinson (1962a, pp. 23–6).
17.   It was independently developed by Gunnar Myrdal and was, of course, to be found in Adam Smith.
18.   My own view veers towards that of Joan Robinson but not completely. I still see a useful and valid role for the classical concept of centres of gravitation as *sometimes* useful

short cuts, especially in short-period analysis; see Harcourt (1981, 1982) for why and Harcourt (1965, 1982) and Harcourt and Kenyon (1976) for applications.
19. For a further statement of my views on all this, see Harcourt (2004, 2006).

REFERENCES

Bliss, C. (2005), 'Introduction: The theory of capital: A personal overview', in Bliss, C., A.J. Cohen and G.C. Harcourt (eds), *Capital Theory*, Vol. 1, Cheltenham, UK and Northampton, MA, USA: Edward Elgar, pp. xi–xxvi.

Bliss, C., A.J. Cohen and G.C. Harcourt (eds) (2005), *Capital Theory*, 3 vols., Cheltenham, UK and Northampton, MA, USA: Edward Elgar.

Bradford, W. and G.C. Harcourt (1997), 'Units and definitions', in Harcourt, G.C. and P.A. Riach (eds), *A 'Second Edition' of The General Theory*, Vol. 1, London: Routledge, pp. 107–31.

Cohen, A.J. and G.C. Harcourt (2003), 'Whatever happened to the Cambridge capital theory controversies?', *Journal of Economic Perspectives*, 17, 199–214.

Cohen, A.J. and G.C. Harcourt (2005), 'Introduction: Capital theory controversy: Scarcity, production, equilibrium and time', in Bliss, C., A.J. Cohen and G.C. Harcourt (eds), *Capital Theory*, Vol. 1, Cheltenham, UK and Northampton, MA, USA: Edward Elgar, pp. xxvii–lx.

Crotty, J.R. (1980), 'Post-Keynesian theory: An overview and an evaluation', *American Economic Review*, 70, 20–25.

Deane, P.M. (1978), *The Evolution of Economic Ideas*, Cambridge: Cambridge University Press.

Dimand, Mary Ann, Robert W. Dimand and Evelyn L. Forget (eds) (1995), *Women of Value: Feminist Essays on the History of Women in Economics*, Aldershot, UK and Brookfield, US: Edward Elgar.

Dixit, A. (1977), 'The accumulation of capital theory', *Oxford Economic Papers*, 29, 1–29.

Dobb, M.H. [1937] (1940), *Political Economy and Capitalism: Some Essays in Economic Tradition*, London: Routledge.

Dobb, M.H. (1973), *Theories of Value and Distribution since Adam Smith*, Cambridge: Cambridge University Press.

Feinstein, C.H. (ed.) (1967), *Socialism, Capitalism and Economic Growth: Essays Presented to Maurice Dobb*, Cambridge: Cambridge University Press.

Goodwin, R.M. (1967), 'A growth cycle', in Feinstein, C.H. (ed.), *Socialism, Capitalism and Economic Growth: Essays Presented to Maurice Dobb*, Cambridge: Cambridge University Press, pp. 54–8.

Hahn, F.H. (1982), *Money and Inflation*, Oxford: Basil Blackwell.

Hahn, F.H. and R.C.O. Matthews (1964), 'The theory of economic growth: A survey', *Economic Journal*, 74, 779–902.

Hamouda, O.F. (1997), 'The general theory of employment, interest and money and prices', in Arestis, P., G. Palma and M. Sawyer (eds), *Capital Controversy, Post-Keynesian Economics and the History of Economics: Essays in Honour of Geoff Harcourt*, Vol. 1, London: Routledge, pp. 226–34.

Harcourt, G.C. (1965), 'A two-sector model of the distribution of income and the level of employment in the short run', *Economic Record*, 41, 103–17, reprinted in Sardoni, C. (ed.) (1992), *On Political Economy and Modern*

Political Economists: Selected Essays of G. C. Harcourt, London: Routledge, pp. 83–98.

Harcourt, G.C. (1969), 'Some Cambridge controversies in the theory of capital', *Journal of Economic Literature*, 7, 369–405.

Harcourt, G.C. (1972), *Some Cambridge Controversies in the Theory of Capital*, Cambridge: Cambridge University Press.

Harcourt, G.C. (1981), 'Marshall, Sraffa and Keynes: Incompatible bed-fellows?', *Eastern Economic Journal*, 5, 39–50, reprinted in Harcourt, G.C. (1982), *The Social Science Imperialists: Selected Essays*, edited by Prue Kerr, London: Routledge, pp. 250–64.

Harcourt, G.C. (1982), *The Social Science Imperialists: Selected Essays*, edited by Prue Kerr, London: Routledge.

Harcourt, G.C. (1987), 'Theoretical methods and unfinished business', in Reese, D.A. (ed.), *The Legacy of Keynes: Nobel Conference*, XXII, San Francisco: Harper & Row, pp. 1–22, reprinted in Sardoni, C. (ed.) (1992), *On Political Economy and Modern Political Economists: Selected Essays of G.C. Harcourt*, London: Routledge, pp. 235–49.

Harcourt, G.C. (1994), 'Kahn and Keynes and the making of *The General Theory*', *Cambridge Journal of Economics*, 17, 11–23, reprinted in Harcourt, G.C. (1995), *Capitalism, Socialism and Post-Keynesianism: Selected Essays of G. C. Harcourt*, Aldershot, UK and Brookfield, US: Edward Elgar, pp. 47–62.

Harcourt, G.C. (1995), *Capitalism, Socialism and Post-Keynesianism: Selected Essays of G.C. Harcourt*, Aldershot, UK and Brookfield, US: Edward Elgar.

Harcourt, G.C. (1997), 'Edward Austin Gossage Robinson, 1897–1993', *Proceedings of the British Academy*, 94, 1996 *Lectures and Memoirs*, 707–31, reprinted in Harcourt, G.C. (2001a), *50 Years a Keynesian and Other Essays*, London: Palgrave, pp. 131–56.

Harcourt, G.C. (2001a), *50 Years a Keynesian and Other Essays*, London: Palgrave.

Harcourt, G.C. (2001b), *Selected Essays on Economic Policy*, London: Palgrave.

Harcourt, G.C. (2003), 'Cambridge economic tradition', in King, J.E. (ed.), *The Elgar Companion to Post Keynesian Economics*, Cheltenham, UK and Northampton, MA, USA: Edward Elgar, pp. 44–51.

Harcourt, G.C. (2004), 'The economics of Keynes and its theoretical and political importance: Or, what would Marx and Keynes have made of the happenings of the last 30 years?' in Magnusson, G. and L. Jespersen (eds), *Keynes's General Theory and Current Views: Methodology, Institutions and Policies*, Reykjavik, Iceland: Faculty of Economics and Business Administration, University of Iceland, pp. 17–32.

Harcourt, G.C. (2006), *The Structure of Post-Keynesian Economics: The Core Contributions of the Pioneers*, Cambridge: Cambridge University Press.

Harcourt, G.C. and P. Kenyon (1976), 'Pricing and the investment decision', *Kyklos*, 29 (3), 449–77, reprinted in Sardoni, C. (ed.) (1992), *On Political Economy and Modern Political Economists: Selected Essays of G. C. Harcourt*, London: Routledge, pp. 48–66.

Harcourt, G.C. and P. Kerr (2003), 'Keynes and the Cambridge School', in Samuels, W.J., J.E. Biddle and J.B. Davis (eds) (2003), *A Companion to the History of Economic Thought,* Oxford: Blackwell, pp. 343–59.

Harcourt, G.C. and M. Kitson (1993), 'Fifty years of measurement: A Cambridge view', *Review of Income and Wealth*, 39(4), 435–47, reprinted in Harcourt, G.C. (2001a), *50 Years a Keynesian and Other Essays*, London: Palgrave, pp. 219–37.

Harcourt, G.C. and P.A. Riach (eds) (1997), *A 'Second Edition' of The General Theory*, 2 Vols, London: Routledge.

Harrod, R.F. (1939), 'An essay in dynamic theory', *Economic Journal*, 49, 14–33.

Harrod, R.F. (1948), *Towards a Dynamic Economics: Some Recent Developments of Economic Theory and Their Application to Policy*, London: Macmillan.

Jevons, W.S. (1871), *The Theory of Political Economy*, London: Macmillan.

Kahn, R.F. [1929] (1989), *The Economics of the Short Period*, Houndmills, Basingstoke: Macmillan.

Kahn, R.F. (1931), 'The relation of home investment to unemployment', *Economic Journal*, 41, 173–98.

Kaldor, N. (1934), 'A classificatory note on the determinates of equilibrium', *Review of Economic Studies*, 1, 122–36.

Kaldor, N. (1939), 'Speculation and economic stability', *Review of Economic Studies*, 7, 1–27.

Kaldor, N. (1955–56), 'Alternative theories of distribution', *Review of Economic Studies*, 23, 83–100.

Kalecki, M. (1936), 'Pare uwag o teorii Keynesa', *Ekonomista*, 3, 18–26, English translation by Targetti, F. and B. Kinda-Hass (1982), 'Kalecki's review of Keynes' *General Theory*', *Australian Economic Papers*, 21, 245–53.

Kalecki, M. (1968), 'Trend and business cycles reconsidered', *Economic Journal*, 78, 263–76, reprinted in Kalecki, M. (1971), *Selected Essays on the Dynamics of the Capitalist Economy, 1933–70*, Cambridge: Cambridge University Press, pp. 165–83.

Kalecki, M. (1971), *Selected Essays on the Dynamics of the Capitalist Economy, 1933–70*, Cambridge: Cambridge University Press.

Keynes, J.M. [1921] (1973), *A Treatise on Probability: Collected Writings*, Vol. VIII, London: Macmillan.

Keynes, J.M. [1923] (1971), *A Tract on Monetary Reform: Collected Writings*, Vol. IV, London: Macmillan.

Keynes, J.M. [1930] (1971), *A Treatise on Money, Collected Writings*, vols. V, VI, London: Macmillan.

Keynes, J.M. [1933] (1972), *Essays in Biography: Collected Writings*, Vol. X, London: Macmillan.

Keynes, J.M. [1936] (1973), *The General Theory of Employment, Interest and Money: Collected Writings*, Vol. VII, London: Macmillan.

Keynes, J.M. (1973a), *The General Theory and After: Part I, Preparation: Collected Writings*, Vol. XIII, London: Macmillan.

Keynes, J.M. (1973b), *The General Theory and After: Part II, Defence and Development: Collected Writings*, Vol. XIV, London: Macmillan.

Keynes, J.M. (1978), *Activities 1939–45: Internal War Finance: Collected Writings*, Vol. XXII, London: Macmillan.

Kregel, J.A. (1976), 'Economic methodology in the face of uncertainty: The modelling methods of Keynes and the post-Keynesians', *Economic Journal*, 86, 209–25.

Kurz, H.D. (1997), 'What could the "new" growth theory tell Smith or Ricardo?' *Economic Issues*, 2, 1–20.

Lawson, T. (1997), *Economics and Reality*, London: Routledge.

Lawson, T. (2003), *Reorientating Economics*, London: Routledge.

Lutz, F.A. and D.C. Hague (eds) (1961), *The Theory of Capital*, London: Macmillan.

Malthus, T.R. (1798), (First Essay) *An Essay on the Principles of Population*, London: J. Johnson.

Malthus, T.R. (1803), (Second Essay) *An Essay on the Principles of Population*, London: John Murray.

Marshall, Alfred [1890] (1961), *Principles of Economics*, London: Macmillan.

McWilliams Tullberg, R. (1990), *Alfred Marshall in Retrospect*, Aldershot, UK and Brookfield, US: Edward Elgar.

McWilliams Tullberg, R. (1991), 'Alfred Marshall and the male priesthood of economics', *Quaderni di Storia dell'Economia Politica*, 9(2–3), 235–68.

McWilliams Tullberg, R. (1992), 'Alfred Marshall's attitude to the *Economics of Industry*, *Journal of the History of Economic Thought*, 14(2), 257–70.

McWilliams Tullberg, R., T. Raffaelli and E. Biagini (eds) (1995), *Alfred Marshall's Lectures to Women: Some Economic Questions Directly Connected to the Welfare of the Laborer*, Aldershot, UK and Brookfield, US: Edward Elgar.

Meade, J.E. (1975), 'The Keynesian revolution', in M. Keynes (ed.), *Essays on John Maynard Keynes*, Cambridge: Cambridge University Press, pp. 82–8.

Meade, J.E. (1982), *Stagflation Volume 1: Wage-Fixing*, London: George Allen and Unwin.

Pigou, A.C. (1920), *The Economics of Welfare*, London: Macmillan.

Robinson, E.A.G. [1931] (1953), *The Structure of Competitive Industry*, Cambridge: Cambridge University Press.

Robinson, E.A.G. (1936), 'Mr Keynes on money', *The Economist*, 24 February, 471–2.

Robinson, E.A.G. [1941] (1956), *Monopoly*, Cambridge: Cambridge University Press.

Robinson, J. (1933a), *The Economics of Imperfect Competition*, London: Macmillan.

Robinson, J. (1933b), 'A parable of saving and investment', *Economica* (N.S.), 13, 75–84.

Robinson, J. (1933c), 'The theory of money and the analysis of output', *Review of Economic Studies*, 1, 22–6.

Robinson, J. [1937a] (1969), *Introduction to the Theory of Employment*, London: Macmillan.

Robinson, J. [1937b] (1947), *Essays in the Theory of Employment*, Oxford: Blackwell.

Robinson, J. [1942] (1966), *An Essay on Marxian Economics*, London: Macmillan.

Robinson, J. (1953a), 'Imperfect competition revisited', *Economic Journal*, 63, 579–93; reprinted in Robinson, J. (1960), *Collected Economic Papers*, Vol. II, Oxford: Basil Blackwell, pp. 222–38.

Robinson, J. (1953b), 'A lecture delivered at Oxford by a Cambridge economist', in Robinson, J., *On Re-reading Marx*, Cambridge: Students Bookshop, reprinted in Robinson, J. (1973), *Collected Economic Papers*, Vol. IV, Oxford: Basil Blackwell, pp. 254–63.

Robinson, J. [1956] (1969), *The Accumulation of Capital*, 3rd edn, London: Macmillan.

Robinson, J. (1962a), *Essays in the Theory of Economic Growth*, London: Macmillan.

Robinson, J. (1962b), 'Review of H.G. Johnson, *Money, Trade and Economic Growth*', *Economic Journal*, 72, 690–92, reprinted in Robinson, J. (1965), *Collected Economic Papers*, Vol. III, Oxford: Basil Blackwell, pp. 100–102.

Sardoni, C. (ed.) (1992), *On Political Economy and Modern Political Economists: Selected Essays of G.C. Harcourt*, London: Routledge.

Skidelsky, R. (2000), *John Maynard Keynes, Volume Three: Fighting for Britain 1937–1946*, London: Macmillan.

Sraffa, P. (1925), 'Sulle relazioni fra costo e quantità prodotta', *Annali di Economica*, II (1), 277–328.

Sraffa, P. (1926), 'The laws of returns under competitive conditions', *Economic Journal*, 36, 535–50.

Sraffa, P. (1930), 'A criticism' and 'A rejoinder' in 'Increasing returns and the representative firm: A symposium', *Economic Journal*, 40, 89–92, 93.

Sraffa, P. (1932), 'Dr Hayek on money and capital', *Economic Journal*, 42, 42–53.

Sraffa, P. (1960), *Production of Commodities by Means of Commodities: Prelude to a Critique of Economic Theory*, Cambridge: Cambridge University Press.

Sraffa, P. (1961), 'Comment', in Lutz, F.A. and D.C. Hague (eds), *The Theory of Capital*, London: Macmillan, pp. 305–6.

Vines, D. (2003), 'John Maynard Keynes 1937–1946: The creation of international macroeconomics', *Economic Journal*, 113, 338–61.

Vines, D., J.M. Maciejowski and J.E. Meade (1983), *Stagflation Volume 2: Demand Management*, London: George Allen and Unwin.

Weale, M., A. Blake, N. Christodoulakis, J. Meade and D. Vines (1989), *Macroeconomic Policy: Inflation, Wealth and the Exchange Rate*, London: Unwin Hyman.

Winslow, T. (2005), *Keynes's Economics: A Political Economy as Moral Science Approach to Macroeconomics and Macroeconomic Policy*, mimeograph, Berlin, 28–29 October, 2005.

2. Heterodox economics: a common challenge to mainstream economics?

Sheila Dow

2.1. INTRODUCTION

Heterodox economics has been going through a period of change. The most noticeable change has been the drawing together of heterodox economists using different approaches into the larger category of 'heterodox economics'. This has had a series of positive outcomes: notably a growing confidence in heterodox economics, and an increasing interchange of ideas among those taking different heterodox approaches. The increasing duality that this has created, between orthodox and heterodox economics, has had both positive and negative outcomes: a growing cohesion among those seeking to put forward a convincing alternative to orthodox economics, on the one hand, but the temptation to slip into a dualistic mode of thought which is more characteristic of the orthodoxy, on the other hand. While orthodox economics has been criticized for its exclusivity, as being the 'right' approach so that all others are 'wrong', there is a danger that heterodox economics might fall into the same habit.

At the same time, orthodox economics has also been undergoing a period of change. In the 1980s it was reasonable to characterize mainstream economics as unified around the commitment to building up a general equilibrium theoretical system (see Weintraub 1985). But there has been increasing evidence of fragmentation, with the development of such apparently diverse research programs as game theory, experimental economics, evolutionary economics, behavioral economics, complexity economics and so on (Davis 2006). While many heterodox economists (such as Lawson 1997, 2003) continue to focus on the common features of orthodox economics, orthodox economists themselves (such as Pencavel 1991) tend to focus on its diversity.

A particular question posed by these developments is whether the different schools of thought in heterodox economics continue to have a useful role to play, and what that role is. It is the purpose of this chapter to address this question. We approach the question in a range of ways, and at a range of levels. (This is an example of a pluralist methodology, something which we will consider explicitly during the discussion.) At the most general level, we can consider schools of thought quite apart from questions of orthodoxy and heterodoxy; is it a good way for promoting the development of knowledge, for knowledge communities and/or ideas to be segmented into schools of thought? In this discussion we bear in mind the importance of issues of meaning; what are the implications of different schools of thought employing different meanings? And, focusing on the orthodoxy/heterodoxy divide, which is the more effective strategy for promoting heterodox ideas – emphasizing or de-emphasizing differences within heterodoxy?

Much of the discussion of the current state of economics has contrasted it with the fierce debates between schools of thought in the 1970s (Pencavel 1991, Colander 2000, Goodwin 2000). The implication has been drawn that economics has moved on from this, regrettable, kind of division. Here already we see issues of meaning arise – perhaps schools of thought are understood differently now – or indeed differently, depending on school of thought? We start therefore by considering a range of traditional views about schools of thought. We then proceed to consider more recent views. Some of these issues have been discussed in more detail elsewhere (Dow forthcoming). The particular contribution of this chapter is to suggest a diagrammatic framework for depicting these different understandings of schools of thought. The case is made that thinking of heterodox economics in terms of schools of thought can be enabling rather than constraining. This argument draws on the argument developed more fully elsewhere (Dow 2004) for structured pluralism. We conclude by considering the strategic issues raised for heterodox economics.

2.2. OPEN AND CLOSED SYSTEMS

In considering how schools of thought have been understood, we will use the concepts of open and closed systems. These concepts can be applied to the different levels of social systems, theoretical systems and systems of thought, and there are connections between the levels (Dow 2001). (Indeed it is the critical realist argument that open social systems require open theoretical systems and open systems of thought; see Lawson 1997, 2003.) But our primary focus here is on systems (or schools) of thought. How we understand the concepts of open and closed systems themselves is a matter for current discussion. For the purposes of this chapter we employ the meaning set out in Chick and Dow (2005), which differs, for example, from the critical realist meaning. We define openness and closure as following from a range of conditions. A closed system has fixed, well-defined bound-aries; all variables within the system, and the structure of their interrela-tions are identified, and their values either knowable or random. (An open *model* is a closed system, since the exogenous variables are well-defined and either known or random.)

Open systems are those in which *any* of these closed-system conditions is not met. There is a range of possibilities therefore for open systems, since all it takes is for one element of the system to be unknowable, one bound-ary not to be fixed, one interrelation to be indeterminate (and non-random). So open systems are not the opposite of closed systems, but rather they are not-closed systems. The conditions for closed systems are very strict. Mearman (2005) has argued that it is more helpful to think in terms of poles than opposites, so that we can think of systems as being more or less close to the extreme closed end of the spectrum. For the pur-poses of the following argument, however, we will simplify by referring to closed and open systems, where a closed system is understood to be 'towards the polar extreme of strict closed systems'.

2.3.   'OLD' VIEWS ON SCHOOLS OF THOUGHT

2.3.1.   The Orthodox Economics Perspective

Let us consider first how schools of thought were understood in the 1980s, starting with the perspective of orthodox economics. The most common example given of differences between schools of thought is the Mon-etarist–Keynesian debate which was conducted in terms of the IS-LM framework. Differences in how the economy functioned were reduced to debates about the relative slopes of the IS and LM curves. To the extent that the differences were not purely technical, they were seen as ideological.

The term 'ideological' in the orthodox literature was always used to dis-parage. It referred to the import of political values into scientific debate. Since it was taken for granted that science in general, and economics in par-ticular, should be value-free, political values had no place. Introductory textbooks were habitually introduced with a discussion of the distinction between positive and normative economics. The economist was to demon-strate the consequences of different policy stances in a positive manner, but it was for the politician to choose between them.

Within orthodox economics, there were different theoretical approaches, as theory moved beyond general equilibrium theory, dealing in different ways with the difficulties encountered with specifying the microfoundations of macroeconomics. Thus Phelps (1990) could identify seven different theoretical approaches to macroeconomics, all within orthodox economics; indeed he referred to them as schools of thought. But these approaches all held in common the key characteristics of orthodox economics: rational, atomistic agents with certainty-equivalent knowledge (or some well-defined constraint on full knowledge), a fixed structure of economic relations which were knowable or random, and could thus be expressed mathematically, and clearly defined exogenous variables which produced random shocks. As a positive discipline, economics itself was value-free; disputes in principle could be tested against objective facts. In other words, positive economics (which was understood as coterminous with orthodox economics, and indeed with economics as a whole) was a closed system.

This closed system is illustrated in Figure 2.1 by a solid line defining the discipline. Within economics, the different theories (New Classical theory, New Keynesian theory and so on) are illustrated as falling within the well-defined boundary of economics. But they are shown with dashed boundaries, to capture the fact that, as evolving systems within the closed system of economics, they are open systems. Since the Monetarist–Keynesian debates were classified as ideological, they fell outside economics proper, belonging rather to normative analysis. The thick closed boundaries illustrate the fixity with which these normative values were associated, and the ferocity with which they were defended. While positive economics was well-defined as orthodox economics, it was recognized that there were other

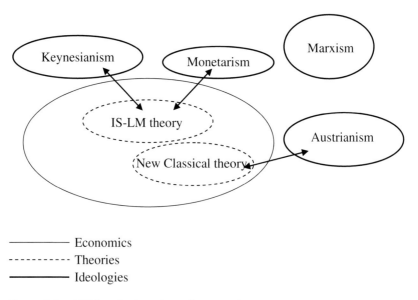

Keynesianism

Monetarism

Marxism

IS-LM theory

New Classical theory

Austrianism

——————— Economics
- - - - - - - - - Theories
——————— Ideologies

Figure 2.1   'Old' orthodox view of economics

schools of thought beyond Monetarism and Keynesianism. Kantor (1979) for example recognized the roots of the rational expectations revolution in Austrian economics. So there was a perception of interplay between ideas developed within an ideological framework and economics-proper (illustrated by the two-way arrows). The most obvious exception was Marxism, which was understood as an ideological system which operated quite independently of economics-proper, so no connecting arrows are shown.

2.3.2 The Heterodox Economics Perspective

This period is referred to by Pencavel (1991) as tyrannical. The implication is that there was excessive criticism, from an ideological perspective. He contrasts this with what he identifies by the 1990s as a greater openness of debate, implicitly conducted within the confines of economics-proper. The period is also often associated with the ideas of Thomas Kuhn, which seemed to have removed the grounds for criticism from an agreed set of principles, exchanging it for an 'anything goes' framework. If we think of schools of thought as paradigms, then each has its own set of principles, and therefore any debate across schools of thought is a debate at cross purposes. These ideas were embraced by heterodox economists as legitimizing their alternative paradigms, taking them outside the ambit of criticism on the basis of the principles of orthodox economics (as making insufficient use of mathematical formalism, for example).

From a heterodox perspective, there was no sharp divide between positive and normative economics. Rather, as Myrdal (1953) argued, ideology, in the sense of values, was embedded in economic thought. This is captured in the range of levels at which Kuhn's paradigms are defined. The distinction then between orthodox and heterodox economics was not, as orthodox economists suggested, the distinction between positive economics and ideology, but rather a distinction between paradigms. Each paradigm was defined by its understanding of the real world (its ontology), its methodological principles and the theories which these supported. It was also defined by the meanings attached to terms; 'rational' for example was taken to mean something very different in Post-Keynesian economics from what it meant in orthodox economics. But there was an element of commonality between the different heterodox schools of thought in that they had all adopted a methodology which, while distinctive, in each case was differentiated from the closed-system methodology of orthodox economics (Dow 1985).

This view of the discipline is shown in Figure 2.2. Orthodox economics is more explicitly seen as a closed system, its boundary being marked by a heavy solid line; the second, lighter, boundary line represents the particularity of

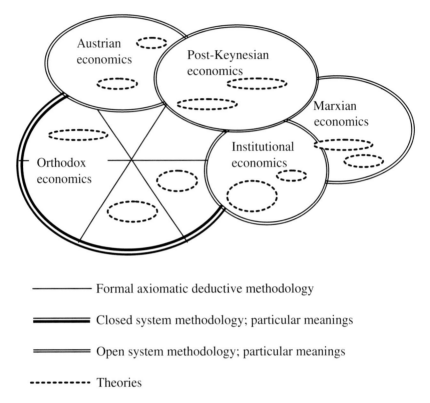

——————— Formal axiomatic deductive methodology

════════ Closed system methodology; particular meanings

═══════ Open system methodology; particular meanings

----------- Theories

Figure 2.2   'Old' heterodox view of economics

meanings associated with that boundary. The radii represent the centrality
of the rationality axioms to orthodox economics. But within the resulting
structure, there were different theories associated with different assumptions
about constraints within the overarching general equilibrium framework (for
example, constraints on expectations formation). Since these theories were
continually evolving, as assumptions were revised, they are shown with
dashed boundaries.

   The different heterodox schools of thought (represented here by four
examples) are shown by light solid lines, with a second line to capture particularity of meaning. The boundary is solid, implying only limited
differentiation from the closed-system approach of orthodox economics.
Indeed in the 1980s there was only limited awareness among heterodox
economists of the closed-system/open–system distinction. Further, schools
of thought were regarded (at least in principle) as reasonably well-defined.
The objections to such definition referred more to the fact that individuals

did not necessarily fit these definitions than that schools of thought could not be understood in terms of a well-defined 'representative individual'. Indeed, the schools illustrated here are shown as overlapping, to reflect the cross-fertilization of ideas facilitated by individual economists whose thought straddled different schools of thought (like Shackle, who was in the interface between Post-Keynesian economics and Austrian economics). Some overlap is also shown with orthodox economics (Hicks being an example of an orthodox economist who nevertheless interacted with Post-Keynesian economics). Again, however, no direct connection is shown between Marxian economics and orthodox economics.[1] Within each school of thought, a range of evolving theories is illustrated by dashed lines. But the heterodox schools of thought do not have an axiomatic structure as is shown for orthodox economics.

While we have seen that orthodox economists associated the 1980s with excessive (and inappropriately ideological) criticism, some heterodox economists (such as Fullbrook 2003) have associated it with insufficient criticism. At the time, Kuhn's framework had been seen as supportive of the whole notion of a range of paradigms offered as alternatives to the dominant, orthodox paradigm. But the suggestion now is that Kuhn's framework had been even more influential in protecting orthodox economics from criticism. Just as orthodox principles had only limited purview as far as heterodox economics was concerned, so the principles of heterodox economics were seen only to apply to heterodox economics. This outcome was reinforced by the emergence of postmodernism, and constructivism more generally, which seemed to remove all grounds for criticism altogether. This development was to change the way in which schools of thought were understood.

2.4. 'NEW' VIEWS ON SCHOOLS OF THOUGHT

2.4.1. The Orthodox Economics Perspective

The view of schools of thought in orthodox economics is colored by the growing theoretical plurality we noted in the introduction to this chapter. The perception of increasing fragmentation in orthodox economics has been welcomed (for example, by Pencavel 1991, Colander 2000 and Goodwin 2000) as an opening-up of the discipline in contrast to the ideological divides of the previous decades. These different theoretical approaches might be called schools of thought, but they were to be differentiated from schools of thought defined by ideology; these new differences were well within the boundaries of 'economics-proper'.

Economics is still seen as well-defined, and there is a consensus that this definition is at the level of method. The same commentators have noted that the increasing plurality of theories has arisen alongside an increasing monism in terms of the method of mathematical formalism. Thus economics is understood to be coterminous with orthodox economics. Since heterodox economics shares the view that economics should not be defined in this way, it is understood as 'non-economics'. Thus, while debate occurred between orthodox and heterodox economics in the 1980s (even if it was frowned upon as being ideological), the connection is now broken.

Figure 2.3 illustrates this perspective. Economics as such is a well-defined (closed) system, defined by method. Anything which does not conform methodologically is treated as non-economics, illustrated by a separate ellipse, with dotted boundary (since it is not well-defined other than in not employing the approved 'economic' method). There is a reluctance to use the term 'heterodox' (see for example Goodwin 2000), in that all economic discourse is now perceived to occur within the 'economics' ellipse. What would once have been heterodox is now seen as just part of the general fragmentation – as long as it employs the appropriate methodology. Anything else by definition falls outside economics. The different theories within economics, as evolving entities, are shown by dashed boundaries. Experimental economics is shown right at the boundary of economics to illustrate its interdisciplinary nature. But experimental economics is defined still in terms of method.

The different approaches within orthodox economics also are not seen as well-defined because of the influence of constructivism, which has affected orthodox economics as much as, if not more than, heterodox economics. Weintraub's (1999) account of twentieth-century economics is a good example of constructivism at work. He shows how different histories may be written from different perspectives; there is no longer any sense that it is possible to identify a 'true' history. Similarly, there is no scope for writing a 'true' account of modern economics.

2.4.2.   The Heterodox Economics Perspective

2.4.2.1.   Pure pluralism

Constructivism has had a more explicit role in the development of heterodox thought. Indeed the launch pad for constructivism in the form of postmodernism was a critique of positivist orthodox methodology. Kuhn's framework provided the basis for a critique of any attempt to establish universal appraisal criteria as inevitably being paradigm-bound. But postmodernists extended the critique to any attempt to establish even paradigm-bound appraisal criteria, a position encapsulated in their embracing

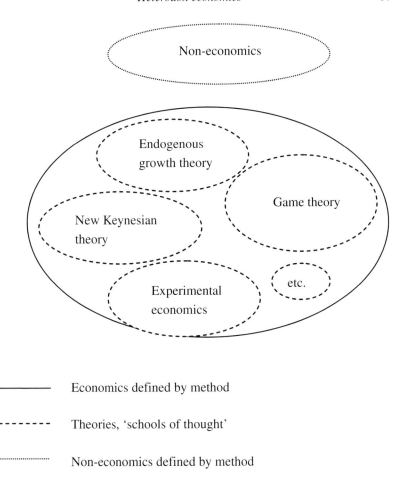

Non-economics

Endogenous
growth theory

Game theory

New Keynesian
theory

Experimental
economics

etc.

—————— Economics defined by method

-------- Theories, 'schools of thought'

.... Non-economics defined by method

Figure 2.3 '*New' orthodox view of economics*

of the term 'nihilism' (see for example Amariglio and Ruccio 1995). There
is no role therefore for methodology as a prescriptive, rather than descriptive exercise. Further, our understanding of the real world is subjective; it
is not even individualistic, since the self itself is fragmented (Amariglio
1988). There is therefore no scope for identifying paradigms defined by
shared understandings of the real world and shared methodologies.

This postmodern reluctance to think in terms of schools of thought, and
indeed of the ontologies and methodological principles which define them,
is shared by the rhetoric approach pioneered in modern economics by
McCloskey (1986, 1994). According to this form of constructivism, knowledge progresses by means of good conversation. Anything which is

thought to impede conversation, like identification with one school of thought or another, or discussion of methodological principles, is to be avoided. McCloskey is not a heterodox economist, and indeed her work arguably has had greater impact on the orthodox reluctance to address methodological issues. Nevertheless she is often cited by heterodox economists (such as Garnett, forthcoming), particularly in support of pluralism within heterodox economics.

While Garnett still sees a role for schools of thought in economics, others who accept constructivist arguments do not. On the one hand, postmodernists see heterodox economics as an open system with ill-defined boundaries, and including a range of approaches, each also having ill-defined boundaries. Problems of meaning are seen as endemic, and contribute significantly to the difficulties with defining boundaries. To define boundaries, that is, to define schools of thought, requires shared meaning and shared methodological principles, which are ruled out by nihilism. This is illustrated in Figure 2.4 by the dashed boundary for heterodox economics and for the approaches within it. Orthodox economics remains well-defined by its mathematical formalist methodology and the consequences for the axiomatic structure, and content, of theory.

Somewhat curiously, the same diagrams may be used to represent critical realism, even though, far from de-emphasizing methodology, critical realists focus on it. The constructivist argument is shared, that there is no basis for demonstrable truth. Further, the difference between orthodox economics and heterodox economics is that the former takes a closed-system approach to knowledge while the latter takes an open-system approach. Schools of thought are given a role in critical realism. But the emphasis is on the overarching open system of heterodox economics, and thus the shared basis for methodological principles. Schools of thought are differentiated merely by their 'ontological commitments', by which is meant their focus of attention within a shared ontology. The distinctions between schools of thought are thus secondary to their shared philosophical principles, and may thus be shown as if they were simply different theories within a single approach, as in Figure 2.4.

2.4.2.2. Structured pluralism

While we have been talking of the constructivist approach to schools of thought as a 'new' view, it could be said in fact to be perpetuating the old view of schools of thought as being rigidly defined, providing the basis for destructive, rather than constructive debate. Or, as in Lawson's view, differences between heterodox schools of thought may be seen as relatively insignificant, and thus the 'old' view of schools of thought was overplayed.

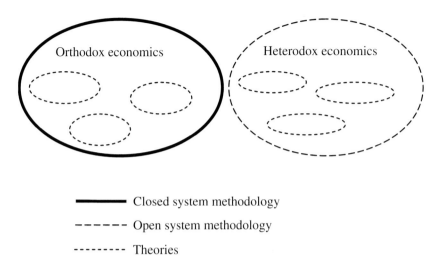

——————— Closed system methodology

— — — — — Open system methodology

‑‑‑‑‑‑‑‑ Theories

Figure 2.4 *'New' heterodox view of economics: unstructured*
pluralism/dualism

But, by considering further the concept of pluralism, we can see a continuing, constructive, role for schools of thought in heterodox economics. The arguments for pluralism have been discussed ever since Caldwell (1982) first proposed it as the way forward, beyond positivism. The Salanti and Screpanti (1997) volume provides a good range of perspectives, with the editors emphasizing both the ethical arguments for openness to a range of approaches as well as the methodological arguments. But there has been less discussion about what pluralism would actually consist of, leaving the impression that what is intended is the pure pluralism discussed above. Caldwell has however always emphasized the role of criticism (see for example Caldwell 1986), which suggests limits to pure pluralism, or 'anything goes'. The difficulty is the grounds on which criticism is to be made.

An answer lies in the study of science, or indeed of a social system like the economy. Pure pluralism is unworkable in practice. Unless there is some shared understanding of reality, some shared meaning of terms, and some shared view about the parameters for argument, then communication cannot take place. There would be no such thing as science. In practice, knowledge communities function by means of some sharing of ontology, meaning and means of argument. There is no need for this sharing to be perfect, and even less for it to be universal. (And we know that there is no basis for any universal standard for knowledge.) What this implies is, rather than pure pluralism, a structured pluralism; rather than an infinite range of approaches to knowledge, a discrete number of knowledge communities (or schools of thought). Further, given the need for open systems of knowledge to address an open-system reality, this structure itself would be open (and thus provisional), with overlap between communities, shifting meanings and methodologies as reality and ideas evolve.

While it has been argued that, for functionality, such communities must form for any shared knowledge to develop, we can see further that identifying these communities can play a constructive part. Classifying economics as a set of communities according to ontology, meanings and methodologies helps us to understand each other better, communicate better (albeit imperfectly) and benefit from each other's ideas, which can then be adapted to different frameworks. Perhaps this argument is best put by means of an anthropological analogy. When traveling to visit a new country, we benefit most (and indeed behave ethically) if we attempt to learn something of the local language and customs. Then we have a better chance of understanding the people and circumstances we come across. What we learn from the experience may not be exactly how matters are understood within that country, but nevertheless can enhance our own experience, just as our encounters may enhance the experience of those we meet.

Figure 2.5 attempts to illustrate this view of identifying schools of thought as a constructive measure, enabling rather than inhibiting the building up of knowledge (however defined). Orthodox economics is still shown as axiomatically structured, with a range of evolving theories. It is defined by a thick line, representing a positivist methodology, with a second line to indicate particularity of meaning. But these are both shown as dashed, to capture the influence of constructivism in encouraging an avoidance of being explicit about methodology, which introduces the possibility of some openness. Mathematical formalism is still taken to define economics, but without methodological justification, and with most decisions (about which techniques to use, and how) being tacit.

Heterodox economics is defined in terms of a range of schools of thought (illustrated here by four schools). Structured pluralism is shown by double boundaries, which indicate that they are reasonably well-defined, although these definitions are provisional and partial. The purpose of defining the boundaries at a particular time is to aid communication; the process of changing these definitions as thought evolves itself is aided by having an initial set of definitions as a point of reference. Again there is overlap between the different heterodox schools of thought, and between some of these and orthodox economics.

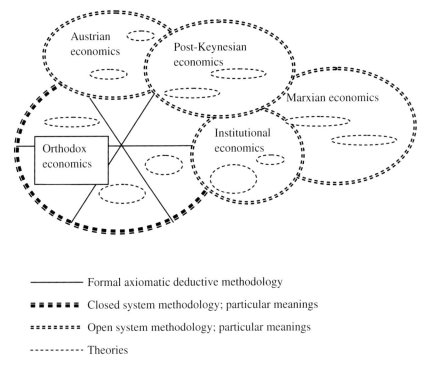

——————— Formal axiomatic deductive methodology

▪ ▪ ▪ ▪ ▪ Closed system methodology; particular meanings

========= Open system methodology; particular meanings

--------- Theories

Figure 2.5   'New' heterodox view of economics: structured pluralism

2.5.   CONCLUSION

We have made the case here for schools of thought to make a constructive contribution to the practice of economics, and to critical debate. The (inevitable) failure of positivism has meant that a range of approaches can be sustained, where none can be demonstrated to be superior to the others. That range is limited by the practical requirement for knowledge to be developed within knowledge communities of a minimum size. Seen in this light, we can continue to move on from the old idea of schools of thought as citadels to be defended at all costs, to a more helpful view of schools of thought as an inevitable feature of the scientific landscape, that is, as a means of organizing knowledge.

There remains however the strategic question. Knowledge communities function in an environment where power can be exercised. Far from the new fragmentation of orthodox economics opening up a new era of free competition between ideas (as suggested by Pencavel 1991), we continue to experience the exercise of market power by the socially-dominant orthodoxy. This power has now been given additional institutional form by such developments as the UK's Research Assessment Exercise, which distorts research programs and hiring decisions according to what is *believed to be* the likely judgment of the panel of peers (see further Gillies 2006). In such an environment, would it be better to downplay divisions within heterodox economics?

Fragmentation as such need not be an issue, in that there is widespread recognition that there has been increasing fragmentation within orthodox economics, and this has been welcomed by many. Indeed heterodox economists are much better placed to handle fragmentation among schools of thought, given the heightened awareness of methodological issues (relative to orthodox economists). The case has been made that using schools of thought as a means of classifying different approaches enables constructive criticism and more effective cross-fertilization of ideas. It is, in contrast, unhelpful for it to be used as an inhibitor of communication. This applies to communication across the heterodox-orthodox divide as much as to communication across divides between heterodox schools of thought. The development of more fora for communication among heterodox economists using different approaches is thus most welcome, and there is no reason why that should not be extended to cover orthodox economics were there to be more awareness there of what is involved in communication across schools of thought.

There is indeed a case, consistent with structured pluralism applied to a plurality of methodologies, for a methodology which is itself structured and pluralist. Specifically this would involve a range of methods. This itself can be applied to strategy for heterodox economics. As argued in more detail elsewhere (Dow 2000), heterodox economics can be promoted in a plurality of ways: developing theory within schools of thought, persuasion, criticism and learning across heterodox schools of thought, and persuasion, criticism and learning with respect to orthodox economics. There is no justification for a monist strategy, any more than a justification for a monist methodology of economics.

The usefulness of the concept of schools of thought therefore rests on how they are understood. As a set of defenses they can no longer be justified. But as long as they are understood as an aid to learning and communication, they have a constructive role to play in the development and communication of heterodox economics in all its diversity.

NOTE

1. The precise details of these figures are of course highly contestable. The priority here is to suggest a framework within which detail can be debated.

REFERENCES

Amariglio, J.L. (1988), 'The body, economic discourse and power: An economist's introduction to Foucault', *History of Political Economy*, 29, 583–613.

Amariglio, J.L. and D.F. Ruccio (1995), 'Keynes, postmodernism and uncertainty', in Dow, S.C. and J. Hillard (eds), *Keynes, Knowledge and Uncertainty*, Aldershot, UK and Brookfield, US: Edward Elgar, pp. 334–56.

Caldwell, B.J. (1982), *Beyond Positivism*, London: Allen & Unwin.

Caldwell, B.J. (1986), 'Towards a broader conception of criticism', *History of Political Economy*, 18, 675–81.

Chick, V. and S.C. Dow (2005), 'The meaning of open systems', *Journal of Economic Methodology*, 12, 363–82.

Colander, D. (2000), 'The death of neoclassical economics', *Journal of the History of Economic Thought*, 22, 127–43.

Davis, J.B. (2006), 'The turn in economics: Neoclassical dominance to mainstream pluralism?', *Journal of Institutional Economics*, 2, 1–20.

Dow, S.C. (1985), *Macroeconomic Thought: A Methodological Approach*, Oxford: Basil Blackwell.

Dow, S.C. (2000), 'Prospects for the progress of heterodox economics', *Journal of the History of Economic Thought*, 22, 157–70.

Dow, S.C. (2001), 'Modernism and postmodernism: A dialectical process', in Cullenberg, S., Amariglio, J. and D.F. Ruccio (eds), *Postmodernism, Economics and Knowledge*, London: Routledge, pp. 61–76.

Dow, S.C. (2004), 'Structured pluralism', *Journal of Economic Methodology*, 11, 275–90.

Dow S.C. (forthcoming), 'A future for schools of thought in heterodox economics', in Harvey, J. and R. Garnett (eds), *Future Directions in Heterodox Economics*, Ann Arbor: University of Michigan Press.

Fullbrook, E. (2003), 'Real science is pluralist', in Fullbrook, E. (ed.), *The Crisis in Economics*, London: Routledge, pp. 118–24.

Garnett, R. (forthcoming), 'Paradigms and pluralism in heterodox economics', in Fullbrook, E. (ed.), *A Handbook of Economic Pluralism*. Cheltenham, UK and Northampton, MA, USA: Edward Elgar.

Gillies, D. (2006), 'Why Research Assessment Exercises are a bad thing', *Post-Autistic Economics Review*, 37, 2–9.

Goodwin, C. (2000), 'Comment: It's the homogeneity, stupid!', *Journal of the History of Economic Thought*, 22, 179–84.

Kantor, B. (1979), 'Rational expectations and economic thought', *Journal of Economic Literature*, 17, 1422–41.

Lawson, T. (1997), *Economics and Reality*, London: Routledge.

Lawson, T. (2003), *Reorienting Economics*, London: Routledge.

Mearman, A. (2005), 'Sheila Dow's concept of dualism: Clarification, criticism and development', *Cambridge Journal of Economics*, 29, 619–34.

McCloskey, D.N. (1986), *The Rhetoric of Economics*, Brighton: Wheatsheaf.

McCloskey, D.N. (1994), *Knowledge and Persuasion in Economics*, Cambridge: Cambridge University Press.

Myrdal, G. (1953), *The Philosophical Element in the Development of Economic Theory*, London: Routledge & Keegan Paul.

Pencavel, J. (1991), 'Prospects for economics', *Economic Journal*, 101, 81–7.

Phelps, E.S. (1990), *Seven Schools of Macroeconomic Thought*, Oxford: Oxford University Press.

Salanti, A. and E. Screpanti (eds) (1997), *Pluralism in Economics*, Cheltenham, UK and Northampton, MA, USA: Edward Elgar.

Weintraub, E.R. (1985), *General Equilibrium Analysis*, Cambridge: Cambridge University Press.

Weintraub, E.R. (1999), 'How should we write the history of twentieth-century economics?' *Oxford Review of Economic Policy*, 15, 139–52.

3. Elements of a monetary theory of production

Trevor Evans, Michael Heine and Hansjörg Herr

3.1. INTRODUCTION

The current dominance of Neoclassical economics continues a tradition of economic analysis characterized by an adulatory attitude to the market that has held sway, almost uninterruptedly, for over 200 years. The idea of a self-regulating market system, of which Adam Smith was one of the most prominent early proponents, has been developed by more recent Neoclassical writers using ever more sophisticated mathematical models, and these are presented today as the last word in economic analysis.

The central concern of Neoclassical economics is the allocation of resources. In this approach, money appears merely as a technical instrument which enables economic processes to function with greater efficiency. The specific forms of social mediation that bind capitalist market economies together and which make it possible for them to function at all are, however, entirely neglected. Neoclassical theory starts by assuming a complete market system, and any notion of uncertainty is excluded by including a set of futures markets which cover every conceivable contingent eventuality that could arise for everything that is transacted. In this approach, a central feature of the process is the hypothetical construct of the Walrasian auctioneer, which ensures that a set of market-clearing prices is established. However, such an auctioneer cannot be regarded simply as a technical aid in constructing a model since it is, in effect, the mechanism which constitutes the market system.

As Keynes noted in his preparatory drafts of the *General Theory*, the theoretical model employed by Neoclassical economics – which he characterized as a 'cooperative economy' – is quite different from the realities of a modern 'entrepreneurial economy'. It is not that the Neoclassical model is different from reality, as is the case with any model, but that it systematically fails to include the central, defining feature of a capitalist economy, namely the advance of money with the aim of making a profit. For this reason, Neoclassical economics is, in effect, concerned with analyzing a dream world.

It is striking that the most sophisticated academic representatives of Neoclassical theory, such as Bliss (1975) or Hahn (1981), repeatedly stress the assumptions that underlie the Neoclassical model, and the limits of applying it to the real world. But the economic experts at business-friendly research institutes and the advisers to governments of virtually every political hue appear to be completely unaware of such limits. On the basis of the Neoclassical dream world, they call for economic policies (the deregulation of markets, cutbacks in welfare provisions) and for individual behavior (flexibility, more self-responsibility, that is, private provision) that are presented as the result of unavoidable economic necessities.

There has, of course, always been opposition to this approach. Perhaps the most systematic criticisms of the Neoclassical approach are those that have been based on the work of Marx and of Keynes. In the case of both, however, the dominant interpretations of their work must be viewed with caution. Thus Marx has frequently been presented as a left-wing representative of the Classical school, who adopted a non-monetary labor theory of value, principally to explain the exploitation of the working class, and a theory of crisis rooted in the questionable (and also non-monetary) law of the tendency of the profit rate to fall. In a comparable way, Keynes's analysis was reduced to the simple IS-LM mechanism, and then, in Samuelson's 'Neoclassical Synthesis', was reincorporated into Neoclassical theory as describing a particular short-term special case – an interpretation which Joan Robinson famously derided as 'bastard Keynesianism'.

For both Marx and Keynes, the dominant interpretations of their work have tended to reduce their analyses to particular cases of, respectively, Classical and Neoclassical theory, and in this way, many of the more innovative features of their thought have become lost. This is particularly true of the importance that both writers gave to the role of money in a capitalist economy. In this chapter, we should like to draw on the ideas of the two writers to suggest a basis for developing a minimum consensus for an alternative to the Neoclassical paradigm.

3.2.   MONEY

Money is a social phenomenon which establishes the specific form of coherence found in a capitalist market economy. This is a notion that is quite missing from most standard Neoclassical approaches to the analysis of money. These begin by positing an economy in which the direct exchange of one commodity for another commodity is already widespread; they then provide some amusing illustration showing the problems faced, for example, by a hungry tailor, who must first search for a baker who happens to need a new jacket before he can satisfy his hunger (the so-called 'double coincidence of wants'); and money is then introduced as a technical medium which can reduce the time involved in such a search procedure, thereby facilitating a reduction in the costs of the exchange process.

Although it is not always made explicit, by introducing money in this way, Neoclassical economics gives analytical priority to money's function as a medium of exchange. Furthermore, this approach is based on the assumption that the introduction of money into a pre-existing exchange economy does not involve any significant change in the basis on which the economy functions. For this reason, money is often referred to as being like a veil, in that it obscures what lies behind it, and Neoclassical economics therefore believes that it is helpful to distinguish between a real and a monetary sphere of the economy. According to this view the most important economic processes occur in the real sphere, and this can be seen and understood most clearly by constructing an analytical model in which money is first left out of the picture. The idea that money does not affect the underlying logic of the economy is captured by the notion of the neutrality of money. Some Neoclassical writers accept that money might have some effect on the real economy in the short run, but all are agreed that, in the long run, money is neutral.

A heterodox view of money has a quite different starting point. According to this approach, there is a fundamental difference between a society which engages in isolated acts of barter and one in which there is an extensive production of commodities for exchange. In an economy where commodities are produced for the purpose of exchange, the decision about what to produce is based on an assessment of the value that the product can realize when it is sold. This presupposes that the society in question has developed some independent means by which the value of the commodity can be expressed – namely money. Accordingly, money is not seen as a something that can be added on to an existing exchange process to reduce the costs of conducting transactions; it is rather viewed as an essential precondition of widespread exchange. In contrast to the Neoclassical approach, it is money's function as a measure of value that is therefore accorded analytical priority (Marx 1867, chapter 3; Keynes 1930, chapter 1). Without a socially accepted means of expressing the value of commodities, it is impossible to establish the proportion in which they should be exchanged. More importantly, once exchange is viewed as a means of obtaining money, it becomes clear that, far from being simply a means of facilitating exchange, the pursuit of money itself becomes a key motivation for economic activity.

For the heterodox approach, the idea that it is helpful to distinguish a real from a monetary sphere of the economy is therefore quite mistaken. On the contrary, the notion of a real economy, devoid of money, will fail to grasp the central, motivating dynamic of a capitalist economy, namely, the advance of money with the aim of making more money. This is the basis for Marx's famous 'general formula' for capital, M – C – M', where money (M) is advanced to purchase commodities (C) which can then be sold for a larger sum of money (M'). Keynes, although he generally disapproved of Marx, quoted this formula approvingly in an early draft of the *General Theory*, and insisted that a monetary economy functions quite differently from what he referred to as a 'real exchange economy' in which money is absent (Keynes 1933).

A key feature of a monetary economy is that the sale of one commodity is not necessarily followed by the purchase of another. In a hypothetical 'real exchange' economy without money, the sale of one product necessarily involves the simultaneous purchase of another product. However, in a monetary economy, it is possible for some producers to sell a product for money and then to hold on to the money, at least for a time. This, of course, implies that some other producers will be unable to sell their products, which may lead them to reduce their level of output and employment. For Marx, the separation of a sale from a purchase in a monetary economy was the basis for what he referred to as *the possibility of crisis*. He used this term because, at the time when he was writing, a generalized inability to sell goods occurred with a certain regularity, and this could set off a chain of payment defaults that led to bank failures and a financial crisis (Marx 1867, p. 209). For Keynes, the possibility that a sale might not be followed by a purchase was the basis for his emphasis on the importance of *uncertainty* in understanding how a capitalist economy functions (Keynes 1936, chapter 12). Uncertainty permeates Keynes's view of capitalism, affecting wealth owners, banks, entrepreneurs and workers, and he believed that the action these groups take to protect themselves from uncertainty can be a major source of economic and financial instability.

The most unstable form of expenditure in product markets is that associated with investment in fixed capital. Such investment invariably involves a considerable risk, since it means taking a position in fixed assets which cannot easily be reversed, except at a substantial loss. Yet firms must make investment decisions on the basis of judgments about the future – in many cases, several years hence – which are subject to considerable uncertainty. The expected profitability of a project is subject, not only to the vagaries of a particular product market, but – and often more so – to the overall macroeconomic situation. Furthermore, a firm must also take a view about the future rate of interest on the capital market. Since neither the future profitability of a project nor the future rate of interest can be known with any certainty, firms are required to make a leap of faith.

In practice, firms' investment decisions are strongly influenced by the overall business climate, and there is, as a result, a marked tendency for investment to bunch. When overall investment is weak, firms will tend to be cautious; when the outlook begins to improve, firms will tentatively increase their investment; when output is rising strongly, investment can boom, perhaps spurred on by rising asset prices in financial or property markets. But declining profitability, rising interest rates, a reversal of asset prices, or simply overcapacity can bring such a boom to an abrupt end and precipitate a renewed downturn in investment. The instability of investment is the principal reason why economic development under capitalism does not occur along a stable growth path, but is rather marked by recurrent cycles, in which periods of growth and rising prosperity are interspersed with periods of recession.

The impact of uncertainty can also be a significant factor in determining the consumption spending of households. The most obvious example of this is that workers who fear that their jobs might be at risk are less likely to undertake discretionary purchases, especially of consumer durable goods. Cuts in a country's unemployment insurance benefits, as recently introduced in Germany, can also increase workers' sense of insecurity, and encourage them to save a larger proportion of their income so as to provide a greater shield against an uncertain future. Where asset prices have an important influence on household consumption – as has been the case with house prices in the US since the 'dot.com' boom ended – uncertainty as to the future course of prices can also have an impact on the level of consumption spending.

In addition to the effects of uncertainty in product markets, it also plays a major role in determining the behavior of financial investors in asset markets. Since the value of financial assets is highly dependent on expectations about the future, they can be subject to large shifts in valuation. As financial investors seek to second-guess the market, this can lead to huge shifts in the holdings of different types of financial asset, as capital is moved back and forth between shares, bonds and bank deposits, and between one currency and another. Such shifts can have a significant impact on interest rates and the availability of finance, and are a major source of financial instability.

3.3.   CREDIT AND BANKING

Just as widespread exchange presupposes the existence of money, so a capitalist economy also presupposes the existence of credit. This is not just a practical matter of the day-to-day functioning of the economy – something that any Neoclassical economist would agree with – enabling, for example, the idle funds of one firm to be put to profitable use by another. Rather the necessity of credit arises as a result of the specific expansionary dynamic of a capitalist economy. A capitalist firm advances a certain amount of money for fixed capital, raw materials and wage costs, and – supposing the process is successful – it produces commodities which can be sold for the original sum of money plus a profit. For the economy as a whole, the sale of the finished products therefore requires more money than was initially advanced, and this need for additional money is met through the creation of credit.

As the profits (or at least a part of them) are reinvested to expand the scale of production, so the economy grows, giving rise to the highly dynamic character displayed by capitalism in certain phases. Credit is able to supply a supremely flexible supply of money that can expand as necessary in accordance with the rhythm of profits, investment and growth. In this way, it avoids the limitations that would be faced by a purely commodity system of money.

The existence of credit in a capitalist economy has two important consequences. The first concerns the rate of interest. A firm that employs credit to finance part of its activities is subsequently required to pay one part of the profit it generates with the borrowed funds in interest. As a result, the rate of interest comes to play a key role in the economy since it sets the minimum rate of return that a firm is normally required to achieve when it invests. The second consequence is that, although credit is a necessary feature of capitalism, it also introduces a significant source of instability into the economy. Credit involves an advance against future expected revenues but, as noted above, the future is uncertain. As with investment in fixed capital, the expansion of credit is strongly cyclical, and as Minsky (1986) has shown, is prone to serious overexpansion when a business upturn is proceeding strongly. The danger is that the onset of a business downturn can lead to payment difficulties, and set off a chain of defaults. This can disrupt the complex web of obligations on which the credit system rests and, because of the central role of money in a capitalist economy, threaten to provoke a major economic crisis.

In response to the experience of financial crises during the nineteenth and early twentieth century, which culminated in the 1929 crash, the monetary system that has emerged as the most adequate in a modern capitalist economy is based on a state-owned Central Bank, and a set of independent commercial banks.

The Central Bank is responsible for issuing currency and it acts as banker to the commercial banks. Commercial banks can obtain currency by making a withdrawal in cash from their account at the Central Bank. The Central Bank provides loans to the commercial banks, predominantly in the form of open market operations. Commercial banks can also borrow additional funds from the Central Bank (typically overnight) on the security of high-grade bonds, but at a slightly higher interest rate as a result of the Central Bank's function as 'lender of last resort'. When the Central Bank provides the commercial banks with loans, it creates deposits at the Central Bank, and these deposits function as the commercial banks' reserves. Because the Central Bank is the ultimate source of finance for the commercial banks, the interest rate that the Central Bank sets for its loans has a decisive influence on the interest rate that the commercial banks charge for loans to their customers.

The defining feature of the commercial banks is that they accept deposits from, and make loans to, firms and households. In a developed capitalist economy, most payments are made by transferring deposits from one bank account to another. Within this system, commercial banks play a key role in determining the total volume of deposits. When a commercial bank extends a loan to a customer, it credits his or her account with a deposit, and this deposit can then be used to make a payment to another account. In this way, commercial banks create deposits and thereby increase the total volume of deposits in the commercial banking system.

Far from the passive role envisaged in simple analyses of the money multiplier, the commercial banks are actively involved on a day-to-day basis in the dynamics of the money supply process. In the first place, it is the commercial banks that have to make the decisions as to whether to extend credit to particular customers. Banks make such a decision on the basis of the information that is available to them but, as Joseph Stiglitz has stressed in his writings on information asymmetry, the banks are always less fully informed than a potential borrower, and this can give rise to the phenomena of credit rationing (Stiglitz and Greenwald 2003). At the same time, the commercial banks have to manage their overall assets, deciding whether to grant further loans, or whether instead to increase their holdings of other assets, such as bonds or short-term securities, that can easily be sold if the bank itself is in need of liquid funds. This process is emphasized by Victoria Chick, who refers to it in terms of banks' liquidity preference (Chick and Dow 2002).

The commercial banks are themselves usually motivated by profit maximization, and this can result in a pattern of extending loans that is strongly pro-cyclical. There is a marked tendency for banks to increase the supply of loans strongly in the expansionary phase of the business cycle, when returns seem more assured, but to adopt a much more restrictive position when the economy is facing a downturn – a time when many firms might be in urgent need of additional finance. In this way, the commercial banks can contribute to exacerbating the uncertain, crisis prone nature of capitalist growth.

In many countries, the Central Bank requires the commercial banks to maintain a minimum amount of reserves in relation to the size of their deposits. Minimum reserve requirements were originally introduced in order to ensure that commercial banks would always have sufficient funds available to meet their customers' withdrawals, but such a requirement is not a necessary feature of the system. In some countries, such as Canada, there are no longer minimum reserve requirements, and in those countries that have reserve requirements, these are very low (3 per cent in the US; 2 per cent in the European Central Bank (ECB) zone). However, commercial banks do need to keep some reserves at the Central Bank in order for them to be able to clear payments from accounts at their own bank to accounts at other commercial banks.

It is important to note that, where the Central Bank imposes a minimum reserve requirement, commercial banks can always borrow additional reserves through the 'lender of last resort' facility. Furthermore, if the Central Bank does not provide the commercial banking system with sufficient reserves, commercial banks will compete with each other in the inter-bank money market for the reserves that are available, and this will drive up the inter-bank interest rate which, in turn, will be reflected in the rate of interest that banks charge their customers for loans. The US Federal Reserve did introduce a policy which attempted to control the supply of reserves to the commercial banking system in 1979, but this led to such great interest-rate volatility that the experiment was effectively ended in 1982, and explicitly abandoned in 1984.

The reality of the modern banking system is sharply at odds with the assumptions of the quantity theory of money. In the first place, the Central Bank does not have direct control over the money supply. The volume of deposits in the banking system will depend on the demand for credit by firms and households, and the extent to which the banks are willing to meet this demand. The Central Bank only has indirect control over the expansion of bank deposits insofar as it can influence the demand for loans through its ability to set short-term interest rates. If the Central Bank raises interest rates, this can sometimes initially lead to an increase in the demand for credit, since the working costs of firms are increased. However, there is always some level of interest rates at which the demand for credit will collapse, thereby leading to a recession. But the opposite is not always true. If the Central Bank lowers interest rates, this will only lead to a monetary expansion if firms or households respond by increasing their demand for loans.

A second problem with the quantity theory arises from making an analytical separation between a real and a monetary sphere of the economy. It is assumed that, provided market forces are allowed to act, the real sphere of the economy will operate at a level of output and employment that is at, or close to full capacity. By contrast, the monetary sphere is viewed principally in terms of money's function as a medium of exchange in product markets. It follows that, if the economy is already working at close to full capacity, a monetary expansion will raise aggregate demand and thereby lead to an increase in the price level. If, however, the economy is working at below full capacity – as has usually been the case under capitalism – an expansion in the supply of credit can have a positive influence on output and employment.

A third problem with the quantity theory arises from its tendency to focus on product markets to the detriment of money's important role in asset markets, in particular, the markets for financial assets. There are two aspects here. One is that, in a modern capitalist economy with a highly developed financial system, money also plays a very important role as a means of exchange in transactions involving bonds or other financial assets. The scale of these transactions is very large, but also far more volatile than is the case in product markets. This is because a change – or even an expected change – in the price of bonds or shares can spark a large shift in the composition of the assets held by financial investors, and lead to a very marked increase in the scale of financial transactions. The second aspect arises because money is not just a means of payment, but also a store of value. This involves conceiving of money in terms of what Keynes referred to as an asset, and what Marx termed capital. In both cases, money is itself a form of holding wealth that can be more attractive than other forms, particularly when other forms of holding wealth threaten a capital loss. This too can lead to large shifts between the holding of financial securities and money, and between one currency and another. Both aspects explain why the velocity of circulation of money is not constant, as assumed by the quantity theory of money.

3.4. PRODUCTION AND EMPLOYMENT

The decision by a firm to advance money for investment is the decisive factor in mobilizing the process of production, in creating employment and in generating income. Income in turn provides the basis for consumer demand, for paying taxes and for savings.

In the short term, output is determined by the expected aggregate demand. In addition to spending on investment and consumption, aggregate demand is influenced by the state, directly through its expenditure on providing public services and infrastructure, and indirectly through its policies on taxation and social insurance contributions. There is also a further important indirect effect on demand through the distribution of income, since a redistribution of income in favor of lower-income groups tends to increase domestic demand, as higher-income groups have a higher propensity to save. Finally, overall demand is also influenced by the net demand for exports from abroad. Saving raises the possibility of a deficiency in aggregate demand. The only condition under which such a deficiency will not occur is if the amount that is saved is compensated for by some other form of expenditure, such as investment.

There are several important points that are raised by this approach. First, it implies that the Neoclassical idea that saving must precede investment is not true. In a capitalist economy, thanks to the banking system, production can be financed by credit, and is not dependent on prior savings. Second, it also challenges the theoretical claim, known as Say's Law, that supply creates its own demand. Since the value of an economy's output corresponds to the income it generates, it is true that, in principal, there is sufficient income to provide a demand for the total output. But Say's Law is premised on the notion of a capital market in which the rate of interest adjusts to ensure that investment and savings are brought into equilibrium. In this way, income that is not spent on consumption will be spent on investment and demand will equal supply. This is, however, an invalid assumption. In a monetary economy characterized by uncertainty, where the banking system plays a key role in making decisions about whether to advance credit, there is no automatic mechanism that brings planned savings and investment into equilibrium.

For the heterodox approach, the relation between supply and demand is exactly the opposite of that proposed by Say's Law. Consequently, an increase in demand will – assuming underutilized capacity – lead to an increase in output and employment. The only exception is when an economy is at, or close to, full capacity utilization, in which case an increase in demand can lead to higher prices.

Once firms have decided to aim for a particular level of output, this will determine their demand for workers in the labor market. If the working time is given, the demand for labor will be determined by the planned level of output, and the level of labor productivity. If planned production is designated with Y, the average productivity per worker with π, and the number of employed workers with N, then it follows that $N = Y/\pi$. Expressed in terms of growth, it follows that $\dot{N} = \dot{Y} - \dot{\pi}$. If the rate of economic growth is higher (or lower) than the rate of growth of labor productivity, employment will rise (or fall).

The relation between economic growth and employment is demonstrated by the rise in unemployment in Western Europe since the 1970s. Although the rate of productivity growth has in fact declined since then, the rate of economic growth has remained even lower. If this trend continues, an employment disaster will only be avoided if working time is reduced, or if the rate of productivity growth is reduced.[1] This problem would become even more acute if, for ecological reasons, a lower rate of economic growth was aimed for.

According to the heterodox analysis, there is no market mechanism which ensures that involuntary unemployment can be avoided. Whether a given level of labor productivity and a given aggregate demand will result in a level of output that provides employment for everyone seeking work is an open question, both theoretically and practically. The history of capitalism has shown this with unmistakable clarity.

This approach is very different from the Neoclassical analysis of the labor market, in which a flexible real wage is able to ensure full employment. In fact, in the heterodox approach, the labor market is not really a market in the normal sense of the word, since the usual market relation between prices and quantities is absent. In the case of the labor supply, the over-whelming majority of workers do not have a choice about whether or not to take a job. At the same time, the demand for labor is determined in a hierarchical system, in which the financial markets stand over the product market, and the product market stands over the labor market.

There are a number of ways in which the Neoclassical analysis can be criticized. First, as Keynes pointed out (Keynes 1936, p. 11), wage negotiations can only agree on nominal wages. The resulting real wage only becomes clear once the price level is known. Real wages are, consequently, not the outcome just of wage negotiations but also of processes involving the complete market system. For this reason, even workers are not able to achieve a reduction in the real wage, should they try to out of a misplaced sense of responsibility for the labor market. This is shown by the case of Japan in the second half of the 1990s, when reductions in nominal wages led to a decline, not in the real wage, but in the price level. For this reason, it is a mistake for workers to restrain their nominal wage demands during a recession.

This leads to a second problem. The Neoclassical analysis of the labor market implies that changes in wages have no effect on prices, even though they are undoubtedly a cost for the firm. It goes without saying that an increase in the price of oil, or of sales taxes, or of any other costs that a firm has to pay will be passed on in higher prices. Quite why this is not also the case with wage costs is unclear. In practice, a close relation between changes in unit labor costs and changes in the price level can be observed in the developed capitalist countries (Heine *et al.* 2006).

A third criticism of the Neoclassical approach to the labor market is its widespread failure to account for the way that capitalism has actually developed historically. With the exception of quite specific instances, such as the post-war 'Golden Age' in the advanced capitalist countries, unemployment has been a persistent feature of all capitalist countries since the rise of industrial capitalism in the 18th and 19th centuries. It is difficult to believe that, whatever the political regime or the economic policy of the day, unemployment is always explained by a labor market failure arising from an incorrect real wage.

On the basis of these criticisms, the Neoclassical analysis of the labor market, and the variations proposed by writers associated with the neoclassical synthesis and, more recently, the so-called New Keynesian approach, must be firmly rejected. The idea that employment policy should focus on real wages carries the danger that it will lead, not to full employment, but rather to deflation.[2]

3.5.   THE PRICE LEVEL AND THE DISTRIBUTION OF INCOME

Following the tradition of Keynes (1930), Kalecki (1954) and Kaldor (1960), in a developed capitalist economy with underutilized capacity the price level is principally determined by costs and firms' mark-up.

For the economy as a whole, wages are the most important component of costs, since wage costs also influence the cost of intermediate products and of fixed capital. In a closed economy, this leads to a close relation between unit wage costs, unit costs and the price level. In the event that unit wage costs rise, firms will usually attempt to maintain their mark-up by raising prices. In the event of a decline in unit wage costs, prices might fall, but this can be a more sluggish process, depending on the degree of competition in product markets. For this reason, a productivity-oriented wage policy is the most appropriate means of ensuring price stability. In practice, this means that nominal wages should rise at a rate equal to the trend growth rate of labor productivity plus the target rate of inflation.

The bargaining power of workers is linked to the level of unemployment. As unemployment falls in the course of a business expansion, firms are only able to attract additional staff if they offer better rates of pay. In such a situation, workers – or their union representatives – are in a stronger position to push for higher nominal wage increases. If wages should increase by more than that associated with a productivity-oriented wage policy, this can lead to firms raising their prices. If workers should then increase their wage demands to compensate, a wage–price spiral can be set in motion.

In addition to wages, the other basic cost that faces firms in the developed capitalist countries is that of imported raw materials. These are produced predominantly in developing countries, and the developed countries have benefited greatly from relatively depressed prices for many primary products for much of the last twenty or so years – something that is closely linked to the policy of expanding raw-material exports that developing countries have been obliged to follow in order to qualify for loans from the World Bank and other international organizations. When primary commodity prices do rise, firms invariably pass this increase on by raising their prices.

There are two other factors that affect costs which can be mentioned here. One concerns sales taxes, any increase in which is virtually always passed on in increased prices. The other is the exchange rate, which affects the cost of imported products, and is particularly serious for small countries and for developing countries, which generally have a relatively high import quota. A depreciation of the currency, by making imports more expensive, tends to reduce the real wage. If workers manage to compensate for this by achieving higher nominal wages, and firms attempt to protect their mark-up by raising prices, it will lead to higher inflation, which in turn can promote a further depreciation of the currency.

The extent to which increases in costs result in increased prices depends on the mark-up, and the ability of firms to maintain their mark-up. Various factors enter into the determination of the mark-up:

- Firms strive to achieve a rate of profit that is not less than the rate of interest.
- Firms will normally only invest in a project if they expect to achieve a premium above the rate of interest to compensate for the risk involved in conducting their business.
- The size of the mark-up is influenced by the market structure, with higher mark-ups in markets characterized by a high degree of oligopoly or monopoly. In such markets, leading firms can benefit from additional profits through strategies of product differentiation and through bringing innovative products to the market before other firms.
- The ability of firms to raise prices is influenced by the extent of international competition in product markets.
- A shift in institutional power within capitalism can lead to a change in the mark-up. An example of this is the way that institutional investors have strengthened their position in the last two decades, effectively pressuring firms to increase their profitability so that the benefits could be distributed to share holders.

The ability of firms to pass on increased costs is also influenced by the degree of capacity utilization. If demand in product markets is strong, and capacity utilization is high, firms are more able to pass on any increase in costs and, indeed, to raise prices by more than the increase in costs, thereby obtaining windfall profits. On the other hand, if demand is relatively weak, and capacity utilization is low, then firms might not be able to pass on increases in costs, and they will be obliged to accept a lower mark-up.

From the analysis presented here, it follows that the distribution of income cannot be explained in terms of the marginal product of labor, or of some fictitious bargaining over the real wage. Rather, it is the result of a complex process which cannot be analyzed without also taking account of the price level. If firms were always able to maintain their mark-up, wage bargaining would have a relatively limited impact on the distribution of income. However, in a dynamic world, where wages and prices are changing at rates which are at least slightly different, and where such changes do not occur with quite the same tempo, then the outcome can lead to changes in the distribution of income. In recent years, this has led to a notable increase in the share of income accruing to profits in many developed countries. Under different conditions, it is possible that the share of income accruing to workers might increase. But in a capitalist economy there is a crucial asymmetry. If workers should increase their share of income beyond a certain point, firms will cease to invest and, as unemployment rises, workers tend to retreat from their wage demands and to focus on defending their jobs.

3.6.   TREND AND CYCLE

In a capitalist economy, there is no underlying, long-term growth path around which actual growth fluctuates in the short term, as a Neoclassical notion of the production function would hold. Rather, it is the pattern of short-term business cycles that determines the way the economy grows in the long term. There is, consequently, also no potential output – even viewed as a long-term tendency – that sets a physical limit to growth. On the contrary, the more that is invested, the more the economy will grow. Consequently, the productive potential of an economy is not something that is given, but is instead the result of the investment process. But investment, as already noted, is subject to marked fluctuations, and so any notion of a stable long-term growth path of the economy's productive potential is quite mistaken.

Attempts to measure an economy's productive potential faces various difficulties. There is, in the first place, a methodological problem, since heterogeneous fixed capital can only be aggregated in monetary units. In this case, however, the value of the capital stock – and hence of the productive potential – would vary with changes in the interest rate and the distribution of income (Sraffa 1960). Partly for this reason, the productive potential is usually measured by simply extrapolating past growth into the future. But this also presents problems. Previous growth was the outcome of the economic policies adopted in the past, as well as a host of one-off factors. In the future, it is possible to adopt different policies that could enable the economy to grow more rapidly. If monetary policy, for instance, is guided by some pre-given notion of an economy's productive potential, then growth might be unnecessarily constrained, and the result would appear to confirm the initial assumption of the economy's potential!

This points to the necessity for an active economic policy that adopts a discretionary approach to actual historical developments. Joan Robinson made this point clearly:

> Keynes was very interested only in very short-period questions (he used to say 'The long period is a subject for undergraduates') and so for him the distinction between making comparisons of the structure of different positions and tracing the consequences of change was perhaps not so very important . . . But when it comes to long-run questions the distinction is indispensable, and those who learnt to float in the smooth waters of equilibrium find the requirements of historical analysis very uncomfortable. We are still slipping and floundering about like ducks who have alighted on a pond and found it frozen over. (Robinson 1962, p. 75)

What is necessary is an economic policy that pays attention to the short- and medium-term stabilization of the economy, rather than simply trusting in the self-regulating capacity of markets.

3.7. THE LIMITS OF ECONOMIC POLICY

Debates about economic policy are generally characterized by two opposing positions. One of these is the Neoclassical position, which stresses the inherent stability of markets, and for which the best economic policy involves leaving as much as possible to the market, with as little intervention as possible. Since this leaves a relatively limited role for the state, taxation and public borrowing should remain low. According to this approach, the efficiency of the market system will, provided markets are sufficiently flexible, of itself ensure full employment and the optimal allocation of resources.

In opposition to this is the standard Keynesian position which held sway after the Second World War, some features of which have been taken up more recently by what are known as New Keynesians.[3] This type of approach emphasizes market imperfections (in particular in financial and labor markets), and therefore supports state intervention in the economy. Low interest rates and credit-financed public investments during a recession are supposed to lead to an economic upturn so that, as tax payments rise in the subsequent expansion, the state can pay back its loans. According to this view, state intervention to stabilize the inherently unstable economy is not only necessary, but also promises success. Full employment and a high rate of return for capital are not seen as mutually exclusive and, if the public investment which is used to stabilize the economy is deployed in the right branches, it is thought that a high level of technical and social development can be promoted.

What both approaches have in common is the idea that, if only the right economic policy is employed, it is possible to achieve a healthy economy without unemployment in which both capitalists and their employees can be satisfied. The approach proposed by the pro-marketeers fails to achieve its goal because markets only function smoothly in a model based on very restrictive assumptions (perfect competition, complete information, existence of a complete set of contingent markets, an auctioneer and so on), which bears little relation to the reality of a capitalist economy. Although the standard Keynesian approach initially appears to be somewhat closer to the reality of capitalism, it too faces serious limits. Whether, and to what extent, low interest rates and public investment will be effective depends on a host of factors, including the degree of capacity utilization, the legacy of inflation, consumer behavior and, perhaps most importantly, the extent to which the economy is internationally integrated, which has major implications for trade, investment and the exchange rate. Expansionary policies, therefore, do not offer a guaranteed recipe for success.

Furthermore, even if full employment, price stability and high profitability were (somewhat exceptionally) to be achieved, this would not be sustainable. Full employment, or at least strongly rising employment, is usually accompanied by rising nominal wages, either because unions take advantage of their stronger bargaining position, or because employers have to compete for increasingly scarce workers. Rising nominal wages can have a number of consequences. If firms are able to pass on the increased wage costs by raising prices, it can lead to a wage-price spiral to which the central bank will at some point react by raising interest rates in order to defend the value of the currency. This can lead to a recession that will successfully reduce inflation, but at the cost of higher unemployment. If firms cannot pass on the cost of higher wages, then profitability will decline. Then firms are likely either to seek for other investment possibilities, in which case economic growth and employment will be reduced, or to increase their investment in fixed capital so as to replace workers, which will also reduce employment.

There is also another major factor that both Neoclassical and standard Keynesian analyses have in common: both fail to take account of the fundamental differences of interest that exist in a capitalist economy. Workers have a direct interest in full employment. This improves their collective bargaining position (both as regards wages and working conditions) as well as the opportunities faced by each individual worker. Capitalists, on the other hand, do not share this interest in full employment. On the contrary, a certain level of unemployment not only dampens the collective bargaining power of the employed; it also serves to exert greater discipline over each individual employee. Since the threat of unemployment is usually enough to persuade workers to make concessions, and since this appears to be the result of objective economic conditions, it is a much more effective form of pressure than even the most favorable laws. The much-loved public appeals for a joint approach to fighting unemployment are therefore misguided.

The owners of financial assets are interested, above all, in maintaining the value of money (that is, low inflation) and a high return on their assets. For low inflation, however, it is not full employment, but a certain degree of unemployment that is most effective, as noted above. And high returns on financial assets must be earned somewhere. This means that – apart from short-term speculative gains – they can only be paid if the rate of profit is high.

Industrial and commercial capitalists also have an interest in a high rate of profit, rather than full employment. From the perspective of an individual firm, a high rate of profit is more likely if wages are as low as possible and workers have minimal legal protection, and if taxes and social security contributions are kept down. Of course, aggregate demand will suffer if wages and public spending are depressed. But, for an individual firm, policies that are motivated by a concern for the overall economy are not very rational. By contrast, an increase in costs (through higher wages, or taxes) raises the prospect of very unwelcome effects.

An adequate rate of profit is, however, not just in the interest of the employers' side; in a capitalist economy, it is a structural necessity that is also apparent to workers. It is only if expected profitability is sufficiently high that firms will invest, that jobs will be created and, in the end, that wages will be increased. While the interest in full employment is limited to the workers' side, strong profitability is a general social interest – so long as we are concerned with a capitalist society.

The structural necessity for profits is also something that affects the policies pursued by the state. Because a high tax take and low social spending are only certain during the expansionary phase of the business cycle, economic policy – especially in a recession – tends to concentrate on measures that can produce a quick improvement in profitability, such as a reduction in the taxation or social security contributions levied on capitalists, or a weakening of employment protection legislation. If this is combined with an obsession with balancing the budget, then lower taxes implies cuts in public spending, which usually leads to reductions in public-sector spending on wages and in social benefits. An improvement in the position of employees, by contrast, is only likely when there is a relatively protracted period of strong growth.

The challenge facing a progressive economic policy is to develop proposals that reduce the financial instability of a capitalist economy; that contribute to improving employment opportunities, working conditions and the distribution of income; and that will point forward towards an economy which is not driven primarily by the incessant search for ways of increasing the profits of a minority of capitalist wealth owners at the expense of the working and living conditions of the great majority of the population.

NOTES

1. Neo-liberal policies strive to lower the rate of growth of productivity by creating low-wage sectors of employment that can meet the rising demand for personal services, such as household help. The development of labor-intensive, but well-paid jobs in the service sector could create employment in various branches of the service sector without resorting to low-paid jobs.
2. For the classic statement of the dangers of deflation, see Fisher (1933).
3. In contrast to Keynes and the standard Keynesians, new Keynesians support the view that macroeconomic analysis should be founded on Neoclassical microeconomic analysis.

REFERENCES

Bliss, C.J. (1975), *Capital Theory and the Distribution of Income*, New York: North Holland Publishing.
Chick, V. and S. Dow (2002), 'Monetary policy with endogenous money and liquidity preference: A non-dualistic treatment', *Journal of Post Keynesian Economics*, 24(4), 587–605.
Fisher, I. (1933), 'The debt deflation theory of the Great Depression', *Econometrica*, 1, 337–57.
Hahn, F. (1981), 'General equilibrium theory', in Bell, D. and I. Kristol (eds), The *Crisis in Economic Theory*, New York: Basic Books.
Heine, M., Herr, H. and C. Kaiser (2006), *Wirtschaftspolitische Regime westlicher Industrienationen,* Marburg: Metropolis Verlag.
Kaldor, N. (1960), *Essays on Value and Distribution*, London: Duckworth.
Kalecki, M. [1954] (1965), *Theory of Economic Dynamics*, New York: Augustus Kelley.

Keynes, J.M. [1930] (1971), *Treatise on Money, Vol. 1: The Pure Theory of Money: Collected Writings, Vol. V*, London: Macmillan.

Keynes, J.M. [1933] (1973), *A Monetary Theory of Production: Collected Writings, Vol. XIII*, London: Macmillan.

Keynes, J.M. [1936] (1973), *The General Theory of Employment, Interest and Money: Collected Writings, Vol. VII*, London: Macmillan.

Marx, K. [1867] (1976), *Capital, Vol. 1*, Harmondsworth: Penguin Books.

Minsky, H.P. (1982), *Can 'It' Happen Again? Essays on Instability and Finance*, Armonk, NY: M.E. Sharpe.

Minsky, H.P. (1986), *Stabilizing an Unstable Economy*, London: Yale University Press.

Robinson, J. (1962), *Economic Philosophy*, Harmondsworth: Penguin Books.

Sraffa, P. (1960), *The Production of Commodities by Means of Commodities*, Cambridge: Cambridge University Press.

Stiglitz, J. and B. Greenwald (2003), *Towards a New Paradigm in Monetary Economics*, Cambridge: Cambridge University Press.

4. The monetary circuit approach: a stock-flow consistent model*

Jean-Vincent Accoce and Tarik Mouakil

The aim of this chapter is to present the stock-flow consistent approach (SFC) developed by Lavoie and Godley (2001–2002) and to show that, in accordance with Lavoie's assertion, this method makes it possible to model and to understand better the so-called Circuit theory.[1] The first section presents the main principles of the Circuit school and some of the criticisms related to this approach: lack of formalism, omission of stocks and only basic analysis of the banking system. The second section proposes a model that tries to represent the Circuit theory and to remedy some of its deficiencies. We use this macroeconomic model in order to study the effectiveness of various policies.

4.1. A CIRCUIT SCHOOL PRESENTATION AND CRITICISMS

The basis of the monetary circuit of production is directly inspired from Books 1 and 2 of John Maynard Keynes's *General Theory of Employment, Money and Interest*, published in 1936. In this work, considered as the core of the Keynesian revolution, the author from Cambridge gives money a key role in economic system regulation. So do the Circuitists. In opposition to the Neoclassicists or the Neo-Keynesians, they reject the idea of an economy based on exchange. They analyze the economy as a monetary economy of production and thus they can be seen as real heirs of the Keynesian theory.

Today, economists and politicians pay little attention to Circuitist analysis. This lack of interest can be explained by the limitations inherent to circuitist analysis. According to Lavoie (1987), the main limitation of this current, which can explain why it collapsed in the early 1990s, is the extreme heterogeneity of Circuitist developments. The Circuitists never managed to agree upon fundamental hypotheses and did not build a real school. Then, even if the Circuitist point of view is very close to John Maynard Keynes's theory, this current failed to gather all Keynesians.

First, we will focus on the shared propositions of the Circuitists. Then we will deal with the limitations or the unanswered questions of this school.

4.1.1 Circuitist Propositions: A Monetary Economy of Production

As Lavoie (1987) argued, the 'Circuitist School' does not really exist. The Circuitists mainly agree upon the importance of money in the economy. They never managed to find common fundamental hypotheses, never found a leader and never induced dissidence. Why do we call them 'Circuitists', if they have not managed to form a joint school versus the Neo-Keynesian school and sometimes do not even consider themselves Circuitists?

As we said, these authors reject the idea of an economy ruled by exchange. In the mainstream conception, the only function of money is to allow for exchange. Dostaler (2005, p. 309) insisted that Keynes rightly remarked that money is not only a 'pivot' as the Classicists and the Neoclassicists think (Keynes 1933, pp. 408–9). In his eyes, money has three functions:

- It helps economic actors to exchange.
- It is a transaction unit.
- It is a store of value.

This last function, ignored by Classicists, is perfectly integrated by Keynes in his theory. According to him, money is the link between present and future. Anyone has the choice to spend his money now or to save it in order to spend it later. The Circuitists emphasize this Keynesian vision of money in their developments. They give money a key role in the economic system. As Parguez shows in his work, if we integrate money into the analysis, we must reject the equilibrium analysis and use a monetary circuit (Parguez and Seccarecia 2000, Parguez and Ducros 1975). Even if the Circuitists do not represent a proper school, they do agree about a number of propositions. We can list two shared ones: endogenous money and priority of macroeconomic laws.

Endogenous money and the finance motive
Endogeneity of money is linked to production needs. As Rochon and Rossi (2004, p. 144) said:

> In a monetary economy of production, credit is needed to enable firms to continue and expand production. There is a definitive link between bank credit and economic growth.

Actually, the Circuitists give a key role to credit and therefore to the finance function in the economy. This function is essential to production. The Circuitists are convinced that finance appears twice in the monetary circuit: before the production process and during the production process (in the circuit).

Before they start producing, entrepreneurs need to borrow money from banks. This is what Graziani (1990) calls *initial finance*. This step is fundamental in Circuitist analysis because it is the first monetary flow that appears in the circuit. In the Circuitists' conceptions, money is created to answer entrepreneurs' anticipations. During the production process entrepreneurs recover part of the income generated by production (investment, consumption, saving). This is *final finance* (Graziani 1990). At this stage, entrepreneurs can pay back their loans.

The endogenous character of money appears at the first step of the circuit. Actually, money creation does not depend on a money supply function but on firms' needs and entrepreneurs' anticipations of sales.

Using a monetary circuit involves a hierarchy between macroeconomic agents and a temporal perspective. In its first phase, money creation and all activities are linked to this creation. Step by step, after money creation, economic activity appears in the circuit and makes possible relationships between macroeconomic agents. This idea is shared by all the circuitists and probably represents the originality of their developments.

Macroeconomic laws
Poulon (1982) argues that the microeconomic method of integrating money is wrong. In his view, we cannot consider money in the economy in the light of a money supply function. This method would be right if money were – as the classicists think – a simple good which enables exchange. But money has a store of value function which can only be considered in a macroeconomic view. Money is a macroeconomic phenomenon so that the integration of money into the analysis cannot take place with a microeconomic method. According to the Circuitists, the correct macroeconomic method to integrate money in the economy is to consider money creation.

The consequences of using this method are important because Circuitist analyses show that the structural relationships that exist between macroeconomic agents are totally independent from rational microeconomic behavior. The most important one is the reversal of the traditional causality between saving and investment. From a microeconomic point of view, investment is dependent on saving. Poulon (2000) underlines that this causality vanishes when we use a macroeconomic method. This macroeconomic law, supposed to be the core of the Keynesian revolution, can be perfectly understood using the monetary circuit of production.

4.1.2 Limitations of Circuitist Developments

Basically, we can point out three limitations of the Circuitist approach: lack of formalism, only a basic analysis of the banking system and omission of stocks.

Lack of formalism
One problem of Circuitist developments is that there is almost no formalization of the monetary circuit approach. In the second section of this chapter we propose a model that tries to represent the circuit theory on the basis of the framework proposed by Poulon (1982). Using Books 1 and 2 of Keynes's *General Theory*, Poulon reduces the economy to three basic functions: finance, production and consumption. The economy is regulated by these three functions and relationships between them are established through monetary flows.

Functions
- Banks: finance.
- Firms: production.
- Households: consumption.

Flows
- ΔF: initial finance.
- U: user cost.
- I: firms' net investment.
- Y: household income. We suppose that household income is composed of wages and shared profit: $Y = W + Pd$.
- C: household consumption.
- S: household saving.

We can follow a representative monetary unit along the circuit in Figure 4.1. This unit is created by banks (ΔF). Once in the production pole it is split into two. The first is a monetary flow oriented to firms themselves. In order to produce, firms need to invest in equipment goods (I), raw material (CI) and in maintenance of their own equipment (CCF). Poulon supposes that these last two costs represent the Keynesian *User Cost* (U), described in Chapter 6 of the *General Theory*. The second monetary flow goes to the consumption pole. As described in this circuit, only households consume, and they get their income from firms. We suppose that households' income is composed of wages (W) and firms' shared profit (Pd). Households consume a part of it (C) and save the rest (S). As we can see, the circuit is closed with this last monetary flow.

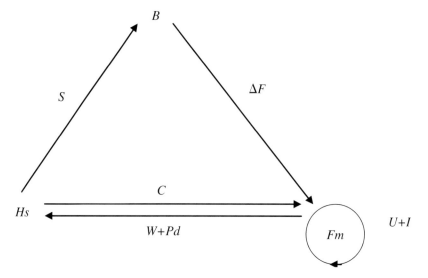

Figure 4.1   Poulon's framework

Poulon's (2000, p. 61) framework expresses rigorously the two shared propositions of circuitists. However, this model is not accepted by all the circuitists. Some feel that this framework is already an extrapolation.

Basic analysis of the banking system
A problem of the framework proposed by Poulon is that it practically ignores the role of the central bank. In fact, the central bank is represented in the finance pole (pole *B* in the previous circuit), but this is not very explicit. Poulon and Marchal (1987) propose a more complex framework that tries to explain the links between the deposit banks (DB) and the Central Bank (CB).

New flows induced by the central bank
- ΔA: Central Bank advances.
- ΔH_b: DB reserves placed at the Central Bank.
- ΔH_h: Households' cash holdings in circulation.
- ΔD: Households' bank deposits.

In this new circuit the government function (*Gvt*) is also considered.

Flows induced by the government
- *G*: Public expenditures.
- *T*: taxes paid both by firms (T_f) and households (T_h).
- ΔB: Public deficit financed by Treasury bills.

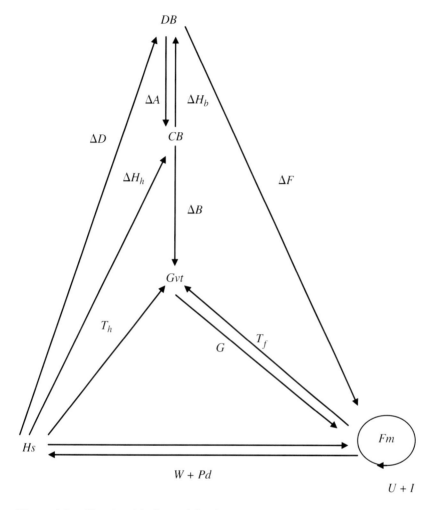

Figure 4.2   Circuit with Central Bank

In the second section of this chapter we will use this framework linking the circuit theory to the post-Keynesian analysis of endogenous money (the so-called horizontalist approach). Another way to introduce a Central Bank in Circuit theory has been proposed by Rochon and Rossi (2004). They note that the existence of multiple banks raises the possibility that a bank may be indebted to another one as a result of the great number of incoming and outgoing payments initiated by the non-bank sector. They also argue that:

inflows or outflows implied by the monetary transactions require that the banking system be complemented by a settlement institution that provides lender-of-last-resort facilities for the bilateral debt-credit relationships born in the interbank market to be settled (Rochon and Rossi 2004, p. 146).

Rochon and Rossi built a circuit which emphasizes the relationships between two banks and a Central Bank. They admit that if the two banks were one and the same bank, the result of the transaction between their respective clients would be simpler and correspond to the case traditionally considered by the theory of the Monetary Circuit (described in our previous circuit).

Their contribution helps Circuit theory to fill an important void because they give to the Central Bank a key role in the economy. They underline that the Central Bank is not only a lender of last resort acting in times of crisis, but that it is 'at the heart of the stability of the financial system on a daily basis' (Rochon and Rossi 2004, p. 150).

Omission of stocks
In Circuitist writers' views, hoarding is considered as a part of the saving flow. Actually they consider liquidity preference as a propensity applied to the saving flow. Van de Velde (2005) argued that this point of view is wrong. According to him, liquidity preference is a function which links the interest rate to stocks of money people want to hold.

The last remark sheds some light on the more important limitation of monetary circuit analyses: the absence of stocks. As we know, the monetary circuit is only composed of flows; stocks are never taken into account. So a part of the information relating to liquidity preference may be missing. Therefore, the circuit theory fails to present properly the Keynesian interest rate theory. The model proposed in the next section tries to incorporate stocks in a circuit analysis framework and to fill that void.

4.2.   THE STOCK-FLOW CONSISTENT (SFC) MODEL

Building an SFC model requires two steps: writing the matrices and defining each unknown with an equation (accounting identity or behavioral equation).

4.2.1   Matrices

We discuss a closed economy without inflation which is essentially the same as the one proposed by Lavoie and Godley (2001–2). Firms issue equities and borrow money from banks to finance investment, but they neither hold money balances nor issue bonds. They have excess capacity but no inventories. Firms use two factors for producing goods (fixed capital and labor), but we deal with a vertically-integrated sector and hence ignore all intermediate goods. Banks have no operating costs and they do not make loans to households. Banks have zero net worth, but contrary to Lavoie and Godley, the rate of interest on money deposits is different from the rate of interest on loans. We postulate that any profits realized by private banks are immediately transferred to households.

The main improvement to Lavoie and Godley's growth model is the introduction of a government and a Central Bank.[2] In the same way as private banks, the Central Bank has neither operating costs nor net worth (the Central Bank pays back all its profits to the government). The government collects taxes from firms and households (but not from private banks) and finances its deficit by issuing treasury bills. Government expenditures are only for final consumption goods: there are neither operating costs (like wages for state employees) nor transfers between households.

Godley's accounting method is based on two tables: a balance sheet matrix and a transactions matrix. Table 4.1 gives the transactions matrix that describes monetary flows between the five sectors of the economy. Every row represents a monetary transaction and every column corresponds to a sector account which is divided, except in the basic case of the government, into a current and a capital account. Sources of funds appear with plus signs and uses of funds with negative signs. So every row must sum to zero; each transaction always corresponds simultaneously to a source and a use of funds. The sum of each column must also be zero since each account (or sub-account) is balanced.

Table 4.2 gives the balance sheet matrix of our postulated economy. Symbols with plus describe assets and negative signs indicate liabilities. The sum of every row is again zero except in the case of accumulated capital in the industrial sector. The last row presents the net wealth of each sector and permits each column to sum to zero.

In our model we must use the accounting identities resulting from the fact that each row and each column sum to zero. A feature of SFC models is that if there are M columns and N non-ordinary rows in the transactions matrix, then there are only $(M + N - 1)$ independent accounting identities in the model. Because of this principle, similar to Walras' Law, one accounting identity must be kept out.

4.2.2 Equations

Now we have to define every variable relating to the five sectors of the economy using an accounting identity or a behavioral equation.

Table 4.1   Transactions matrix

	Govt	Firms current	Firms capital	Households current	Households capital	Private banks current	Private banks capital	Central Banks current	Central Banks capital	Σ
Consumption		$+C$		$-C$						0
Govt expenditures	$-G$	$+G$								0
Net investment		$+I$	$-I$							0
Wages		$-W$		$+W$						0
Taxes	$+T$	$-T_f$		$-T_h$						0
Interest on T. bills	$-r_{b-1}B_{-1}$			$+r_{b-1}B_{h-1}$		$+r_{b-1}B_{b-1}$		$+r_{b-1}B_{cb-1}$		0
Interest on bank deposits				$+r_{d-1}D_{-1}$		$-r_{d-1}D_{-1}$				0
Interest on loans		$-r_{l-1}L_{-1}$				$+r_{l-1}L_{-1}$				0
Interest on CB advances						$-r_{a-1}A_{-1}$		$+r_{a-1}A_{-1}$		0
Profits of firms		$-P$	$+P^u$	$+P^d$						0
Profit of banks				$+P_b$						0
Profits of CB	$+P_{bc}$							$-P_{bc}$		0
Hous. savings				$-S$	$+S$					0
ΔHPM					$-\Delta H_h$		$-\Delta H_b$		$+\Delta H$	0
ΔT. bills	$+\Delta B$				$-\Delta B_h$		$-\Delta B_b$		$-\Delta B_{cb}$	0
ΔEquities			$+\Delta ep_e$		$-\Delta ep_e$					0
ΔBank deposits					$-\Delta D$		$+\Delta D$			0
ΔLoans			$+\Delta L$				$-\Delta L$			0
ΔCB advances							$+\Delta A$		$-\Delta A$	0
Σ	0	0	0	0	0	0	0	0	0	0

Table 4.2   Balance sheet matrix

	Government	Firms	Households	Private Banks	Central Bank	Σ
Capital		$+K$				$+K$
HPM			$+H_h$	$+H_b$		0
T. bills	$-B$		$+B_h$	$+B_b$	$+B_{cb}$	0
Equities		$-ep_e$	$+ep_e$			0
Bank deposits			$+D$	$-D$		0
Loans		$-L$		$+L$		0
CB advances				$-A$	$+A$	0
Net wealth	$+B$	$-V_f$	$-V_h$	0	0	$-K$
Σ	0	0	0	0	0	0

Government

We assume that public expenditures G are growing at the same rate gr_y as national income Y:

$$G = G_{-1}(1 + gr_{y-1}) \qquad (4.1)$$

$$gr_y = \Delta Y / Y_{-1} \qquad (4.2)$$

$$Y = C + I + G \qquad (4.3)$$

When we solve the model using a computer, this assumption makes it easier to find a steady state, although we think that it would have been better to model the growth rate of public expenditure as an exogenous parameter.

In this model, the government collects taxes from firms T_f and households T_h:

$$T \equiv T_h + T_f \qquad (4.4)$$

where taxes on firms are composed of indirect taxes on sales Y and direct taxes on profits:[3]

$$T_f = T_y + T_p \qquad (4.5)$$

$$T_y = \tau_1 Y \qquad (4.6)$$

$$T_p = \tau_2 P_{-1} \qquad (4.7)$$

and households pay direct taxes on wages and wealth:

$$T_h = T_w + T_y \tag{4.8}$$

$$T_w = \tau_3 W_{-1} \tag{4.9}$$

$$T_y = \tau_4 V_{h-1}, \tag{4.10}$$

with τ_i: constants.

The government finances any deficit issuing bills, so that the supply of bills B in the economy is identical to the stock of government debt. In other words, government debt is given by the pre-existing stock of debt plus its current deficit DG:

$$B \equiv B_{-1} + DG \tag{4.11}$$

$$DG = G + r_{b-1}B_{-1} - T - P_{cb} \tag{4.12}$$

Firms

The investment function is the most important one in a growth model. In their paper, Lavoie and Godley (2001–2) use the Post-Keynesian investment function tested empirically by Ndikumana (1999). In the Ndikumana model there are four variables that explain the rate of accumulation gr_k: the ratio of cash flow to capital r_{cf}, the ratio of interest payments to capital $(r_l \cdot L)/K$, Tobin's q ratio and the rate of growth of sales. Lavoie and Godley use the first three of these and replace the fourth by the rate of capacity utilization u:

$$I = gr_k K_{-1} \tag{4.13}$$

$$K = K_{-1} + I \tag{4.14}$$

$$gr_k = \gamma_0 + \gamma_1 r_{cf-1} - \gamma_2 r_{l-1} l_{-1} + \gamma_3 q_{-1} + \gamma_4 u_{-1} \tag{4.15}$$

with γ_i: constant.

In order to make this function compatible with the Circuit theory, we have decided to suppress the constant γ_0 and Tobin's q and to replace the rate of cash flow r_{cf} by its expected value r_{cf}^a. Therefore equation (4.15) is replaced by equation (4.15a):

$$gr_k = \gamma_1 r_{cf}^a - \gamma_2 r_{l-1} l_{-1} + \gamma_3 u_{-1} \tag{4.15a}$$

with γ_i: constant.

According to the Post-Keynesian theory, it is the expected rate of cash flow r_{cf}^a which enters into the investment decision. As it is impossible to measure empirically these expectations, Ndikumana's function only contains the rate of cash flow of the previous period while the residue γ_0 is understood as the 'animal spirits' of the entrepreneurs, including expectations. However, there is no place for such a residue in a theoretical model. We must have an investment function that contains the expectations explicitly although we know that the question of modeling them has still not been answered satisfactorily. Even if it does not make the slightest difference with Lavoie and Godley's formulation, it is better to introduce an expected rate of cash flow defined by a basic mechanism. In this model, the expected value of any variable for the current period (represented with the superscript *a*) depends on its value from the previous period plus an error correction mechanism where θ represents the speed of adjustment in expectations:[4]

$$r_{cf}^a = r_{cf-1} + \theta_f(r_{cf-1} - r_{cf-1}^a) \tag{4.16}$$

with θ_f: constant

where the rate of cash flow is the ratio of retained earnings to capital:

$$r_{cf} = P^u / K_{-1} \tag{4.17}$$

As for Tobin's *q*-ratio, it would be hard to justify its utilization from a Circuitist point of view. Lavoie and Godley themselves recognize that

> Tobin's *q* ratio is not usually incorporated into heterodox growth models with financial variables. . . . Kaldor himself did not believe that such a ratio would have much effect on investment. (Lavoie and Godley 2001–2, pp. 286–7)

Due to the presence of Tobin's *q*, Lavoie and Godley's model could generate non-intuitive results in what they call a *puzzling* regime.

On the other hand, we have retained the negative impact of interest payments on investment and Lavoie and Godley's change concerning the replacement of the growth rate of sales by the utilization rate. The negative impact of firms' interest payments on investment reflects credit constraints by banks that appear at the beginning of the monetary circuit:

> Credit constraints thus appear at the stage of initial finance [as in equation (4.16)], not at the stage of final finance [as in equation (4.48)]. (Lavoie 2001, p. 14)

In equation (4.16) the leverage ratio *l* is the debt-to-capital ratio of the firms:

$$l = L/K \qquad (4.18)$$

The adoption of Lavoie and Godley's investment function may seem strange considering that the Circuitists mention the impact of the growth rate on investment (through the traditional accelerator effect), but never analyze the impact of the utilization rate. However, this change is the consequence of reintroducing stocks into the analysis. As they do not pay attention to the stock of capital, the Circuitists do not use any rate of capacity utilization. Contrary to that, in a Kaleckian model, an increase in demand will generate an increase of production and of the utilization rate. This rise leads the entrepreneurs to accelerate accumulation. Thus, any rise in effective demand will induce an increase in the growth rate of the economy. This is a variant of the traditional accelerator effect. The rate of capacity utilization is defined as the ratio of output to full capacity output Y_{fc}:

$$u = Y/Y_{fc} \qquad (4.19)$$

where the capital-to-full capacity ratio σ is defined as a constant:

$$Y_{fc} = K_{-1}/\sigma \qquad (4.20)$$

with σ: constant.

Wages can be decomposed into a unit wage w and the level of employment N:

$$W = w \cdot N \qquad (4.a)$$

where employment is determined by sales given productivity μ:[5]

$$N = Y/\mu \qquad (4.b)$$

with μ: constant.

Following Lavoie and Godley, it is assumed, as is usual in Post-Keynesian models, that prices are set as a mark-up ρ on unit direct cost UDC:

$$p = (1 + \rho)UDC \qquad (4.c)$$

with ρ: constant,

where unit direct costs is the ratio of direct costs (that consist entirely of wages) on net sales (gross sales minus indirect taxes on sales):

$$UDC = W/(Y - T_y) \qquad (4.d)$$

Under these assumptions we have:

$$p = (1 + \rho)w/(\mu(1 - \tau_1)) \qquad (4.e)$$

In this model there is no inflation, and prices are set to 1 so equation (4.e) can be rewritten:

$$w = \mu(1 - \tau_1)/(1 + \rho) \qquad (4.e')$$

Finally, equations (4.a), (4.b) and (4.e') can be condensed in equation (4.21), that determines wages:

$$W = Y(1 - \tau_1)/(1 + \rho) \qquad (4.21)$$

with ρ: constant.

Total profits P of firms are the difference between their sales and their expenditures (wages, taxes and interest payments):

$$P \equiv C + I + G - W + T_f - r_{l-1}L_{-1} \qquad (4.22)$$

Distributed dividends P^d are a fraction of profits realized in the previous period:

$$P^d = (1 - s_f)P_{-1} \qquad (4.23)$$

with s_f: constant

and retained earnings P^u are determined as the residue:

$$P^u = P - P^d \qquad (4.24)$$

Equations concerning issues of equities by firms are usually over-simplified in SFC models. We assume that firms finance a percentage x of their investment expenditures with equities, regardless of the price of equities or of the value taken by usual valuation ratios. With a lag our function is:

$$\Delta e p_e = x I_{-1}$$
$$\Leftrightarrow e = e_{-1} + x I_{-1}/p_e \qquad (4.25)$$

with x: constant.

Households

We assume that households determine their consumption expenditure C on the basis of their expected disposable income and their expected wealth V_h^a:

$$C = \alpha_1 Y_w^a + \alpha_2 Y_v^a + \alpha_3 V_h^a \tag{4.26}$$

with α_i: constants, $1 > \alpha_1 > \alpha_2 > \alpha_3 > 0$.

$$Y_w = W - T_w \tag{4.27}$$

$$Y_w^a = Y_{w-1} + \theta_h(Y_{w-1} - Y_{w-1}^a) \tag{4.28}$$

with θ_h: constant.

$$Y_v = r_{d-1}D_{-1} + r_{b-1}B_{h-1} + P^d + P_b - T_v \tag{4.29}$$

$$Y_v^a = Y_{v-1} + \theta_h(Y_{v-1} - Y_{v-1}^a) \tag{4.30}$$

where Y_w^a is the expected disposable income of workers, Y_v^a the expected disposable financial income and each α_i is a propensity to consume. We assume, following the Kaleckian tradition, that wages are mostly consumed while financial income is largely devoted to saving ($1 > \alpha_1 > \alpha_2 > 0$).

This consumption decision determines the amount that households will save out of their disposable income Y_h:

$$S \equiv Y_h - C \tag{4.31}$$

$$Y_h = Y_w + Y_v \tag{4.32}$$

The change in total households' wealth ΔV_h is equal to these savings plus the capital gains of the period:

$$V_h = V_{h-1} + S + CG \tag{4.33}$$

where CG are capital gains arising from the fluctuations in the price of equities:[6]

$$CG = \Delta p_e e_{-1} \tag{4.34}$$

In the same way, the expected wealth of households V_h^a is a function of their expected disposable income Y_h^a and of their expected capital gains V_h^a:

$$V_h^a = V_{h-1} + Y_h^a - C + CG^a \tag{4.35}$$

$$Y_h^a = Y_{h-1} + \theta_h(Y_{h-1} - Y_{h-1}^a) \tag{4.36}$$

$$CG^a = CG_{-1} + \theta_h(CG_{-1} - CG_{-1}^a) \tag{4.37}$$

We assume that households' holdings of cash money are a fixed share of their consumption:

$$H_h = \eta_h C \tag{4.38}$$

with η_h: constant.

In this model the central bank provides all the cash money demanded by households.

We now come to the equations defining the portfolio behavior of households. We follow the methodology developed by Lavoie and Godley and inspired by Tobin (1969). On top of cash money, households can hold three different assets: treasury bills B_h, equities $E = e.p_e$ and bank deposits D. We first present portfolio behavior in the form of matrix algebra:

$$\begin{vmatrix} B_h \\ E \\ D \end{vmatrix} = \begin{vmatrix} \lambda_{10} \\ \lambda_{20} \\ \lambda_{30} \end{vmatrix} \times (V_h^a - H_h) + \begin{vmatrix} \lambda_{11} & \lambda_{12} & \lambda_{13} \\ \lambda_{21} & \lambda_{22} & \lambda_{23} \\ \lambda_{31} & \lambda_{32} & \lambda_{33} \end{vmatrix} \times \begin{vmatrix} r_b \\ r_e^a \\ r_d \end{vmatrix} \times (V_h^a - H_h).$$

Households are assumed to hold a certain proportion λ_{i0} of their expected wealth V_h^a (net of cash holdings H_h) in the form of asset i, but this proportion is modified by the rates of return on these assets. Households are concerned about r_b and r_d, the rates of interest on treasury bills and on bank deposits to be determined at the end of the current period, but which will generate the interest payments in the following period. We have further assumed that it is the expected rate of return on equities r_e^a that enters into the determination of portfolio choice:

$$r_e^a = P^{da} + CG^a(p_{e-1}e_{-1}) \tag{4.39}$$

$$P^{da} = P_{-1}^{da} + \theta_h(P_{-1}^d - P_{-1}^{da}) \tag{4.40}$$

The three assets demand function described with the matrix algebra are thus:

$$B_h = (\lambda_{10} + \lambda_{11}r_b - \lambda_{12}r_e^a - \lambda_{13}r_d)(V_h^a - H_h) \tag{4.41}$$

with λ_{ij}: constants.

$$E = (\lambda_{20} - \lambda_{21}r_b + \lambda_{22}r_e^a - \lambda_{23}r_d)(V_h^a - H_h) \qquad (4.42)$$

$$D = (\lambda_{20} - \lambda_{21}r_b - \lambda_{22}r_e^a + \lambda_{23}r_d)(V_h^a - H_h) \qquad (4.43)$$

As is the case with every matrix, we cannot keep all these equations in the model, because each one of them is a logical implication of the others. We have decided to model bank deposits as the residual equation, because, when there is imperfect foresight, the amount of deposits held will be the residual. So equation (4.43) has been dropped and replaced by (4.43a):

$$D \equiv V_h - H_h - B_h - E \qquad (4.43a)$$

The only price clearing mechanism of this model occurs in the equity market. The price of equities will allow the equilibrium between the number of shares e that has been issued by firms (the supply) and the amount of shares E that households want to hold (the demand):

$$p_e = E/e \qquad (4.44)$$

Banking system
It is assumed that banks are obliged by the government to hold reserves H_b that do not generate interest payments and that must always be a fixed share (the compulsory ratio η_b) of deposits:

$$H_b = \eta_b D \qquad (4.45)$$

with η_b: constant.

The bank reserves together with cash in the hands of households H_h make up what is called base money or high powered money H:

$$H \equiv H_h + H_b \qquad (4.46)$$

Following the theory of endogenous money (the so-called *horizontalist* view) we assume that private banks are fully accommodating. They (i) fix a rate of interest on loans r_l applying a mark-up m_l on the key rate of the Central Bank r_a and then (ii) provide whatever loans L are demanded by credit-worthy firms at this rate: [7]

$$r_l = r_a + m_1 \qquad (4.47)$$

with m_1: constant.

$$L \equiv L_1 + I - P^u - \Delta e p_e \tag{4.48}$$

Credit-worthy firms are firms that can provide financial guarantees. In this model, credit constraints imposed by banks at the stage of initial finance (as analyzed in the circuit theory) are incorporated within the investment function, with the latter being sensitive to the weight of debt payments $r_{l-1} l_{-1}$.

> The initial finance provided by banks to allow production is in all cases larger than the final finance requirements of firms at the end of the period. If finance has been granted to start the production process, problems of credit restraints cannot arise at the end of the accounting period. (Lavoie 2001, p. 14)

In the same way, the Central Bank (i) fixes a key rate r_a and (ii) provides whatever advances A are demanded by banks at this rate:

$$r_a = r_{a0} \tag{4.49}$$

with r_{a0}: constant.

$$A \equiv B_b + L + H_b - D \tag{4.50}$$

The latter equation corresponds to an overdraft financial system as in continental Europe. However, our model does not describe a pure overdraft economy: private banks wish to hold a certain proportion of their assets in the shape of safe treasury bills. We assume that they demand bills on the basis of an exogenous banking liquidity ratio BLR that expresses their liquidity preference:

$$B_b = BLR \cdot L \tag{4.51}$$

with BLR: constant.

When their liquidity preference is increasing, banks wish to hold a higher proportion of safe assets and the bills-to-loans ratio BLR is rising. In this model, if banks wish to hold more bills, everything else being equal, they will need to borrow more from the Central Bank. This assumption explains that when the model is subjected to simulation, the value of BLR does not play any role.

In our model without inflation, the rate on treasury bills is the same as the Central Bank key interest rate:

$$r_b = r_a \tag{4.52}$$

How is the Central Bank able to sustain a fixed rate of interest whatever the demand for bills of households and private banks and whatever the fluctuations in the government deficit? It is possible because the Central Bank is the residual buyer of bills: it purchases however many of the bills issued by the government that households and private banks are not willing to hold at the given interest rate. In other words, 'the central bank clears the market at the price of its choice by providing an endogenous demand for bonds' (Lavoie 2001, p. 15):

$$B_{cb} \equiv B - B_h - B_b \tag{4.53}$$

This is another feature of the Post-Keynesian theory. In the Neoclassical view the bills rate is endogenous and the money supply exogenous so that the Central Bank decides arbitrarily about the proportion of the deficit that will be financed by bonds issues and by the creation of high powered money:

> In the post-Keynesian view, cash is provided on demand to the public. The government, or the central bank does not decide in advance on the proportion of the deficit that will be 'monetized'. This proportion is set by the portfolio decisions of the households, at the rate of interest set from the onset by the monetary authorities. (Lavoie 2001, p. 15)

Banks apply a spread m_2 between the rate on loans and the rate on deposits in order to realize profits P_b:

$$r_d = r_l - m_2 \tag{4.54}$$

with m_2: constant.

$$P_b \equiv r_{l-1} L_{-1} + r_{b-1} B_{b-1} - r_{d-1} D_{-1} - r_{a-1} A_{-1} \tag{4.55}$$

Since the Central Bank is collecting interest payments on bills and advances while paying out no interest on the notes, it is also making profits P_{cb}:

$$P_{cb} \equiv r_{a-1} A_{-1} + r_{b-1} B_{cb-1} \tag{4.56}$$

It is assumed, in line with current practice, that any profits realized by the Central Bank are reverted to the government.

Our model is now closed. The missing identity is the one related to the capital account of the Central Bank:

$$H \equiv A + B_{cb} \qquad (4.57)$$

This identity reflects the fact that base money is supplied to the economy through two channels: purchases of treasury bills and advances to private banks. Of course, this accounting identity must invariably hold. When we solve the model we have to verify that the numbers issued from simulations do generate $H \equiv A + B_{cb}$. As Lavoie and Godley have underlined:

> it is only when an accounting error has been committed that the equality given by the missing equation will not be realized. With the accounting right, the equality must hold (Lavoie and Godley 2001–2, p. 294).

When we solve our model numerically, identity (4.57) holds perfectly.

4.2.3 Experiments[8]

Given the complexity of the model, it would be difficult to find analytical solutions. We therefore make simulation experiments using the E-views 4.0 software and following the methodology used by Lavoie and Godley:

> First we assigned values to the various parameters using reasonable stylized facts. Then, we solved the model and found a steady-state solution through a process of successive approximations. Having found a steady state, we conducted experiments by modifying one of the exogenous variables or one of the economically significant parameters of the model at a time. (Lavoie and Godley 2001–2, p. 296)

There is nothing original about this methodology: It is the one used by orthodox economists for their dynamic models.[9] As for Post-Keynesian economists in general and Circuitists in particular, they show some distance from the notion of steady state. In fact, Lavoie and Godley use it only as an analytical tool, but they themselves recognize that such a theoretical construct is never reached in practice because parameters and exogenous variables are continuously changing (Lavoie and Godley 2007, introduction). That is why, when running a simulation, it is important to make a distinction between initial effects of some change (in the early periods of the dynamic response) and terminal effects (in the steady state).

Space considerations prevent us from discussing experiments for each parameter. For each sector, we have just selected the experiments corresponding to the main results of the circuit theory and we explain them briefly. Further explanations on similar experiments can be found in Lavoie and Godley (2001–2) or Dos Santos and Zezza (2004).

Government: gr_g $(=\Delta G/G_{-1})$

In our model, there is no parameter corresponding to government expend-iture because the search for a steady state requires postulating that public expenditures are growing at the same rate as national income. However, once we have obtained a steady state, we can study what happens if the gov-ernment raises the growth rate of its expenditures gr_g slightly. This perman-ent increase pushes the economy to a higher growth path, generating both a rise in the utilization rate and in the ratio of cash flows. This is coherent with Circuit theory: public expenditures correspond to sure receipts for firms and can reduce the lender's risk from private banks. In our model, the increase in government receipts due to taxes on higher national income, is not sufficient to balance the increase in government payments due to higher expenditure and to an increase in payments of the stock of bills which rise initially to finance the increase in expenditure: in the long run, the govern-ment deficit turns out to be higher, as a ratio to output, than in the base case. All of these effects are shown in Figure 4.3, where, as in all the fol-lowing figures, the various series are expressed as a ratio of the steady-state base case.

Households: α_1, λ_{20}

In our Post-Keynesian model, an increase in the propensity to consume α_1 leads to a higher rate of utilization and higher rates of profit, both of which encourage entrepreneurs to increase the rate of accumulation (Figure 4.4). Hence, a drop in the propensity to save brings about faster growth. This is the famous paradox of thrift which is a feature of Keynesian models in contrast to Neoclassical models of endogenous growth where the opposite occurs.

Banking system: r_a, m_1, γ_2

Let us consider now an increase in the interest rate on Central Bank advances r_a. With such a rise, it is in fact the entire structure of interest rates that shifts upwards. The rise in the Central Bank key rate increases the rates on loans, deposits and bills. Households therefore increase their demand for bank deposits and treasury bills while reducing their demand for equi-ties, thus generating a fall in the price of equities.

Basically, the increase in the structure of interest rates has two effects on effective demand. On the one hand, the increase in the rate on loans has a negative impact on investment through higher interest payments and smaller retained profits. But on the other hand, an increase in interest rates has a favorable effect on consumption demand and hence on the rate of capacity utilization, since more income is now being distributed to house-holds. However, the drop in the price of equities generates negative capital gains with a negative impact on wealth and consumption.

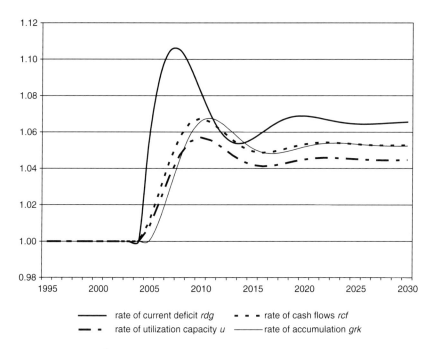

Figure 4.3   Higher government expenditure

In our model, the negative effects are initially stronger: an increase in the interest rate on Central Bank advances generates adverse effects on all determinants of investment. But in the long term, the positive effects tend to play a greater role and the evolution of all these determinants is reversed. Finally, our virtual economy stabilizes on a lower growth path (in accord-ance with the Keynesian literature) characterized by a lower rate of cash flows but also by a higher capacity rate and a lower leverage ratio (Figure 4.5).

Post-Keynesian economists have generalized the concept of liquidity preference to private banks. Such a liquidity preference is an indication of banks' prudence, a measure of their confidence in the future. When banks become more pessimistic, their liquidity preference increases with two consequences.

On the one hand, the interest rate on loans rises higher. As banks fear that more borrowers could become insolvent, they try to protect their rate of return, applying a higher mark up m_1 on the central bank's key rate (Figure 4.6). As we have just seen, this increase in the rate on loans has a negative impact on investment through higher interest payments and smaller retained profits. It also generates higher bank profits: since bank profits are

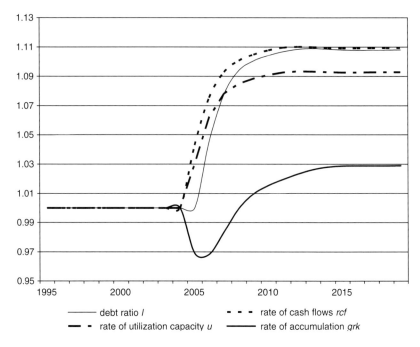

Figure 4.4   Higher propensity to consume (α_1)

transferred to households, this can induce a positive effect on consumption demand and hence on the rate of capacity utilization (because sales growth rate becomes higher than capital growth). That is why the steady-state rate of utilization ends up at its starting value. As for the debt ratio, it first increases since more loans are required to balance the reduced retained profits but it decreases in the long term with the drop of investment.

On the other hand, banks will apply stronger requirements with respect to credit-worthyness and credit rationing will rise at the stage of initial finance. In our model the effect of this is a rise in the value of the parameter γ_2 in the investment function. Such an increase leads to a smaller debt ratio and has a negative impact on investment, cash flows and capacity utilization.

4.3.   FINAL REMARKS

In this chapter, we intended to solve some problems of Circuit theory: lack of formalism, omission of stocks and only basic analysis of the banking

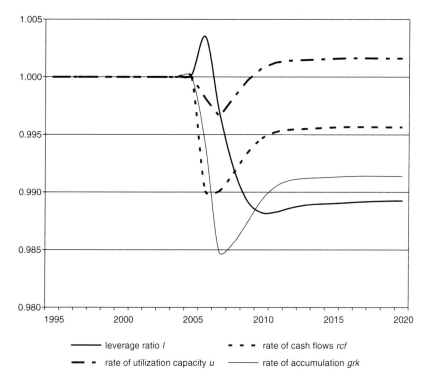

Figure 4.5   Higher rate on central bank advances (r_a)

system. However, since the Circuitists have never managed to agree upon fundamental hypotheses, we do not pretend that our model is representative of all their different works and ideas. We have used some results from Poulon but we cannot even claim that our model is a 'Poulonian' one for at least two reasons.

The first reason is that we have not introduced user costs in our model. According to Poulon (2000, p. 57), these costs, described by Keynes in Chapter 6 of the *General Theory* (1936), are fundamental to the explanation of economic crisis. Poulon thinks, like Marx, that crisis appears when entrepreneurs do not properly anticipate the rise of these costs and so do not anticipate properly the competition intensity in the economy. From a 'Poulonian' point of view there is a real problem linked to the absence of user costs in our model, because errors in anticipation of competition are not considered. These errors are supposed to have consequences in the determination of such variables as investment. Actually, an unanticipated rise in competition (which raises the user costs through the depreciation of

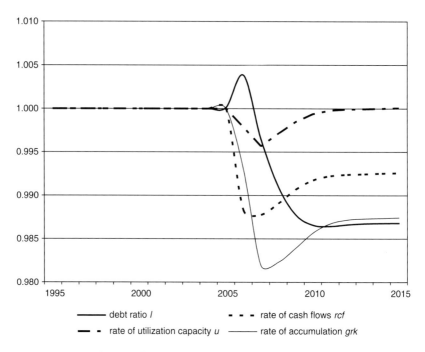

Figure 4.6   Higher mark up (m_1) on the central bank's key rate

capital) will have consequences for the firms' capital value and hence for investment.

The second reason is the integration of time into our dynamic model. Every Circuitist mentioned the importance of time in economic activity. They show that some decisions are taken before or after others and describe a hierarchy in economic decisions. But Poulon (2000, p. 105) goes further: he isolates a crisis condition related to time. Like Marx, he thinks that crisis appears when entrepreneurs do not have the time to recover their loans. Our model does not integrate this consideration either.

NOTES

*   The authors are grateful to Marc Lavoie and Frédéric Poulon for their helpful comments. Tarik Mouakil also thanks Jung-Hoon Kim for providing him the technical support on simulation programming during his stay in Ottawa University.
1.   In 1999, Marc Lavoie, Professor at the University of Ottawa and author of *Foundations of Post-Keynesian Economic Analysis* (1992), invited Wynne Godley, former Director of the Department of Applied Economics at Cambridge University (1970–1994), to present

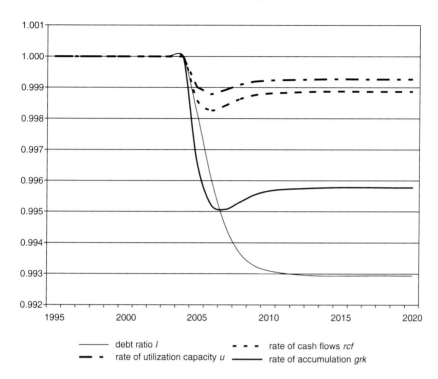

——— debt ratio *l*	- - - rate of cash flows *rcf*
▬ ▬ rate of utilization capacity *u*	——— rate of accumulation *grk*

Figure 4.7   Stronger credit rationing (γ_2)

in Canada's capital what Godley considered to be his most important and radical work to date. Godley had been Deputy Director of the Economics Section at HM Treasury (1956–1970). He is perhaps best known in the UK for his role as one of the 'six wise men' that provided independent advice to successive Chancellors of the Exchequer between 1992 and 1995. Godley had finally managed to represent his macroeconomic theory in a stock-flow consistent accounting framework linking stocks and flows together and integrating money in the best Cambridge Post-Keynesian tradition (Godley 1996, 1999). Most of Godley's ideas had already been presented 16 years ago in Godley and Cripps (1983). Godley's accounting framework was inspired by the works of Tobin and some of his associates at Yale University (Tobin 1969, Tobin and Brainard 1968; Backus *et al.* 1980). For his part, Lavoie was trying to build a Post-Keynesian growth model incorporating money and equities but did not know exactly how to do it, especially for representing choices in the composition of portfolios. He found with Godley's work the method he was missing and Godley found in him the heterodox economist who would help to make his work more pedagogical, linking it to the rest of Post-Keynesian theory. As a French Canadian and a former student of the University of Paris 1 (Panthéon-Sorbonne), Marc Lavoie is well up on French economics and, according to him, the 'matrix method proposed by Godley makes it possible to formalize the circuit theory and to justify the main assertions of the thesis of endogenous money' (Lavoie 2003, p. 159).

2.   This work is also inspired by the model by Dos Santos and Zezza (2004).
3.   In this closed economy, sales are equal to the national income.
4.   Note that with this expectation mechanism, if the variable to be forecasted is stationary, its expected value will always be correct on average.

5. Here we assume implicitly that there is no overhead or fixed labor. However, additional outlays on unproductive labor could have a significant impact on economic activity.
6. As capital gains do not appear in the transactions matrix, it is important to remember that any change in the value of an asset may be made up of two components: a component associated with a transaction involving additional units of the asset in question and a component with a change in the price of the asset. In our model, shares are the only assets of households' portfolio whose price can change. The change in the value of equities arising from the transactions is $\Delta e \, p_e$ while the change in the value of equities arising from capital gains is $\Delta p_e \cdot e_{-1}$. The global change in the value of equities is $\Delta(e \, p_e) = \Delta e \, p_e + \Delta p_e \, e_{-1}$.
7. In June 2005 in France, r_a (bottom rate) is 2 per cent and r_l (ten-years rate) is 4.8 per cent.
8. Values of our parameters and exogenous variables and the E-views program are available from Tarik Mouakil on request.
9. For example, Mercado *et al.* (1998) describe the same methodology for modeling orthodox dynamic macro models with the GAMS software.

REFERENCES

Backus, D., Brainard, W.C., Smith, G. and J. Tobin (1980), 'A model of U.S. financial and non-financial economic behavior', *Journal of Money, Credit, and Banking*, 12(2), 259–93.

Dos Santos, C.H. and G. Zezza (2004), 'The role of monetary policy in Post-Keynesian stock-flow consistent macroeconomic growth models', in Lavoie, M. and M. Seccarecia (eds), *Central Banking in the Modern World*, Cheltenham, UK and Northampton, MA, USA: Edward Elgar, pp. 183–208.

Dostaler, G. (2005), *Keynes et ses Combats*, Paris: Albin Michel.

Godley, W. (1996), *Money, Finance and National Income Determination: An Integrated Approach*, WP No. 167, Annandale-on-Hudson: Jerome Levy Economics Institute of Bard College.

Godley, W. (1999), 'Money and credit in a Keynesian model of income determination', *Cambridge Journal of Economics*, 23(2), 393–411.

Godley, W. and F. Cripps (1983), *Macroeconomics*, London: Fontana.

Graziani, A. (1990), 'The theory of the monetary circuit', *Economies et Sociétés*, 24(6), 7–36.

Keynes, J.M. (1936), *The General Theory of Employment, Interest and Money*, London: Macmillan.

Keynes, J.M. (1973 [1933]), 'A monetary theory of production', in *The Collected Writings of J.M. Keynes, vol. XIII, The General Theory and After: Part I Preparation*, London: Macmillan for the Royal Economic Society, 408–11.

Lavoie, M. (1987), 'Monnaie et production: Une synthèse de la théorie du circuit', *Economies et Sociétés*, 9, 65–101.

Lavoie, M. (1992), *Foundations of Post-Keynesian Economic Analysis*, Aldershot, UK and Brookfield, US: Edward Elgar.

Lavoie, M. (2001), *Endogenous Money in a Coherent Stock-Flow Framework*, WP No. 325, Annandale-on-Hudson, NY: Jerome Levy Economics Institute of Bard College.

Lavoie, M. (2003), 'La monnaie endogène dans un cadre théorique et comptable cohérent', in Piegay, P. and L.-P. Rochon (eds), *Théories Monétaires Post-Keynésiennes*, Paris: Economica, pp. 143–61.

Lavoie, M. and W. Godley (2001–2002), 'Kaleckian models of growth in a coherent stock-flow monetary framework: A Kaldorian view', *Journal of Post Keynesian Economics*, 24(2), 277–311.

Lavoie, M. and W. Godley (2007), *Monetary Economics: An Integrated Approach to Credit, Money, Income, Production and Wealth*, Basingstoke: Palgrave Macmillan.

Mercado, P.R., Kendrick, D.A. and H. Amman (1998), 'Teaching macroeconomics with GAMS', *Computational Economics*, 12, 125–49.

Ndikumana, L. (1999), 'Debt service, financing constraints, and fixed investment: Evidence from panel data', *Journal of Post Keynesian Economics*, 21(3), 455–78.

Parguez, A. and B. Ducros (1975), *Monnaie et Macroéconomie: Théorie de la Monnaie en Déséquilibre*, Paris: Economica.

Parguez, A. and M. Seccarecia (2000), 'The credit theory of money: The monetary circuit approach', in Smithin, J. (ed.), *What is Money?*, London: Routledge, pp. 101–23.

Poulon, F. (1982), *Macroéconomie Approfondie: équilibre, Déséquilibre, Circuit*, Paris: Cujas.

Poulon, F. (2000), *La Pensée Économique de Keynes*, Paris: Dunod.

Poulon, F. and J. Marchal (1987), *Monnaie de Crédit dans l'Économie Française*, Paris: Cujas.

Rochon, L.-P. and S. Rossi (2004), 'Central banking in the monetary circuit', in Lavoie, M. and M. Seccarecia (eds), *Modern Banking in the Modern World*, Cheltenham, UK and Northampton, MA, USA: Edward Elgar, pp. 144–163.

Tobin, J. and W.C. Brainard (1968), 'Pitfalls in financial model building', *American Economic Review*, 58(2), 99–122.

Tobin, J. (1969), 'A general equilibrium approach to monetary theory', *Journal of Money, Credit, and Banking*, 1(1), 15–29.

Van de Velde, F. (2005), *Monnaie Chômage et Capitalisme*, Villeneuve d'Ascq: Presses universitaires du Septentrion.

PART II

Distribution and aggregate demand

5. What drives profits? An income-spending model

Olivier Giovannoni and Alain Parguez

INTRODUCTION

This chapter is an attempt to inquire into the role and determinants of aggregate profits. It has been partly motivated by what has been dubbed the New Consensus in growth theory (see Romer 2000, Taylor 2000, Lavoie and Kriesler 2005), which relies on the fundamental postulate of a dual temporal nature of the economy. In the short run, the economy is seen as in a Keynesian (or demand-led) disequilibrium, but in the long run, supply factors *only* drive the economy along a natural growth path. The focus of the New Consensus approach is to study the conditions, such as economic policy rules, under which short-run disequilibria would disappear in favor of a 'Classical' or a 'New Wicksellian' equilibrium path.

On this long-run growth path, capital accumulation (investment) is given the preponderant role of the leading variable. Here the classical law of thriftiness rules: investment needs to be financed out of *prior* savings. Since the primary source of such savings is profits, the amount of profits determines savings, therefore investment, therefore growth. The bottom line of this approach is that profits are the exogenous, leading factor which propels the rest of the economic system. Demand is left aside and consumption, in particular, is the residual of the saving pattern.

From this set of theoretical propositions a whole policy agenda stems, which seems to be espoused by a growing fraction of the American business community (Ferguson 1995). The New Consensus typically views economic policies as curative action in the short run *only* because the economy is believed to be on its equilibrium path over the long run. In a sense, economic policies should only be done to correct for the short-run market imperfections which are brought by Keynesian-style deviations. The role of monetary and fiscal policies is to enforce a smooth short-run adjustment of the economy towards its natural long-run, supply-led, growth path. This is commonly understood as a zero-inflation target for monetary policy, because such is the natural level of the interest rate which reconciles savings (profits) with investment (capital accumulation). It also implies a supplementary fiscal policy aiming at balanced budgets or even surpluses – as they are (public) saving. This is especially true in the case of 'excess consumption' leading to a shortage of private savings.

Another view of the relationship between profits and macroeconomic policy, when the economy operates in excess capacity, has been spelled out as the 'Profit Paradox' (Parguez 2002, 2005). This approach challenges the New Consensus view of economic policy on the basis that the savings target will merely generate a smaller amount of consumption and is far from certain to raise investment in return. In the end, aggregate demand and production and employment are squeezed, so that the New Consensus theory is likely to miss its long-run equilibrium target – should its policy recommendations be effectively implemented.

Starting from a generalized Post-Keynesian approach, the Profit Paradox spells out three fundamental and interrelated propositions: (1) 'in the long run you are still in the short run', (2) profits are demand-driven in the short run *as well as in the long run*, and therefore (3) the New Consensus theory raises a deep Profit Paradox in the sense that its agenda is more likely to squeeze profits than to promote them.

Such is the conflicting framework of the New Consensus and Profit Paradox theories. This chapter leaves theoretical debates aside for a time and concentrates upon shedding a new light from an empirical perspective. Our goal is to study the real-world behavior of profits through the lens of a large-scale econometric model that relies upon the least possible theoretical and restrictive assumptions. Our research focuses on the post-war US economy, from 1954 to 2004 (quarterly data), and our data sources are the National Income and Product Accounts (NIPAs).

Not much previous work has been done in that particular empirical direction. A noticeable exception is Asimakopulos (1983), who provides an empirical investigation of American profits. His study, however, is conducted in a statistical accounting way and lacks the dynamics approach permitted by modern econometrics. The profit theme frequently appears in the papers of the Federal Reserve (see Burke 1973, Uctum 1995, Himmelberg *et al.* 2004, McGrattan and Prescott 2005 and the references therein), yet many of those contributions are more centered around distributional or measurement implications than we presently are.

The rest of the chapter is organized as follows. Section one presents the motivation behind the choice of variables, their properties and the econometric model which make up the non-partisan framework of the analysis. Section two addresses the dynamics of the model and especially the issue of causality through the various channels and meanings allowed for by the model. Section three sums up the results and provides concluding directions in terms of economic theory and policy.

5.1. BUILDING A REAL-WORLD MODEL FOR PROFITS

This section is devoted to building a framework that is empirical in nature and global in perspective. We model profits and related variables but, for space requirements, we will concentrate almost exclusively upon profits. Three crucial decisions have to be made: choosing the variables affecting profits, choosing a technique allowing information to be extracted from the data, and choosing the parameters of that technique.

5.1.1 The Data: Choice, Sources and Properties

Virtually all schools of thought have addressed the issue of profits. However, theoretical propositions are generally of little help because they often represent a schematized vision of reality, they typically rely upon *a priori* knowledge and do not always make explicit all the variables involved (Sims 1980). The fact that profits are one variable among many other aggregates makes it hard, from an empirical perspective, to choose the variables to which profits may be empirically related.

A major challenge underlying the process of variable selection has its econometrics counterpart known as the 'omitted variable' case. Keynes (1939) for instance was highly skeptical of Tinbergen's early econometric work, partly because Tinbergen did not make it clear on what basis he decided to include, or not to include, some variables in his models. Yet, as is well documented now, we know that statistical inference depends crucially on which variables are included in the model.

Here we will analyze profits as stemming from a definition stated in the National Accounts. In the National Income and Product Accounts of the United States (NIPAs) a 'corporate income' line appears which we shall rename as 'profits' throughout the rest of the text. Profits are reported in the accounting identity relating the income decomposition to the demand decomposition of national income. The general income-spending identity featuring profits and thirteen related variables is the following, with magnitudes in billions of current US dollars as of the first quarter of 2005:

$$\underset{8538}{C} + \underset{2084}{I} + \underset{2259}{G} + \underset{1249}{X} - \underset{1940}{M} - \underset{1405}{CFC} + \underset{31}{IncRW}$$
$$\equiv \underset{6977}{W} + \underset{961}{PI} + \underset{1345}{\Pi} + \underset{557}{NI} + \underset{834}{T} + \underset{155}{R} + \underset{83}{BTr} + \varepsilon \qquad (5.1)$$

where C stands for private consumption, I for total private investment, G for total government spending, X for exports, M for imports, CFC for consumption of fixed capital (private and public), $IncRW$ for net income from the rest of the world, W for aggregate employee compensation, PI for proprietors' income, Π for corporate profits, NI for net interest, T for taxes on production and imports (less subsidies and surplus of government enterprises), R for rental income and BTr for business transfers. Finally, ε stands for a statistical discrepancy which we will not include in the model because it is not directly interpretable and because it is negligible most of the time. This discrepancy is likely to be attributable to misreporting or measurement issues on the income side.

Equation (5.1) is a definitional identity. It holds true every time the data is collected. What is at the core of the present analysis is the study of the macroeconomic relationships among the variables of definition (5.1), with particular emphasis on the place and role of profits. The interesting feature of such a point of departure is that it avoids the pitfalls of model selection based upon theoretical considerations. However, any time series analysis based upon (5.1) can only be a statistical analysis of realized profits (or of any other variable of the model for that matter) yielding *ex post* results. Before proceeding to the study of the dynamic properties of such an income-spending system, a lot of knowledge is to be gained, as a pre-analysis exercise, from the statistical properties of each variable.

The data comes from the 2003 revision of the NIPA Tables 1.5.5, 1.7.5 and 1.12. All variables in identity (5.1) are reported in billions of current US dollars; all income variables are before tax and are log-linearized. For notational simplicity we shall refer to X_t as the set of all such variables, except for the discrepancy. The data is available on a quarterly basis since 1947 but due to the accumulation of specific events – the Korean War, the Treasury–Fed accord[1] and the price control experience – we choose to start our analysis at the later date of 1954q1. The final observation is 2004q3, leaving 203 quarterly observations.

We turn first to the time plots of the variables. Figure 5.1 presents a comparison of the amount of profits (and its linear trend) together with a selection of income and outlays. Two observations ought to be made. The first observation is that of the smooth evolution of most variables, so that a more-or-less pronounced trend appears in retrospect. In any case many variables have decelerated since the eighties – a pattern absent from profits. The exceptions here are trade variables and rents. The second observation is that corporate profits appear as the most stable of all variables, apparently reverting around their linear trend.[2]

The stability of profits is indeed a result that is both puzzling and rarely mentioned in the economic literature. Yet the business literature provides

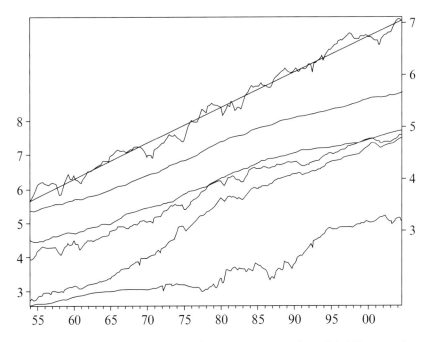

Notes: All variables in logs. From top to bottom: corporate profits and their linear trend, compensation, government spending, investment, imports and rents. All variables are on the left scale except for profits and their time trend. The trend is obtained from a regression of corporate profits on time and a constant.

Source: NIPAs.

Figure 5.1 *Plot of corporate profits and selected variables*

disseminated ideas which may explain this stability; one may think for instance about financial markets' preference for smooth profit reports. This potential explanation is further reinforced by accounting techniques allowing firms to (temporarily) hide, convert or even transfer profit earnings. Yet the weight of such explanations is hard to assess at the present stage; for now we will take the stability of profits as an empirical fact and will account for that through the rest of the paper.

We now turn to the order of integration of the variables to inquire deeper into the question of trends; as widely known, this pre-test has important implications for theoretical and applied economists. For the purpose of the present study we recall that the key difference between processes integrated of order zero and one is that exogenous shocks persist in the latter case while they have merely transitory effects in the former case. The $I(0)$ case is that of stationary, linear variables while the $I(1)$ case is that of non-stationary, stochastically-dominated variables. Indeed, we know since the early eighties that most macroeconomic aggregates fall into the $I(1)$ category, notwithstanding some controversies about the generality of this result when alternative methods or samples are used (Nelson and Plosser 1982).

The classic way to discriminate between $I(0)$ and $I(1)$ variables is through testing for unit root(s). We performed two unit root tests with different spirits (the 'old' ADF and the 'newer' DF-GLS) as well as the KPSS stationarity test on each variable of the model, considered both in log levels and in log changes on 1954–2004. Because of model size and space requirements we will not report the results here. Instead we point to two comments which stand out from the results.

First, the ADF test reports a significant trend for three series (Π, PI and I) and does not appear irrelevant for six other series (R, BTr, C, X, CFC and $IncRW$, at the 15 per cent significance level). We are thus dealing with a set of variables featuring quite a significant trending pattern in log levels. But are the series fluctuating significantly around their trend? The unit root test results indicate unambiguously that this is not the case for any series *with the notable exception of corporate profits*. Note that those results are in line with the time plots of the variables.

Second, all series become highly stationary when log changes are considered. Equivalently we find that shocks have had persistent effects on all series in log levels except on profits, for which shocks have proven to be merely transitory. This translates into profits featuring as some sort of attractor set, from which profits have not deviated persistently in time.

The puzzling finding of profits' trend-stationarity reminds us of the quote by Newbold *et al.* (2001, p. 97) about real GNP:

> Faith in the hypothesis of trend-stationarity in RGNP over the period 1875–1993 would imply a belief that, at the beginning of time, God stretched out Her hand and drew a (straight) line in the sky, ordaining that henceforth (or at least from 1875) RGNP (measured in logarithms) would not wander arbitrarily far from that path.

Indeed, the nature of real GNP (trend-stationarity or not) is a recurring topic in the applied literature. However, we will not get into that debate for the present case of profits and we will content ourselves with a conclusion similar to that of Newbold *et al.* We document the puzzling stability of profits over fifty years, but we consider that taking profits as stable through time, whatever happens, is an overly restrictive, barely credible assumption.

5.1.2 VECMs: Dynamic Econometrics with a Rich Structure

Equation (5.1) is disappointing in several respects because it is just a static accounting identity. It does not allow us to deal with the dynamics of the system itself. In addition, the variables under study are income and spending variables, and a general modeling strategy would be to allow for the possibility of interaction between the variables.

A classic starting point for the study of economic relationships is the one initiated by Sims (1980). Sims's idea was that econometric models could 'not be taken seriously' because they relied too often upon restrictive and arbitrary theoretical assumptions. Instead, Sims proposed vector autoregressions (VAR models) to discuss relationships in terms of the dynamics that prevail in an estimated system. Sims's goal was to build a general a-theoretical framework which would broaden the scope of analysis by relying on fewer assumptions.

Our preceding section showed that the variables we are dealing with are better understood as $I(1)$ variables. Those variables are *a priori* not unrelated to each other, and Figure 5.1 provided empirical evidence of co-movements. Such co-movements between the variables provide important information which is better not left out of the modeling process.[3] Economically speaking, those co-movements can be intuitively thought of as proportionality between variables. Econometrically speaking, the co-movements call upon the classic works of Granger (1981), Granger and Weiss (1983) and Engle and Granger (1987) on cointegration, that is, the idea that there exist common stochastic trend(s) which cancel out in the long run or 'on average'. The present case therefore calls upon an extension of Sims's original VAR model made to accommodate the case of cointegration.

The cointegrated VAR model has been extensively studied since the pioneering works of Johansen (1988, 1991) and Johansen and Juselius (1990). It is also known as the vector error-correction model (VECM), and is a classic VAR model (in levels and with Gaussian errors) extended to account for possible cointegration. The most general representation of VECMs is given by (5.2):

$$\Delta X_t = \underbrace{\alpha\beta' X_{t-1}}_{long-run} + \underbrace{\sum_{i=1}^{k-1}\Gamma_i\Delta X_{t-i}}_{short-run} + \underbrace{\Phi D_t + \mu_0 + \mu_1 t}_{deterministics} + \underbrace{\varepsilon_t}_{error} \qquad (5.2)$$

where X_t stands for the set of variables being modeled, Δ is the difference operator[4] and D_t is a set of dummy variables intended to account for exceptional events. The weights $\alpha, \beta, \Phi, \Gamma, \mu_0, \mu_1$ are coefficients of the model which are freely estimated. However, the researcher has choices to make about the deterministic component, as well as k, the number of relevant past values to be included. We will return to that in the next section.

For now we will outline a few interesting features of VECMs. We will not discuss the VEC model from an econometrics perspective – interested readers can refer to the excellent exposition of Johansen (1995), among many other places. We will instead discuss the most interesting feature of a VECM, its structure, and the subsequent various causality tests one can perform on it.

A foremost interesting feature of a VECM is that there is no assumption made from the outset about the nature of the variables. As equation (5.2) shows, each variable of a VECM is in turn endogenous and exogenous (in the sense of being a consequence and a cause). Every variable depends upon each and every variable with no *a priori*.

Second, and as a result of the above property, VECMs make up systems of variables. Time matters and is explicitly taken into account by the lagged terms ΔX_{t-i}. Tests performed on their coefficients Γ allow temporal causality to be dealt with in the Granger sense. A sequence of Granger tests performed on each equation of the model results in an exogeneity/endogeneity ranking.

Third, VECMs are comprised of distinct 'short-run' and 'long-run' parts whose link is made through the adjustment coefficients α. Null values of α for a given variable translate into that variable featuring 'no long-run' feedback. The significance of that adjustment effect for each and every variable of the model gives rise to a second measure of causality.

Fourth, those systems are dynamic systems: one can simulate shocks on the system and see how a given variable reacts. There are two relevant measures here: a shock may affect a variable in variance or magnitude. Those are alternative measures of causality: no significant effect in either magnitude or variance can be interpreted as 'no causality'. They make up two additional measures of causality, namely 'variance causality' and 'impact causality'.

5.1.3 Limitations and the Choice of the Parameters

The VEC models provide a particularly rich structure, which makes them desirable tools. They nonetheless suffer from potentially severe limitations. The usual criticisms are their lack of theoretical underpinnings and the high number of coefficients to be estimated, which decrease the explanatory power.

However, the most important problem with VECMs is that they suffer from high sensitivity to the parameters involved. There are three major parameters to choose: the lag length k, the deterministic specification in μ_0, μ_1 and the number of cointegrating relationships r. Those are indeed tough choices, for at least three reasons: (1) different parameters are likely to change the results, (2) the choice of a parameter has consequences for the choices of the other parameters and (3) the statistical procedures involved in helping to choose the parameters are perfectible. Here we will refer the interested reader to the works of Johansen (1995) and Lütkepohl (2005).

Because of those limitations we spent a considerable amount of time searching for the best model available over the sample. For space requirements we will not supply the detailed parameterization procedures or the fully estimated system. Following Sims (1980) we provide instead causality tests, variance decompositions and impulse/response functions as a description of the estimated system. Below are some comments about the choice of the model parameters.

Lag structure

The value of the lag length k has to be set so that the errors of the time series in levels included in the VAR are Gaussian, that is, neither autocorrelated nor heteroscedastic, and normally distributed. Those requirements have been tested for with the Breush-Godfrey test, the White test and the Jarque-Bera test respectively. We avoided using the usual information criteria to set k (FPE, LR, AIC, BIC and so on), since all failed to provide Gaussian errors.

We consequently checked the properties of the residuals sequentially in a specific-to-general manner, starting with value $k = 1$. It turned out that no major serial autocorrelation was present when $k = 2$ or 7 or possibly 4 lags were used. The White test for homoscedasticity for those three candidates indicated that $k = 7$ was an overall better choice. However, the errors could not be made normally distributed for any reasonable choice of k, including $k = 7$. Non-normality is a far less serious issue than autocorrelation.

Deterministic component and tests for the cointegration rank

Given $k = 7$, the number of linearly independent cointegrating relationships r has been tested for with Johansen's two cointegration tests, the trace test and the maximum eigenvalue test. The results of those tests depend on the deterministic specification of the model in μ_0, μ_1, however. Johansen provides five cases all nested one into another, with case five featuring the most general deterministic specification. The choice of the deterministic component can be made on the basis of the significance of the extra deterministic component using an LM test (Johansen 1995).

In the following, we employed Johansen's cointegration test as implemented in JMulti and Eviews, which feature different critical values. Case five was consistently rejected on the basis that (1) it is known for providing unreliable out-of-sample forecasts (Johansen 1995), (2) there do not appear to be quadratic trends in the data, and (3) the trend coefficients in the VAR are not significant. Case four was accepted instead, yielding eleven cointegrating relationships at the 1 per cent level according to Johansen's trace test. That specification features a linear trend in each cointegrating relationship, which all simultaneously turned out to be significant. This result corroborates the visual inspection of the series in (log) levels in Figure 5.1 which showed smoothly trending variables. This is also compatible with the finding of significant trends when performing the unit root tests.

At this stage all parameters have been chosen consistently and the model can be fully estimated. A battery of tests has been applied to check for the robustness of the results subject to alternative parameter choices. The general result is that the results do not change by much, even if other relevant parameter combinations appear to exist. In its present form, the model explains (R^2) between 60 per cent and 80 per cent of the variance of all variables in Δlogs (approximately growth rates), but those figures drop to the 20 per cent – 60 per cent range when degrees of freedom are accounted for (adjusted R^2).

5.2.   THE DYNAMICS OF THE MODEL

We may now turn to the study of the model's dynamics quite confidently. Our goal here is not so much to discuss the structure of the model as to analyze the direction and magnitude of the causal relationships involving profits.

As often noted, the concept of causality has different meanings which may or may not coincide with (economists') conventional views on the subject. The same applies to exogenous and endogenous and to the short- and long-run dichotomies. For those reasons we will define precisely several econometric concepts before discussing the results. In the three sections below we should in turn distinguish between temporal 'short-run' causality (5.2.1), 'feedback causality' (5.2.2), 'variance causality' (5.2.3) and 'impact causality' (5.2.4).

5.2.1   Exogeneity and 'Short-Run' Temporal Causality

The first measure of causality we address is that of temporal causality, better known as 'Granger causality' (Granger 1969, 1988). In our model the equation for profit is the following:

$$\dot{\Pi}_t = \alpha\beta' X_{t-1} + \sum_{k=1}^{6} \Gamma_{\Pi C} \dot{C}_{t-k}$$

$$+ \sum_{k=1}^{6} \Gamma_{\Pi I} \dot{I}_{t-k} + \ldots + \sum_{k=1}^{6} \Gamma_{\Pi BTr} \dot{BTr}_{t-k} + C + \varepsilon_{\Pi t} \tag{5.3}$$

where a dot above a variable indicates its transformation in $\Delta\log$, that is roughly the variable's growth rate (quarterly rates here).

Granger causality tests for the significance of all the lagged terms in the equation for profits, that is, the significance of each and every Γ_{Π}. coefficient. Here, we test whether the past growth rates of consumption C affect the present growth rate of profits, and do so for each and every variable of equation (5.1). We will thus end up with the significance level of each and every spending and income variable in the profit equation. A low significance level, say $<10\%$, means that the basic hypothesis, that the independent variable does *not* Granger-cause profits, is rejected. Alternatively such a low probability is an indication that there is significant causality towards profits. The joint significance levels of all independent variables may be used to deduce a Granger causal ordering, from the most leading to the most lagging variable (that is, from the most exogenous to the most endogenous).

Note that causality in the Granger sense covers a specific definition of causality. First and as widely noticed, it is a precedence or predictability test. It thus helps determine the significance of the direction of causality (which may run both ways), but does not provide any weight of the impact. Second, note the temporal nature of Granger's test: The test is that of past values causing present values. Yet since the model features a long-term part (the 'long run', or 'steady state' part $\alpha\beta' X_{t-1}$), Granger causality is only one side of the temporal causality coin. It measures only precedence when the long run has been accounted for, so that Granger causality is only indicative of precedence during the business cycle. Third, Granger causality is better thought of as 'short-run' causality, for it measures precedence between variables taken in quarter-to-quarter growth rates.

We have performed Granger tests on the whole system. Because of space requirements we will only present the following results:

- The significance of each variable as a determinant of profits.
- The significance of profits when explaining each other variable.
- The ranking of profits in the exogeneity/endogeneity scale.

Those results are summed up in Table 5.1.

A quick comparison between columns (a) and (b) of Table 5.1 reveals that profits have been caused by virtually every other variable of the model,

Table 5.1   Results of Granger causality and weak exogeneity

X_i	(a) $X_i{\rightarrow}\Pi$	(b) $\Pi{\rightarrow}X_i$	(c) Granger ordering (prob. [rank] χ^2)			(d) Weak exog. tests		
C	**0.04**	0.66	**0.05**	**[3]**	*113.6*	0.00	[10]	*45.4*
I	0.13	0.52	**0.00**	**[11]**	*144.9*	0.00	[3]	*29.9*
G	**0.08**	0.91	**0.01**	**[7]**	*123.6*	0.00	[12]	*56.4*
X	**0.00**	0.92	0.29	[2]	*97.8*	0.00	[9]	*44.8*
M	**0.01**	0.58	0.11	[3]	*107.6*	**0.22**	**[1]**	*14.2*
CFC	**0.03**	0.12	**0.00**	**[13]**	*169.4*	0.00	[8]	*43.9*
IncRW	**0.01**	0.43	**0.00**	**[11]**	*141.2*	0.00	[7]	*43.5*
W	0.16	0.99	**0.08**	**[3]**	*110.5*	0.00	[6]	*42.0*
PI	**0.00**	**0.00**	**0.00**	**[10]**	*132.6*	0.00	[11]	*48.2*
Π	–	–	**0.00**	**[14]**	*175.8*	0.00	[14]	*70.9*
NI	0.45	0.82	0.85	[1]	*77.3*	0.03	[2]	*21.8*
T	**0.03**	0.52	**0.01**	**[7]**	*125.6*	0.00	[5]	*33.6*
R	**0.04**	0.77	**0.08**	**[3]**	*110.5*	0.00	[4]	*30.8*
BTr	0.84	0.73	**0.01**	**[7]**	*125.3*	0.00	[13]	*63.3*
All *jointly*	**0.00** *175.8* **[14]**							

Note: Values are probabilities of 'not being a cause in Granger's sense'. Bold figures
indicate causality up to the 10 per cent level. Values in brackets indicate the ranking
position, from most exogenous [1] to most endogenous [14].Values in italics are the
chi-squared statistics.

while being the cause of almost no variable. As a result, profits are highly
jointly caused by the remaining variables of the model with probability 0.00
and a chi-square statistic 175.8. This same type of measure is provided in
column (c) for each and every variable of the model. As compared to the
other variables, profits are ranked last at position 14, indicating that profits
are given the highest degree of endogeneity.

Quite unambiguously, Granger causality results give profits the 'consequence' role rather than the 'cause' role. Profits are being significantly predicted by the past growth rates of each and every variable of the model,
while at the same time the rate of growth of profits does not help in pre-
dicting them. This is true whether the income and spending variables are
taken as individual or joint regressors of profits. Remember, however, that
Granger causality is only one specific measure of causality, that of precedence in the 'short run', during the business cycle.

5.2.2 'Feedback Causality' and Weak Exogeneity

The rich structure of VEC models reveals an additional channel of temporal causality, that through the $\alpha\beta' X_{t-1}$ terms. If those terms are null, that is, if the estimated α coefficients are zero, then profits do not participate in the long-run realignment of the variables. Note that this measure of causality is that of causality towards the long run. Together with causality in the Granger sense, both measures are indicative of temporal causality, either during the business cycle or towards the steady state.

The test for the nullity of the adjustment coefficients α is presented in Johansen and Juselius (1990) and labeled the weak exogeneity test. The term 'weak' refers to the fact that exogeneity is with respect to the long-run parameters β only. The test hypothesis is that all $\hat{\alpha}_i$ for a given variable i are jointly null. The results are reported in the last column of Table 5.1.

Imports turn out to be the only weakly exogenous variable of the model. All other variables have a test significance level below 5 per cent, indicating that they are endogenous with respect to the long run. As a result the weak exogeneity tests do not help much in discriminating between causes and consequences.

One may, however, still order variables by degree of exogeneity. The ranking is given in the last column of Table 5.1, and is broadly identical to the Granger causality ranking. There are exceptions,[5] but of particular interest is that profits, again, appear on the last rank. Profits are thus found to be highly endogenous with respect to the long run.

Profits appear very much endogenous by the two measures of causality discussed thus far. Note that those measures are temporal measures so that profits follow in time the movements of the other income and spending variables of the model. One way to make sense of those results is to think of profits as a consequence of the consumption, imports, compensation, and so on.

Another result stemming from the Granger and feedback measures of causality is that the system we consider is highly causal. This is in line with what should be expected from an income-spending model. However, as an important property of the model, the high levels of causality make it hazardous to discriminate among leading and lagging variables on the *sole* basis of the previous tests.

5.2.3 FEVD and 'Variance Causality'

Another way to measure causality can be constructed with reference to the variability of a variable (see Masih and Masih 1997 for instance). In VAR and VECM models, it can be shown that the variance (of the forecast error) of any variable can be decomposed into parts attributable to each and every variable of the model. This is called forecast error variance decomposition, or FEVD. The intuition here is that, trivially, an exogenous variable will have none of its variance being explained by the remaining variables.

Just like temporal causality, FEVD describes a particular definition of causality. The idea behind FEVD is to simulate a 'typical' shock on the fully-estimated system, realize a forecast up to some chosen horizon and then decompose the variance of the forecast error. This procedure can be thought of as resulting in a degree of exogeneity or, equivalently, as a measure of the strength of the leading role. Note at this stage that, contrary to Granger causality, the nature of causality implied by FEVD is not of the temporal sense. Instead, FEVD is an out-of-sample definition of causality since it relies upon forecasts.

A drawback of FEVD is precisely the fact that a 'typical' shock has to be simulated. This is done on the residuals, but those in turn are typically contemporaneously correlated. As a result, the impact of a simulated shock is likely to incorporate the degree of correlation between the error terms. In that case the influence of a shock cannot be completely attributable to a precisely-defined variable of the model. A classic way to overcome this problem is the Cholesky orthogonalization of the error terms. This is essentially a convenient way of rewriting the system in order to avoid residual cross-correlation. However, that procedure is sensitive to the way the variables enter the system: the first variable in the model is allowed to affect all variables, whereas the second variable affects all variables except for the first one, and so on. This is equivalent to imposing a shock hierarchy in order to make sense of the FEVD interpretation.

Unfortunately, there is no universally better way to assess the prevalence of a hierarchical chain in any model (Sims 1980). A reasonable choice is to assume that shocks occur according to the degree of exogeneity of the variables, for example, according to the Granger ordering. Highly ranked variables (for example, (5.1)) are the most exogenous/autonomous variables and are thus the variables most likely to lead rather than to lag the remaining variables, hence the most likely to act as causes rather than consequences. However, using Granger ordering in VEC models may be misleading, precisely because VECMs uncover an additional channel of feedback causality.

In the following we have estimated six 'typical shocks' of a magnitude equal to one standard deviation. Three of them are based upon the precedence orderings evidenced in our results of Granger causality (shock I), 'feedback causality' ordering (shock II) and 'joint temporal' causality orderings (shock III).[6] The three remaining shocks are simulated to check the robustness of our results when changes are made in the orderings

Table 5.2 Decomposition of variance in profits

Ordering	Percent of profits' variance accounted for by own innovations		FEVD at $h = 12$	FEVD at $h = 32$
	at $h = 1$	at $h = 8$		
I	29.8	4.1	I, C, X, W	*65%:* R, C, W, M
II	29.8	4.1	C, W, M, I	*68%:* R, C, M, W
III	32.6	4.1	C, I, M, W	*65%:* W, CFC, R, M
IV	29.8	4.1	C, I, M, W	*67%:* R, C, M, W
V	32.6	4.1	I, C, M, W	*69%:* R, C, M, T_{YMS}
VI	100	19.9	Π, W, C, M	*51%:* I, R, W, PI

Notes: Italics are the percentage of profits' FEVD being accounted for by the top 4 variables
  I: 'business cycle' Granger causality ordering
  II: weak exogeneity ordering
  III: 'joint temporal causality' ordering
  IV: Alternative temporal causality ordering: M, W, C, R, TYMS, NI, X, I, G, CFC, PI, IncRW, BTr, Π
  V: Alt. ordering (policy variables first, then labor and capital variables): M, R, TYMS, NI, X, G, W, C, I, CFC, PI, Π, IncRW, BTr
  VI: Reverse of ordering III.

(shocks IV and V), and when the ordering is reversed (shock VI is the converse of shock III). The main results of FEVD for each of those orderings are presented in Table 5.2. Since the effects of a shock may take time to materialize, we have reported the FEVD of profits at $h = 12$ quarters (3 years) as well as at $h = 32$ quarters (8 years) after the shock has been simulated.

The first two columns of Table 5.2 show that, for the first five orderings, profits do not account for much of their own variance. Typically, profits account for 30 per cent of their own variance at $h = 1$ quarter, and this figure steadily drops to about 4 per cent two years after the shock has been simulated. This means that the variance of profits has some exogeneity in the short run, but the variability of profits becomes highly endogenous over the long run. The last two columns of Table 5.2 give us a hint as to which variables affect the variability of profits most. The general result is that, whatever the type of shock hitting the system, the variability of profits is attributable to the same three variables (consumption, compensation, imports) either in the short run (12 quarters) or in the long run (32 quarters). Note that in addition to those three variables, investment spending is an important contributor to the variance in profits, but in the short run only. Rental income is also an important contributor but shows up significant only over the long run. Altogether, the top four most important variables typically account for about two-thirds of the variability in profits. This is especially high in a fourteen-variable model.

Quite worth noting, those FEVD results are in line with our previous temporal causality measures. The 'core three' variables affecting profits evidenced here as consumption, compensation and imports are indeed good predictors of profits according to our previous tests. Also, profits are given a very endogenous role according to both measures. Profits quickly become endogenous even in the unlikely case of a shock of type VI hitting the system (a profit-dominated shock).

5.2.4   Impulse–Response Functions and 'Impact Causality'

So far we have discussed causality in terms of temporal precedence and variability. We have not addressed it in terms of magnitude of impact, that is, by how much a variable is likely to change following an increase in another variable.

Following Sims (1980), the signs and magnitudes of shocks can be assessed through the computation of impulse–response functions or IRFs. The idea behind IRFs is again to simulate a one-time shock on the system and then keep track of the effect of a response variable when an impulse is simulated on another variable. The issue of correlated residuals has been removed by using the 'generalized impulses' described in Pesaran and Shin (1998). This avoids getting into Cholesky factorization and simulating different shocks to assess the robustness of the results. In the present context, the responses can be interpreted as dynamic multipliers because they account for the interactions and feedback properties of the model. Note however, that the IRFs represent a 'spot' value at different horizons after the shock has taken place. To capture the overall effect of a shock at horizon h, one has to accumulate all the dynamic multipliers before quarter h.

A one-time shock has been simulated on the unrestricted VECM using the Pesaran–Shin method with a 'typical' magnitude equal to one standard deviation. Figure 5.2 presents the 'spot' responses of profits for 100 quarters (25 years) after the simulated shock, a time when the system is roughly at rest. The responses show different patterns in time and it is difficult to have an encompassing view. One can, however, distinguish, at least in the long run, between three different groups of responses (as in Figure 5.2).

A first group of variables having a positive impact on profits consists of consumption, proprietors' income, government spending and imports. The second group of variables which have an overall neutral effect on profits comprises investment, net interest and exports. Finally, compensation, taxes on production and imports, and rents have a negative effect on profits.

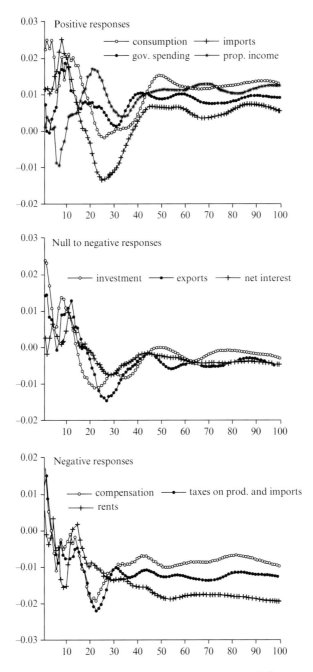

Figure 5.2 Responses of corporate profits to shocks in different variables

We will not discuss at length here the magnitude and sign of the responses of profits. Those are generally intuitive. There are, however, a few interesting facts which ought to be noticed.

1. Note that the groups affecting profits significantly (top and bottom panels) are not without meaning. Clearly, there is a set of variables related to private consumption (consumption, proprietors' income, imports, compensation) together with a set of policy-related variables (government spending and taxes). In addition to those two types of variables are rents, which exert the most powerful drag on profits.
2. There is a puzzle in consumption fostering profits and compensation dragging them. The reconciliation between the two findings could be that a growing share of American consumption is being funded by credit, a well-known phenomenon. This amounts to stating that the major source of profits, consumption, actually hides an increased indebtness trend.
3. There is a perplexing positive effect of imports on profits. This could be explained through the influence of a third-party variable, consumption. When consumption is high, imports are high, and when consumption is high, profits are high. This would explain that the signs of the responses of profits to consumption and import stimuli are the same. This seems an especially plausible explanation when one thinks of the large amounts of goods being imported into the US by American corporations, which make a profit selling them.
4. Investment having a somewhat neutral impact on profits is at odds with the New Consensus theories. The neutral impact can, however, be explained by the proposition that investment does not generate profits in itself, but rather increases production capacity, therefore *potential* profits.
5. Rents have a negative effect on profits. This result is in line with virtually all theoretical propositions. The magnitude of the negative effect, however, is about twice as large as the positive effect of consumption and related variables. Clearly then, money used in non-productive investments is an important leakage in the system in general, and a major loss for profits in particular.

5.3. CONCLUSIONS: THEORY AND POLICY

This chapter has attempted to provide an answer to the question of what drives profits from a mostly empirical perspective. While profits are indeed one of the main concerns of theoretical economics, there is a lack of empirical studies in the literature, comparatively speaking. The fifty-year-long stable trend of profits documented here testifies that theoretical economics has a lot to gain from empirical investigations.

Some data and technical limitations affect our consideration of the robustness of the results. In particular we have discussed *corporate* profits only, leaving aside the question of what amount of profit is contained in proprietors' income. The large size of our model, also, creates a problem with the degrees of freedom. We believe that, unless those issues have been dealt with satisfactorily, it is wise to understand the present findings as schematized results. We do believe, however, that there is a rationale underlying our results. This is motivated by the fact that they are coherent among themselves and across the various techniques used, in addition to comply with well-known documented, real-world facts.

In the course of the chapter we have primarily addressed the dynamics of all income and spending variables. Our attention has been set on the causal relationships pertaining to corporate profits, the word 'causal' having been discussed and measured along four different definitions. Two main results have emerged from our study.

The first one is that profits are better thought of as a consequence rather than a cause. *We find that profits are more likely to have a lagging role in the system, as opposed to a leading role.* As such, we do not find empirical support for the New Consensus claim, according to which profits are the autonomous, leading factor which economic policy should target. To the contrary, we find that profits have behaved in a highly endogenous way, as compared to other income and spending variables. This result is consistent throughout all our measures of causality and holds true even according to our long-run measures. This casts doubts on the plausibility of successful policies of the New Consensus type and provides empirical support for the Profit Paradox view.

The second major finding is that profits are driven by two well-identified groups of variables: consumption-related and policy-related. The first group appears to exert a more powerful force and comprises consumption, proprietors' income, imports and compensation. The second group comprises government spending and taxes. In addition, rents are found to affect profits greatly in the long run.

We have studied the signs of the relationships between profits and all those variables, and we have provided a few plausible interpretations. In particular, we uncovered signs of increased credit-financed consumption being a major source of profits. Again, such explanations are more in line with the Profit Paradox view than with the New Consensus tradition.

The finding about credit financing raises concerns over the future. The American economy is presently highly indebted, savings are at historic lows and Federal support is *de minima*. The increasing indebtness of American households cannot go on forever. In those conditions there would be upward pressures on the interest rate to slow the pace of consumer borrowing. But this is a risky path: a credit crunch in the American economy will not only depress consumption and profits but also drive the country into a recession. And, because the United States is such a great importer, this gloomy outcome is likely to spread to US trading partners. As a result, the interest rate policy tool ought to be utilized with great care.

However, we do not believe in a gloomy outcome. This is partly motivated by the high capacity of resilience in the American economy, and partly by our result that policy variables such as government spending and taxes have a role to play. There is still room for government action, even if the recent episodes go in the opposite direction. Another policy channel which may come out as being even more efficient is the exchange rate tool. The largely open American economy may well take advantage of this in the present globalized world. Currency issues may well be the next challenges for the United States.

NOTES

1. Treasury-Fed Accord (1951): an arrangement between the US Department of Treasury and the Federal Reserve that restored the independence to the Fed after the Second World War.
2. The remarkable stability of corporate profits also holds when deflated by the GDP price level (implicit price deflator).
3. See Toda and Phillips (1993) and Yamada and Toda (1998) for the implications of the loss of that information in the typical case of Granger causality.
4. Since variables are considered in logs, ΔX_t is roughly equal to growth rates.
5. A most notable exception is that investment gains exogeneity by this long-run measure, by moving up from position 11 to position 3. Equivalently, investment is found to respond more to the levels of the income and spending variables than to short-run growth rates.
6. This ordering, not presented here, is derived from a Fisher test on the adjustment coefficients jointly with the Γ coefficients.

REFERENCES

Asimakopulos, A. (1983), 'A Kaleckian profits equation and the United States economy 1950–1982', *Metroeconomica*, 35 (1–2).

Burke, W. (1973), The Bottom Line, *Federal Reserve Bank of San Francisco Weekly Newsletter*, 23 February, 1–3.

Engle, R. and C. Granger (1987), 'Co-integration and error correction: Representation, estimation, and testing', *Econometrica*, 55, 251–76.

Ferguson, T. (1995), *Golden Rule: The Investment Theory of Party Competition and the Logic of Money-Driven Political Systems*, Chicago: University of Chicago Press.

Granger, C. (1969), 'Investigating causal relations by econometric models and cross-spectral methods', *Econometrica*, 37, 424–38.

Granger, C. (1981), 'Some properties of time series data and their use in econometric model specifications', *Journal of Econometrics*, 16, 121–30.

Granger, C. (1988), 'Some recent developments in the concept of causality', *Journal of Econometrics*, 39, 199–211.

Granger, C. and A. Weiss (1983), 'Time series analysis and error correcting models', in Karlin, S. (eds), *Studies in Econometrics, Time Series and Multivariate Statistics,* London: Academic Press.

Himmelberg, C., Mahoney, J., Bang, A. and B. Chernoff (2004), 'Recent revisions to corporate profits: What we know and when we knew it', *Current Issues in Economics and Finance*, 10(3), 1–7.

Johansen, S. (1988), 'Statistical analysis of cointegration vectors', *Journal of Economic Dynamics and Control*, 12(2–3), 231–54.

Johansen, S. (1991), 'Estimation and hypothesis testing of cointegration vectors in Gaussian vector autoregressive models', *Econometrica*, 59, 1551–80.

Johansen, S. (1995), *Likelihood-Based Inference in Cointegrated Vector Autoregressive Models: Advanced Texts in Econometrics*, Oxford: Oxford University Press.

Johansen, S. and K. Juselius (1990), 'Maximum likelihood estimation and inference on cointegration with applications to the demand for money', *Oxford Bulletin of Economics and Statistics*, 52, 169–210.

Keynes, J.M. (1939), 'Professor Tinbergen's method', *Economic Journal*, 49, 558–68.

Lavoie, M. and P. Kriesler (2005), *Capacity Utilisation, Inflation and Monetary Policy: Marxian Models and the New Consensus*, paper presented at the 31st Annual Conference of the Eastern Economics Association, New York, 4–6 March.

Lütkepohl, H. (2005), *New Introduction to Multiple Time Series Analysis*, Berlin: Springer-Verlag.

McGrattan, E. and E. Prescott (2005), *Productivity and the Post-1990s U.S. Economy*, Staff Report No. 350. Minneapolis: Federal Reserve Bank of Minneapolis.

Masih, A. and R. Masih (1997), 'On the temporal causal relationship between energy consumption, real income, and prices: Some new evidence from Asian energy-dependent NICs based on a multivariate cointegration/vector error-correction approach', *Journal of Policy Modeling*, 19(4), 417–40.

National Income and Product Accounts (NIPAs), available at www.bea.gov/bea/dn1.htm, 30 August 2006.

Nelson, C. and C. Plosser (1982), 'Trend and random walks in macroeconomic time series: Some evidence and implications', *Journal of Monetary Economics*, 10, 139–62.

Newbold, P., Leybourne, S. and M. Wohar (2001), 'Trend-stationarity, difference-stationarity, or neither: Further diagnostic tests with an application to US real GNP', *Journal of Economics and Business*, 53(1), 85–102.

Parguez, A. (2002), *The Paradox of Fiscal Discipline in Contemporary Capitalist Economies: An Inquiry into the Poverty of Nations*, presented at the 7th International Post Keynesian Workshop, Kansas City, July.

Parguez, A. (2005), 'The absolute paradox of economic policy in contemporary capitalism', in Gnos, C. and L.P. Rochon (eds), *Post Keynesian Principles of*

Economic Policy, Cheltenham, UK and Northampton, MA, USA: Edward Elgar.

Pesaran, M. and Y. Shin (1998), 'Impulse response analysis in linear multivariate models', *Economics Letters*, 58, 17–29.

Romer, D. (2000), 'Keynesian macroeconomics without the LM curve', *Journal of Economic Perspectives*, 14(2), 149–69.

Sims, C. (1980), 'Macroeconomics and reality', *Econometrica*, 48(1), 1–48.

Taylor, J. (2000), 'Teaching modern macroeconomics at the principles level', *American Economic Review*, 90(2), 90–94.

Toda, H. and P. Phillips (1993), 'Vector autoregressions and causality', *Econometrica*, 61(6), 1367–93.

Uctum, M. (1995), *The Evolution and Determinants of Corporate Profits: An International Comparison*, Research Paper No. 9502, March, New York: Federal Reserve Bank of New York.

Yamada, H. and H. Toda (1998), 'Inference in possibly integrated vector autoregressive models: Some finite sample evidence', *Journal of Econometrics*, 86, 55–95.

6. Wages and aggregate demand: an empirical investigation for France*

Stefan Ederer and Engelbert Stockhammer

6.1. INTRODUCTION

In recent policy debates the suggestion of a reduction of wage costs as a means to increase employment and growth has figured prominently. For instance, in Germany the *Hamburger Appell* (IWK 2005), an appeal signed by 241 economists before national elections in 2005, demands wage cuts especially for the low-wage sector to reduce unemployment.[1] Of course, the EU jargon for this is not wage cuts, but 'employment-friendly wage policies', by which is meant employment lagging behind productivity growth.[2] But is it clear that lower wages would actually foster growth and employment?

Indeed, in economic theory the hypothesis that a wage cut, that is, a more unequal distribution of income, will stimulate aggregate demand, is contested. The Keynesian view of the interaction between the goods market and the labor market differs fundamentally from Neoclassical economics. For Keynesians, unemployment is the result of demand deficiencies in the goods market. For Neoclassical economists, unemployment is a labor market phenomenon. There exists a real wage which would clear the labor market. If the real wage is too high, unemployment will arise. Therefore Neoclassical economists emphasize the necessity of flexible wages and wage cuts as political measures to bring the economy back to full employment.

Keynesian economists see wages not only as the cost of labor, but also as a determinant of the level of aggregate demand (Keynes [1936] 1973). Keynes, of course, was mostly concerned with changes in nominal wages. In this paper, however, a redistribution of income, that is, a real wage change, is of interest. A wage increase, while raising costs of inputs, possibly promotes a higher level of demand and employment. Even for Keynesians, however, the effect of changes in the functional income distribution cannot be determined *a priori*. A wage increase stimulates consumption, but on the other hand reduces the expected future rate of profits

119

and dampens the demand for investment goods. Furthermore, it raises the costs of inputs and therefore reduces the demand for net exports. Whether the negative effects will offset the positive, is an empirical question (Bhaduri and Marglin 1990).

There is a small but growing literature (to be discussed below) that tries to identify the effects of changes in income distribution on demand empirically. This chapter aims at contributing to this literature by decomposing the effects of a rise in the profit share on the components of aggregate demand for one country, France, in order to determine the overall effect and identify the nature of the growth regime. The choice of this country is arbitrary and our results are preliminary. This country study forms part of a larger research project, in which the major European countries will be investigated.

It is worth noting that at first glance it is far from self-evident that the French economy, much indeed like other European countries, is profit-led as Neoliberal economics implies. The adjusted wage share fell from around 75 per cent in the early 1980s to some 65 per cent in the early 1990s (where it has remained since) without any discernable increase in trend growth (which is stagnating at around 2 per cent per annum)

The chapter is structured in the following way: Section 2 outlines the theoretical background and the existing empirical literature relating to this subject. Section 3 presents the econometric estimations and the empirical results for the components of aggregate demand. Finally, section 4 summarizes the results and draws some conclusions and policy implications.

6.2. THEORETICAL BACKGROUND

In order to analyze the effects of changes in the functional income distribution on aggregate demand we utilize a Post-Keynesian model based on Marglin and Bhaduri (1990). They formulated a general neo-Kaleckian model which allows for profit-led as well as wage-led growth regimes.

In our model, total aggregate demand (Y) is the sum of consumption (C), investment (I), net exports (NX) and government expenditure (G). All of these variables, except government expenditure, are a direct or indirect function of the profit share (π). The model (summarized in Table 6.1) is of a basic private open economy type and has several limitations. Because of our focus on the effect of changes in the functional income distribution, fiscal policy is ignored in the analysis. Income distribution, that is, the profit share (π)[3] is taken as exogenous. Thus feedbacks from, say, growth on

Table 6.1   Overview of the model

GDP	$Y = C(\pi) + I(\pi) + NX(\pi) + G$
Consumption	$C = f(W, R)$
Investment	$I = f(R, Y, i)$
Exports	$X = f(ULC, P_{IMP}, Y_{EU})$
Imports	$M = f(ULC, P_{IMP}, Y)$

Notes: Y: GDP, C: private consumption, I: private investment, NX: net exports, G: government expenditure, π: profit share, W: wage sum, R: profits, i: long-term real interest rate, X: exports, M: imports, ULC: unit labor costs, Y_{EU}: GDP Euro-12 countries. See Appendix 6.A for the definition of the variables.

income distribution via lower unemployment and a better bargaining position of labor are ignored at this stage.[4]

The effect of the increase in the profit share on aggregate demand and production is indeterminate and will depend on the sum of the reaction of the components of GDP, namely consumption, investment and net exports.

In order to determine the effect of changes in functional income distribution on consumption, total income is divided into wages (W) and profits (R), and their marginal consumption propensities are estimated. Because the savings rate of capitalists is higher than the savings rate of workers, consumption is expected to decrease when the profit share rises. The investment function depends on profits (R), output (Y) and the long-term real interest rate (i). Investment will probably increase when raising the profit share because expected future profits will rise. In agreement with standard theory, the effect of output is expected to be positive and that of interest rates negative.

In an open economy, exports and imports have to be included in the analysis. Exports are a function of unit labor costs (ULC), which indicate the competitiveness of the domestic economy on the world market. If unit labor costs increase, demand for domestic products will decrease both at home and abroad, because prices relative to foreign prices will rise. Exports also depend on the GDP of the trading partners. For France, these are mainly the Euro-12 countries, therefore their GDP is included in the exports function. Unit labor costs are negatively related to the profit share (see section 6.3.4). Imports also depend on unit labor costs relative to foreign prices and on domestic GDP.

Exports are expected to react positively to a rise in the profit share, because raising the profit share leads to a decrease in unit labor cost by definition. Reducing unit labor costs relative to foreign prices will make domestic goods more competitive in the world market. Thus, exports will be stimulated. Imports, for the same reason, are expected to react negatively to an increase in the profit share. As net exports are exports minus imports, the overall effect on net exports is probably positive.

The expected partial effects of changes in the income distribution on demand in an *open economy* are summarized below:

- $\partial C / \partial \pi < 0$
- $\partial I / \partial \pi > 0$
- $\partial NX / \partial \pi > 0$
- $\partial Y / \partial \pi = ?$

The overall effect of changes in the functional income distribution on aggregate demand and GDP depends on the magnitudes of the partial effects and can only be determined empirically. If it is positive ($\partial Y/\partial \pi > 0$), the demand regime is profit-led. If the effect is negative ($\partial Y/\partial \pi < 0$), it is wage-led.

Empirically, given the high levels of international trade, one would expect net exports to play a major role in determining the overall outcome. However, while individual countries can increase demand by increasing output, the world as a whole of course cannot. Therefore it is important to distinguish between the domestic sector of the economy and the open economy. The domestic sector in this case is defined with respect to consumption and investment only, assuming that the net export position does not change (as would be the result if wages were to change simultaneously in all countries). If consumption reacts more sensitively to an increase in the profit share than investment, the domestic demand will be wage-led.

The estimation strategy adopted is similar to that of Bowles and Boyer (1995). The model will be estimated by means of separate single equations for savings, investment and net exports. The key differences are the following. First, the econometric specifications differ. In particular, Bowles and Boyer fail to discuss the time series properties of the economic variables and ignore the issue of unit roots. As a consequence, they do not apply differences or error correction models (see section 6.3.1), that form the core of modern time series econometrics. To check the robustness of results, several plausible specifications will be reported. Second, Bowles and Boyer use the employment share as a proxy for capacity utilization. For European countries with a high persistence of unemployment this may be a misleading indicator, so output growth will usually be used instead. Third, Bowles and Boyer's period of estimation was 1961–1987; here this period is extended to 2004. The result obtained by Bowles and Boyer was that the growth regime was weakly profit-led, whereas excluding the foreign sector they derived a weakly wage-led regime.

Other related literature is only briefly mentioned here. Gordon (1995a) estimates consumption and investment as a function of income distribution for the USA. In a vector autoregression (VAR) model, various exogenous shocks are simulated. Gordon (1995b) extends the model for an open economy and investigates reactions of aggregate demand on changes in income distribution empirically for the USA. His conclusion is that the growth regime of the USA is profit-led.

Hein and Krämer (1997) as well as Hein and Ochsen (2003) in their studies employ a model for a closed economy based on Marglin and Bhaduri (1990). Hein and Ochsen (2003) extend the model with the monetary interest rate as exogenous variable and elaborate various accumulation regimes, depending on the sensitivity of the savings function and the investment function to the interest rate. In the empirical part, they estimate savings and investment econometrically and try to characterize the accumulation regimes of France, Germany, the USA and the UK.

Stockhammer and Onaran (2004) estimate a structural VAR model consisting of the variables capital accumulation, capacity utilization, profit share, unemployment rate and labor productivity growth for the USA, UK and France. Employing a VAR model, the mutual interaction of the variables is incorporated. The goods market is simulated by a model based on Marglin and Bhaduri (1990). It is supplemented by an equation for income distribution, a productivity function and a function for unemployment. From the empirical investigation it is concluded that unemployment is determined by the goods market, but that the impact of income distribution on demand and employment is very weak. Technical progress is shifting income distribution in favor of profits. Onaran and Stockhammer (2005) employ a similar model for Turkey and Korea.

Naastepad (2006) presents and estimates a richer model for the Netherlands, in which productivity growth is modeled explicitly. Productivity, savings, investment and exports are estimated by single equations. She finds that 'the Dutch demand regime during 1960–2000 is . . . wage-led' (Naastepad 2006, p. 24), but only narrowly so. Overall, she concludes that 'the growth rate of Dutch aggregate demand is relatively insensitive to changes in real wage growth' (Naastepad 2006, p. 29) in the postwar period.

6.3. EMPIRICAL RESULTS

6.3.1. Method

The model is estimated for the period from 1960 to 2004, based on annual data provided by the OECD Economic Outlook Database (2005). Unless indicated otherwise, variables are in real terms and logarithms in order to estimate elasticities instead of direct partial effects.

Regressions with non-stationary time series, as most of the macro-economic variables are, may produce misleading ('spurious') results. They show high R^2- and t-values, indicating erroneously a significant relationship between the variables. If variables are integrated of order one, employing first differences in the regression can solve this problem. However, using differences only investigates the short-run effects, losing all the information about long-run relationships. In order to avoid this problem, a structural model can be formulated including the long-run relationships postulated by the economic theory as well as the dynamic adjustment process when deviating from the equilibrium. These models are called Error Correction Model (ECM). If the economic long-run relationship is characterized by

$$y_t = \alpha x_t, \tag{6.1}$$

then the ECM has the form

$$\Delta y_t = \beta_0 + \beta_1 \Delta x_t + \beta_2 (y_{t-1} - \alpha x_{t-1}) \tag{6.2}$$

In order to employ an ECM, the existence of a long-run relationship is required. If this is true, the variables are both integrated of order one, but their linear combination according to equation (6.1) is stationary and the variables are referred to as being cointegrated. Thus, applying a unit root test on the residuals of the estimation of equation (6.1) permits the acceptance or rejection of cointegration.[5]

Following these arguments, in the econometric estimation the following steps are applied:

- Testing the variables for existence of a unit root (ADF test).
- Formulating the long-run relationship and testing the residuals of the estimation for stationarity (ADF test).
- If cointegration can be accepted, an ECM is estimated.
- If there is no cointegration relationship, the equation is estimated employing first differences of the variables.

In the following, the results of the econometric analysis for consumption, investment, exports and imports are described and the overall effect is calculated.

6.3.2. Consumption

The consumption function estimated econometrically has the following general form:

$$C = f(W, R) \tag{6.3}$$

C is real private consumption, *W* is the wage sum of both the private and the public sector, and *R* indicates operating surplus. Wages are calculated at the base of compensation rates; the operating surplus represents gross profits. Both wages and profits are pre-tax values. They are divided by the GDP deflator in order to obtain the real values. Dividing total income in wages and profits and estimating their consumption propensities separately permits the calculation of the effect of changes in income distribution.

ADF tests fail to reject the null hypothesis of a unit root at the five per cent level for private consumption, wages and profits.[6] Therefore it is very likely that the variables are not stationary and their first differences have to be used in the econometric estimations.

In order to estimate the function econometrically, three different specifications were adopted (see Table 6.2). Firstly we estimate an error correction model (ECM) supposing a long-run relationship between consumption on the one side and wages and profits on the other. However, testing the residuals of the long-run relationship shows that the null hypothesis of non-cointegrated variables cannot be rejected at a significance level of five per cent. The assumption of the cointegration relationship therefore cannot be confirmed.

Second, a pure differences specification without any presumed long-run relationship was estimated. The only explaining variables are the first differences of wages and profits. For the purpose of comparing the results, a partial

Table 6.2 Estimation results for the consumption function

	ECM		Differences		Shares	
	coefficient	prob.	coefficient	prob.	coefficient	prob.
c	3.814	0.000	0.006	0.033	0.023	0.452
$\Delta\ln(W)$	0.348	0.001	0.506	0.000		
$\Delta\ln(R)$	0.294	0.000	0.212	0.000		
$\ln(C(-1))$	−0.682	0.000				
$\ln(W(-1))$	0.424	0.000				
$\ln(R(-1))$	0.197	0.000				
R/Y					0.117	0.046
W/Y					0.235	0.006
$C(-1)/Y(-1)$					0.726	0.000
Adj. R-squared	0.763		0.663		0.892	
DW statistic	1.821		2.346		2.139	
Dep. Variable	$\Delta\ln(C)$		$\Delta\ln(C)$		C/Y	

Table 6.3   Results for consumption function

	ECM		Differences		Shares	
	W	R	W	R	W	R
Estimated coefficient	0.424	0.197			0.235	0.117
Elasticity lr $(\partial C/C)/(\partial W/W)$	0.622	0.289	0.506	0.212		
$(\partial C/Y)/(\partial W)$	0.675	0.510	0.549	0.374	0.858	0.427
$(\partial C/Y)/(\partial \pi)$	−0.165		−0.175		−0.431	

adjustment model employing the consumption share as dependent variable and the wage and profit shares as explanatory variables was estimated as the third function. To avoid the problem of perfect multicollinearity, only wages in the business sector are considered. The estimation results are satisfactory with respect to diagnostic statistics for all three equations. All of them show a substantial difference between the coefficient on wages and profits.

The resulting effects of changes in the profit share on consumption are presented in Table 6.3. For the ECM, the long-run elasticities $(\partial C/C)/(\partial W/W)$ and $(\partial C/C)/(\partial R/R)$ respectively, are calculated by dividing the corresponding estimated coefficients of W and R by the estimated coefficient of the error correction term.

For both the ECM and the differences specification, the elasticities are converted into direct partial effects according to equation (6.4).

$$\frac{\partial C/Y}{\partial \pi} = \frac{\partial C/C}{\partial R/R} * \frac{C}{R} - \frac{\partial C/C}{\partial W/W} * \frac{C}{W} \tag{6.4}$$

Regarding the shares specification, the estimated coefficient has to be corrected only for the long-run effect, dividing it by one minus the coefficient for the lagged dependent variable.

The total effect is calculated as the difference between the effects of wages and profits according to equation (6.4). Results for ECM (−0.165) and differences specification (−0.175) are quite close, but the result of the shares specification (−0.431) is remarkably different from the other two. Considering that testing the long-run relationship for cointegration does not produce a satisfactory outcome, the result of the differences specification appears to be the most plausible. It is also the median of the three results; therefore we chose to use it for calculating the overall effect.

An estimated coefficient of –0.175 means that raising the profit share by 1 percentage point (for example, from 30 per cent to 31 per cent) will lead to a reduction of private consumption of 0.175 percentage points of GDP (for example, from 55 per cent to 54.825 per cent of GDP).

Table 6.4   Estimation results for the investment function

	Unrestricted business GDP		Restricted total GDP		Restricted business GDP	
	coefficient	*prob.*	coefficient	*prob.*	coefficient	*prob.*
C	−0.437	*0.118*	−0.693	*0.000*	−0.454	*0.000*
ln(Inv(−1))	−0.188	*0.006*				
ln(*Y*(−1))	0.184	*0.023*				
ln(Inv(−1)) − ln(*Y*(−1))			−0.191	*0.004*	−0.187	*0.005*
ln(R(−1))	0.022	*0.701*	0.038	*0.013*	0.018	*0.233*
Δln(*Y*)	2.439	*0.000*	2.906	*0.000*	2.450	*0.000*
Δln(*R*)	−0.073	*0.699*	−0.063	*0.730*	−0.076	*0.669*
Δ*i*	−0.005	*0.983*	0.006	*0.980*	−0.010	*0.965*
Adj. R-squared	0.836		0.833		0.841	
Durbin-Watson statistic	1.415		1.376		1.421	
Dep. variable	Δln(Inv)		Δln(Inv)		Δln(Inv)	

6.3.3.   Investment

Private investment (*I*) is a function of operating surplus (*R*), real GDP (*Y*) and the long-term real interest rate (*i*) deflated by last year's GDP inflation (equation (6.5)).

$$I = f(R, Y, i) \tag{6.5}$$

Following the methodical steps discussed in section 6.3.1, the tests indicate that the variables are not stationary. Thus, for the econometric estimation, three slightly different ECM specifications were applied (see Table 6.4). All of them include profits and GDP as explanatory variables for long-run as well as short-run effects. The error correction term varies within the three specifications. In a first step, the coefficients for lagged private investment and lagged GDP are estimated separately (named 'unrestricted'). Because the coefficients for private investment and GDP are very close, in a second and third specification (labeled 'restricted') we estimate them with a common coefficient. The first and the third equation are estimated with the GDP of the business sector, whereas the second employs total GDP. All three equations contain the long-term real interest rate as explanatory variable.

The estimation results of all three equations are very similar. The coefficients of the ECM term are very close for all three specifications. The

Table 6.5　Results for the investment function

	Unrestricted business GDP	Restricted total GDP	Restricted business GDP
Estimated coefficient	0.022	0.038	0.018
Elasticity lr $(\partial I/I)/(\partial R/R)$	0.117	0.199	0.096
$(\partial I/Y)/(\partial \pi)$	0.062	0.105	0.051

long-run coefficient for profits ranges from 0.018 to 0.038. The short-run effect of profits is negative in all three specifications, a fact that is surprising. At this point we are still unable to offer an explanation. The estimated parameter for the interest rate is near zero and statistically insignificant in all three specifications.

Table 6.5 presents the effect of changes in the profit share on investment. Similarly to the ECM specification of private consumption (see section 6.3.2), the estimated coefficients have to be divided by the coefficient of the error correction term in order to get the long-run elasticities $(\partial I/I)/(\partial R/R)$. The elasticities are converted into direct partial effects according to equation (6.6).

$$\frac{\partial I/Y}{\partial \pi} = \frac{\partial I/I}{\partial R/R} * \frac{I}{R} \tag{6.6}$$

The calculated effects range from 0.051 to 0.105, with a median of 0.062. A partial effect of 0.062 means that raising the profit share by 1 percentage point (for example, from 30 per cent to 31 per cent) will have a positive effect on private investment of 0.062 percentage points of total GDP (for example, from 17 per cent to 17.062 per cent of GDP). Thus, the reaction of investment on changes in the functional income distribution is very small.

6.3.4.　Exports

Exports (X) are a function of domestic unit labor costs (ULC) in proportion to foreign prices and total foreign income. The foreign price level is included in our estimations through the import price deflator (P_{IMP}). Total foreign income is represented by real GDP of the Euro-12 countries (Y_{EU}), because the majority of French exports go to these countries (equation (6.7)).

$$X = f(Y_{EU}, ULC, P_{IMP}). \tag{6.7}$$

Table 6.6   Estimation results for the export function

	Indirect		Direct	
	coefficient	*prob.*	coefficient	*prob.*
C	0.007	*0.351*	0.001	*0.916*
$\Delta\ln(Y_{EU})$	1.836	*0.000*	1.935	*0.000*
$\Delta\ln(P_X/P_{IMP})$	−0.291	*0.015*		
$\Delta(ULC)$			−0.345	*0.463*
$\Delta(P_{IMP})$			0.002	*0.026*
Adjusted R-squared	0.635		0.644	
Durbin-Watson statistics	1.823		1.624	
Dependent variable	$\Delta\ln(X)$		$\Delta\ln(X)$	

Changes in the functional income distribution will affect exports, because they directly raise unit labor costs in relation to import prices. *ULC* are defined as real wages per person employed, divided by output per worker (equation (6.8)). Employing a definition which takes into account the employment structure of an economy, we avoid distortions which result from a reduction of the self-employed rate.[7]

$$ULC = \frac{W/E_D}{Y/E_T} = \frac{W}{Y} * \frac{E_T}{E_D} = (1 - \pi) * \frac{E_T}{E_D}. \tag{6.8}$$

Changes in unit labor costs in reaction to changes in functional income distribution, according to equation (6.8), only depend on the structure of employees ($\partial ULC/\partial\pi = -E_T/E_D$).

Alternatively, exports are estimated as a function of export prices instead of unit labor costs. An auxiliary equation for export prices as a function of unit labor costs has to be estimated additionally in order to determine the reaction of export prices to a rise in unit labor costs and thus the effect of changes in functional income distribution. The second estimation strategy is labeled 'indirect', whereas the first one is called 'direct' (see Table 6.6). Because the ADF test indicates non-stationarity for all variables, we employ first differences in all estimation specifications. No cointegration relationship between the variables can be confirmed, so we do not estimate any error correction model.

The estimated coefficient of the indirect specified equation is an export price elasticity $((\partial X/X)/(\partial P_X/P_X))$. It has to be converted into a unit labor costs elasticity according to equation (6.9). The elasticity $(\partial P_X/P_X)/(\partial ULC)$ was estimated through the auxiliary equation for export prices.

$$\frac{\partial X/X}{\partial ULC} = \frac{\partial X/X}{\partial P_X/P_X} * \frac{\partial P_X/P_X}{\partial ULC}. \tag{6.9}$$

The obtained unit labor costs elasticity has to be converted into direct partial effects of a change in the profit share according to equations (6.10) and (6.11). The same calculation is done with the estimated coefficient of the direct specified equation.

$$\frac{\partial X/X}{\partial \pi} = \frac{\partial X/X}{\partial ULC} * \left(-\frac{E_T}{E_D} \right). \tag{6.10}$$

$$\frac{\partial X/Y}{\partial \pi} = \frac{\partial X/X}{\partial \pi} * \frac{X}{Y}. \tag{6.11}$$

Table 6.7 shows the results for exports. According to equation (6.11), the resulting effect depends on the export share. Because the French export share increased from 8.1 per cent in 1965 to 28.6 per cent in 2004, two bench-mark values were calculated. First we calculated the partial effect using the average export share for the whole period from 1965 to 2004 (17.7 per cent). The corresponding values for the indirectly and the directly estimated partial effect are 0.075 and 0.092. Second, the export share for 2004 (28.6 per cent) was applied. The resulting partial effect ranges from 0.121 to 0.149, which is remarkably higher. This result corresponds to our expectations. Because we estimate constant elasticities, the reaction of exports relative to GDP should be higher, the greater the export share. The intuition of this is clear. An increase in unit labor costs relative to foreign prices make domestic goods less competitive in the world market as well as in the domestic market. If a large share of aggregate demand is made up by exports, the impact on GDP must be higher than in a relatively closed economy.

The average effect calculated with the export share for 2004 can be interpreted as an increase of exports of 0.135 percentage points of GDP (for

Table 6.7   Results for the export function

	Average export share (17.7%)		Export share 2004 (28.6%)	
	indirect	direct	indirect	direct
Estimated coefficient	−0.291	−0.345	−0.291	−0.345
Elasticity lr $(\partial X/X)/(\partial \pi)$	0.519	0.425	0.519	0.425
Export share X/Y	0.177	0.177	0.286	0.286
$(\partial X/Y)/(\partial \pi)$	0.092	0.075	0.149	0.121
Average	0.084		0.135	

example, from 28.6 per cent to 28.735 per cent) when the profit share is raised by 1 percentage point (for example, from 30 per cent to 31 per cent).

6.3.5. Imports

The same strategies as for exports were used in order to calculate the effects for imports (Tables 6.8 and 6.9). Imports are therefore estimated as a function of domestic unit labor costs relative to foreign price level and total domestic income. As in the export function, foreign prices are represented by the import price deflator (P_{IMP}) (see equation (6.12)).

$$M = f(Y, ULC, P_{IMP}) \qquad (6.12)$$

The alternative estimation strategy corresponds to exports. Instead of unit labor costs, the domestic price level (represented by the GDP deflator) in relation to foreign prices is applied. This estimation strategy is supported by a similar auxiliary equation for prices as a function of unit labor costs. Also, first differences are employed in the econometric specifications due to the non-stationarity of the variables, and there is no ECM estimated.

In order to obtain the effect of changes in the profit share, we calculate the price elasticity of imports estimated through the indirect specification according to equation (6.9), applying the domestic price level instead of export prices. After that, the corresponding calculations to equations (6.10) and (6.11) for imports are realized. The elasticities estimated through the direct specification are immediately converted according to equations (6.10) and (6.11). Because, in the same way as for exports, the impact of

Table 6.8 Estimation results for the import function

	Indirect		Direct	
	coefficient	*prob.*	coefficient	*prob.*
C	−0.002	*0.811*	0.011	*0.202*
$\Delta\ln(M(-1))$	−0.306	*0.001*	−0.228	*0.011*
$\Delta\ln(Y)$	2.709	*0.000*	2.732	*0.000*
$\Delta\ln(P(-1)/P_{IMP}(-1))$	0.253	*0.002*		
$\Delta\ln(P_{IMP}(-1))$			−0.279	*0.000*
$\Delta(ULC(-1))$			0.793	*0.114*
Adjusted R-squared	0.744		0.822	
Durbin-Watson stat	1.226		1.569	
Dependent variable	$\Delta\ln(M)$		$\Delta\ln(M)$	

Table 6.9   Results for the import function

	Average import share (17.5%)		Import share 2004 (29.2%)	
	indirect	direct	indirect	direct
Estimated coefficient	0.253	0.793	0.253	0.793
Elasticity lr $(\partial M/M)/(\partial\pi)$	−0.655	−0.798	−0.655	−0.798
Import share M/Y	0.175	0.175	0.292	0.292
$(\partial M/Y)/(\partial\pi)$	−0.115	−0.140	−0.191	−0.233
Average	−0.127		−0.212	

changes in income distribution and corresponding changes in unit labor costs is greater the higher the import share in total GDP, the effects are calculated both for an average import share (17.5 per cent) for the whole period and with the import share for 2004 (29.2 per cent).

The resulting effect of changes in functional income distribution on imports calculated for the average import share ranges from −0.115 to −0.140. Employing the import share for 2004, we obtain an income effect on imports of −0.191 and −0.233 (Table 6.9). The effect (for example, for the import share for 2004) can be interpreted as a reduction of imports by 0.212 percentage points of GDP (for example, from 30 per cent to 29.798 per cent) when profit share is raised by 1 percentage point (for example, from 30 per cent to 31 per cent).

6.3.6.   Total Results

Tables 6.10 and 6.11 represent the total results of changes in the functional income distribution on aggregate demand, adding up the effects on consumption, investment, exports and imports $(\partial Y/\partial\pi = \partial C/\partial\pi + \partial I/\partial\pi + \partial X/\partial\pi - \partial M/\partial\pi)$. As consumption responds strongly to changes in the profit share whereas the effect for investment is very small, the resulting effect for the 'domestic sector' (consumption plus investment) is clearly negative (−0.113). If there were no exports and imports, the French economy would contract when income distribution is changed in favor of profits. On the contrary, it could be stimulated by raising real wages.

The 'foreign sector' (exports minus imports) reacts in a strongly positive way to a rise of the profit share. Reducing unit labor costs makes domestic goods more competitive in relation to foreign goods. Therefore, every shift of functional income distribution in favor of profits will lead to an increase in exports and a decrease in imports, thus raising net exports and stimulating aggregate demand.

Table 6.10   Total results, average exports and import shares 1960–2004

	Average export/import shares		
	median	min	max
Consumption	−0.175	−0.165	−0.431
Investment	0.062	0.051	0.105
Exports	0.084	0.075	0.092
Imports	−0.127	−0.115	−0.140
Total effect	**0.098**		

Table 6.11   Total results, export and import shares for 2004

	Export/import shares 2004		
	median	min	max
Consumption	−0.175	−0.165	−0.431
Investment	0.062	0.051	0.105
Exports	0.135	0.121	0.149
Imports	−0.212	−0.191	−0.233
Total effect	**0.234**		

Calculating the total effect for average export and import shares (Table 6.10), we see that the positive reaction for net exports slightly over-compensates the negative one for the domestic sector. The total effect is 0.098, thus raising the profit share by 1 percentage point (for example, from 30 per cent to 31 per cent), will increase total aggregate demand by 0.098 per cent (for example, from 1.5 to 1.50147 billion euros).

As the effect on net exports is calculated in percentage points of GDP, it is higher, the larger the export and import shares are (see section 6.3.4). Thus, applying the values calculated for the export and import shares for the year 2004, the positive reaction of net exports to a rise of the profit share is much greater than the negative effect on the domestic sector. The total effect therefore is clearly positive (see Table 6.11). A total effect of 0.234 stands for an increase in total aggregate demand of 0.234 per cent (for example, from 1.5 to 1.5035 billion euros) when the profit share rises by 1 percentage point (for example, from 30 per cent to 31 per cent).

In summary, the main results of the investigation are the following: first, the (negative) effect of a change in the profit share on consumption is substantially larger than the (positive) effect on investment. The domestic sector of the French economy is therefore clearly wage-led. Second, the reactions of exports and imports depend on the size of the foreign sector relative to GDP; the more open the economy, the more dominant will be the role played by exports and imports. With the export and import shares for 2004, the foreign sector outbalances the domestic sector.

6.4. CONCLUSIONS

The starting point for this investigation of the relation between income distribution and demand was skepticism against what Howell (2005) called the 'IMF–OECD orthodoxy' which implies that wage cuts would improve economic performance (Stockhammer 2006). The skepticism is grounded in theoretical as well as empirical considerations. Empirically it is remarkable that France, much like other European countries, experienced substantial reductions in the wage share without a corresponding improvement in economic performance. Theoretically, Keynes and Kalecki had highlighted that an increase of profits at the expense of wages may have positive effects on investment and net exports, but it will also have negative effects on consumption expenditures.

To evaluate the net effect of the partial effects on consumption, investment and net exports, a post-Kaleckian model was estimated econometrically. The conclusion of this was that, overall, the French economy is now profit-led. At first this may seem at odds with the stylized fact that the wage cuts of the 1980s have failed to deliver growth. However, to understand this seeming contradiction, one has to look at the results in more detail. Indeed, the key factor that makes the French economy profit-led is the foreign sector. Domestically, the French economy is wage-led because the effect (of an increase in the profit share) on consumption is clearly stronger than that on investment.

Therefore, wage cuts and a redistribution of income in favor of profits would stimulate economic growth only because it stimulates net exports. Wage cuts would lead to higher economic growth at the cost of the trading partner countries, which is a kind of 'beggar thy neighbor' policy via wage constraint and competitive real devaluation (rather than exchange rate manipulation or tariffs).

In other words, a 'growth through wage cuts' strategy cannot work for all countries, even though it may work for any single country. To stimulate the world economy, or at least larger economic units, wage increases may be necessary. Thus wage coordination is needed to prevent prisoners' dilemma situations. Although worldwide wage coordination is far from being realistic, it is at least conceivable at the European level, where collective bargaining systems, if diverse, do already exist in all countries. The EU, with export and import shares well below those of France, may well constitute a wage-led economy and could conceivably stimulate economic growth by a more egalitarian distributional policy. Of course, this last point is presently speculation which needs to be backed by further research.

NOTES

*   This paper received support from the Project 'Asset and Labor Markets in Economic Growth' by the Austrian Science Fund (FWF P18419-G05).
1.   'The unpleasant truth consists mainly in the fact that an improvement of the situation of the job market is only possible through lower wage compensation of the low-wage employees' (IWK 2005, own translation)
2.   EU documents usually emphasize the role of wage flexibility more than that of general wage cuts. However, while wage developments below productivity growth in order to foster profitability are occasionally mentioned, wage growth above productivity growth seems not to be worth mentioning.
3.   Functional income distribution and its measure, the profit share, are used synonymously throughout this paper.
4.   This raises substantial theoretical as well as econometric issues. Econometrically we ignore the issue of simultaneity.
5.   The above discussion is standard now in time series econometrics and can be found in any recent time series econometrics textbook. Charemza and Deadman (1997) is a particularly readable one.
6.   The results of the ADF tests for all variables are reported in Appendix 6.B.
7.   See Marterbauer and Walterskirchen (2003) for further discussion.

REFERENCES

Bhaduri, A. and S. Marglin (1990), 'Unemployment and the real wage: The economic basis for contesting political ideologies', *Cambridge Journal of Economics*, 14, 375–93.

Bowles, S. and R. Boyer (1995), 'Wages, aggregate demand and employment in an open economy: An empirical investigation', in Epstein, G. and H. Gintis (eds), *Macroeconomic Policy after the Conservative Era*, Cambridge: Cambridge University Press, pp. 143–71.

Charemza, W. and D. Deadman (1997), *New Directions in Econometric Practice: General to Specific Modelling, Cointegration and Vector Autoregression*, Cheltenham, UK and Lyme, USA: Edward Elgar.

Gordon, D. (1995a), 'Putting the horse (back) before the cart: Disentangling the macro relationship between investment and saving', in Epstein, G. and H. Gintis (eds), *Macroeconomic Policy after the Conservative Era*, Cambridge: Cambridge University Press, pp. 57–108.

Gordon, D. (1995b), 'Growth, distribution, and the rules of the game: Social structuralist macro foundations for a democratic economic policy', in Epstein, G. and H. Gintis (eds), *Macroeconomic Policy after the Conservative Era*, Cambridge: Cambridge University Press, pp. 335–83.

Hein, E. and H. Krämer (1997), 'Income shares and capital formation: Patterns of recent developments', *Journal of Income Distribution*, 7(1), 5–28.

Hein, E. and C. Ochsen (2003), 'Regimes of interest rates, income shares, savings and investment: A Kaleckian model and empirical estimations for some advanced

OECD economies', *Metroeconomica*, 54(4), 404–33.

Howell, D. (ed.) (2005), *Fighting Unemployment: The Limits for Free Market Orthodoxy*, Oxford: Oxford University Press.

IWK (2005) *Hamburger Appell*, Hamburg: Institut für Wachstum und Konjunktur, Universität Hamburg, www1.uni-hamburg.de/IWK/appell.htm, 10 April 2006.

Keynes, J. [1936] (1973), *The General Theory of Employment, Interest and Money: The Collected Writings of John Maynard Keynes, Volume VII*, Cambridge: Macmillan.

Marglin, S. and A. Bhaduri (1990), 'Profit squeeze and Keynesian theory', in Marglin, S. and J. Schor (eds), *The Golden Age of Capitalism: Reinterpreting the Postwar Experience*, Oxford: Clarendon Press, pp. 153–86.

Marterbauer, M. and E. Walterskirchen (2003), 'Bestimmungsgründe der Lohnquote und der realen Lohnstückkosten', *WIFO Monatsberichte*, 2, 151–9.

Naastepad, R. (2006), 'Technology, demand and distribution: A cumulative growth model with an application to the Dutch productivity slowdown', *Cambridge Journal of Economics*, 30(3), 403–34.

OECD (2005), *Economic Outlook Database*, No. 76.

Onaran, Ö. and E. Stockhammer (2005), 'Two different export-oriented growth strategies: Accumulation and distribution a la Turca and a la South Korea', *Emerging Markets, Finance and Trade*, 41(1), 65–89.

Stockhammer, E. (2006), *Still Unemployment . . . After All These Wage Cuts*. Paper presented at the Conference of the Allied Social Sciences Associations, Boston, 6–8 January.

Stockhammer, E. and Ö. Onaran (2004), 'Accumulation, distribution and employment: A structural VAR approach to a Kaleckian macro model', *Structural Change and Economic Dynamics*, 15, 421–47.

APPENDIX 6.A   DATA DEFINITIONS

Model notation	OECD notation	Name	Formula
–	CFKG	Govt. consumption of fixed capital, value	–
–	CGW	Govt. final wage consumption expenditure, value	–
C	CPV	Consumption private, volume	–
E_D	EEP	Dependent employment business sector	$EEP = ETB - ES$
–	ES	Self employed	–
E_T	ETB	Employment business sector	–
–	GDP	GDP, value	–
–	GDPB	GDP business sector, value	$GDPB = GDP - CGW - (TIND - TSUB) - CFKG$

Model notation	OECD notation	Name	Formula
Y	GDPV	GDP, volume	–
I	IPV	Private investment, volume	–
–	IRL	Interest rate, long-term	–
i	IRLR	Interest rate, long-term, real, based on GDP deflator (-1)	IRLR = IRL – 100 * (PGDP(-1) / PGDP (-2) – 1)
M	MGSV	Imports, volume	–
R	OSB	Operating surplus, value	OSB = GDPB – WSB
P	PGDP	GDP deflator	PGDP = GDP / GDPV * 100
P_{IMP}	PMGS	Import price deflator	–
P_X	PXGS	Export price deflator	–
–	TIND	Indirect taxes, value	–
–	TSUB	Subsidies, value	–
ULC	ULC	Unit labour costs real	ULC = (WSB/EEP) / (GDPB/ETB)
–	WSB	Wage sum business sector	WSB = WSSE*EEP
–	WSSE	Compensation rate, business sector	WSSE = (WSSS – CGW) / EEP
W	WSSS	Compensation of employees, value	WSB + CGW
X	XGSV	Exports, volume	–

APPENDIX 6.B   ECONOMETRIC TESTS

6.B.1   Result of ADF tests

	with Intercept		without Intercept	
	ADF	crit. value (5%)	ADF	crit. value (5%)
ln (GDPV)	−5.687	−2.935	2.525	−1.949
Δln (GDPV)	−3.377	−2.935	−2.045	−1.949
ln (CPV)	−2.683	−2.935	2.469	−1.949
Δln (CPV)	−3.227	−2.935	−1.875	−1.949
ln (IPV)	−1.700	−2.935	1.714	−1.949
Δln (IPV)	−3.614	−2.935	−3.082	−1.949
ln (XGSV)	−3.109	−2.935	8.560	−1.949
Δln (XGSV)	−4.116	−2.935	−2.198	−1.949
ln (MGSV)	−2.029	−2.935	6.456	−1.949
Δln (MGSV)	−6.210	−2.935	−3.684	−1.949

	with Intercept		without Intercept	
	ADF	crit. value (5%)	ADF	crit. value (5%)
ln (WSB+CGW)	−2.722	−2.935	1.001	−1.949
Δln (WSB+CGW)	−1.739	−2.935	−1.435	−1.949
ΔΔln (WSB+CGW)	−6.403	−2.935	−6.442	−1.949
ln (OSB)	−1.472	−2.935	4.967	−1.949
Δln (OSB)	−4.265	−2.935	−3.190	−1.949
ln (GDPV_EU12)	−4.445	−2.935	10.245	−1.949
Δln (GDPV_EU12)	−3.752	−2.935	−2.072	−1.949
ULC	−0.580	−2.935	−1.194	−1.949
ΔULC	−3.901	−2.935	−3.711	−1.949
PIMP	−1.467	−2.935	0.561	−1.949
ΔPIMP	−3.880	−2.935	−3.602	−1.949

6.B.2   Results of Cointegration Tests

	with intercept			without intercept		
	ADF	crit. value (5%)		ADF	crit. value (5%)	
		lower	upper		lower	upper
Consumption	−3.735	−4.07	−4.01	−3.789	−3.80	−3.71
Investment	−2.603	−4.07	−4.01	−2.634	−3.80	−3.71

PART III

Economic policies

7. New institutions for a new economic policy

Jesús Ferreiro and Felipe Serrano

7.1. INTRODUCTION

The main feature of modern Neoclassical economic theory is that it includes some of the information problems that agents face when they try to optimize their market decisions into its equilibrium models. The inclusion of asymmetric information problems in these models has enriched economic theory. Besides this, it has put the analysis of the institutional framework surrounding the working of markets back into the core of its empirical and theoretical studies.

Nevertheless, one of the main problems faced by the agents, the problem of uncertainty, as defined in Post-Keynesian thought, has not received the same attention. The rational expectations hypothesis is still dominant in most of the new equilibrium models. Modern Neoclassical macroeconomics, that is, New Keynesian economics, departs from Lucas and Sargent's New Classical macroeconomics not because of the rejection of that hypothesis, but because of the rejection of the hypothesis of perfect flexibility of wages and prices. The problems of asymmetric information are used to explain the existence of rigidities that generate market failures. These rigid-ities allow government intervention to be defended, from the point of view of economic equilibrium theory.

However, the problems created by the existence of Post-Keynesian uncertainty not only cannot be ignored but they must be at the centre of any theory that tries to understand the real working of market economies. In this sense, the objective of this chapter is to expose some elements that are behind the current theoretical debate on the analysis of information problems. We have focused on the institutional side of that debate, leaving aside those aspects with a higher microeconomic dimension. Our aim is to stress that the economic policy that must be implemented in the current situation, which is defined by an intense uncertainty, is an economic policy connected with the design of institutions.

7.2.   THE NEOCLASSICAL APPROACH TO INSTITUTIONS: THE NEW INSTITUTIONAL ECONOMY

The classical view of welfare economics, as formed by the two equivalence theorems, is a static model: a representation of the 'state of the economy' at a certain moment in which the agents' decisions and the resource allocation only depend on the initial endowment of resources and the state of technology. The information that the agents need to make optimizing decisions is, by definition, available to all of them, that is, there is perfect information. Stiglitz (1994) refers to this classical version as the 'Neoclassical paradigm' and proposes an alternative version that he names the 'information paradigm'. In order to grasp the main differences between these paradigms, that is, between both Neoclassical dialects, we must first remember some of the key elements of equilibrium theory related to the aim of this chapter.

In the first neoclassical approaches, there was an absolute absence of institutional elements or an institutional framework. The only institution required for the economic decision-making process was the market. Traditional Neoclassical economic analysis was 'non-institutional', as Joskow stated in his presidential address to the Annual Conference of the International Society of New Institutional Economics (Joskow 2004). The institutions simply did not exist or, at the very most, their working was perfectly compatible with the restrictions imposed for the existence of economic equilibrium.

This way of understanding institutions was the logical consequence of the assumption of perfect information that allows agents to make optimizing decisions and, consequently, to reach an outcome of economic equilibrium.[1] The role of the institutions was to provide the information that agents need to make efficient decisions.

The hypothesis of perfect information means that *all* the individuals: i) have an exact knowledge of the (past, present and future) values of the relevant variables in their decision-making processes, ii) are able to process the information without making systematic errors, iii) obtain all the information they need at zero cost, iv) share the same information (the information is symmetrically distributed), and, v) have the certainty that all the other individuals make the same decisions in the presence of the same event.

Overcoming this Neoclassical tradition is the result of two lines of research that arose within the Neoclassical paradigm itself. First, the works of the so-called New Institutional Economy (NIE), whose ultimate aim is to extend the Neoclassical approach to the analysis of institutions (Coase 1937,

1960, North 1990, Williamson 1985, 1993, 2000). The dissatisfaction with welfare economics comes from the contradiction between the significance of institutions in the real world and their absence in the equilibrium models. The works of this new school of thought try to incorporate institutional variables in the equilibrium models with the aim of enriching these models. In this approach, the analytical tools of the Neoclassical paradigm are used to study the institutional framework (Matthews 1986).

Second, the contributions of the information paradigm have also helped to revitalize Neoclassical institutional analysis (Stiglitz 2002). The incorporation of the problems related to asymmetric information generates new forms of disequilibrium that may have deep effects on the working of markets and on the existence of economic equilibria. Small information problems can generate deep disequilibria that the market cannot correct. The works of this school have helped to revitalize the analysis of institutions by showing how the working of markets (and equilibrium) is determined by the incentive structures faced by agents, which can be partially determined by the nature of the institutions existing at a given point of time and space.

But, what is the nature of the Neoclassical analysis of institutions? From a theoretical perspective, we could say that its ultimate aim is to complete the model of economic equilibrium by incorporating the institutional dimension. The proposed institutional analysis, however, still depends very much on the myths of Neoclassical efficiency and equilibrium (Rutherford 2001). Institutions are, on some occasions, presented as answers to a market failure, and, in most cases, as constraints on the agents' behavior that allow them to make optimal or, at least sub-optimal decisions.

Institutions, from a broader perspective, can influence economic behavior in different ways. First, they can constrain behavior, showing what can and cannot be done. Second, they are a source of information, since, by inducing certain behaviors, they inform the agents about the decisions that other agents will adopt, helping to remove problems of asymmetric information. Third, they are an even deeper source of information, because the institutional framework can influence the definition of the individuals' objectives, and the way they select and interpret the information.

Although the first two functions are fully compatible with the existence of a rational agent that maximizes her utility, the third function is contrary to an atomist approach to society, since this function involves the individuals' behavior being influenced by customs, the social norms of the environment in which they live and the ethical values prevailing in their society.

If we take into account Williamson's model of institutional analysis (Williamson 2000), where four levels of institutional analysis are defined, most of the papers of the NIE are located in levels 2 and 3. In level 1

Williamson locates norms, traditions, customs, ideology and religion. For most economists of the NIE, this level is considered as 'given', and it changes only in the very long term. In level 2 we find what Williamson calls 'the formal rules of the game', that is, the analysis of constitutions, political systems, property rights, currencies, financial institutions and, in general, the economic, political and legal mechanisms that facilitate economic exchanges. In level 3 we find what Williamson calls 'the play of the game', that is, given the rules of the game, how agents play within these rules. Finally, level 4 is the level in which Neoclassical economic theory operates: that is, once the institutional framework needed for markets to work has been defined, level 4 shows how the interaction among agents brings about optimum equilibrium outcomes.

For the authors belonging to the NIE, their compromise with neoclassical equilibrium theory is behind the choice of the institutions on which they focus their work (and the type of analysis proposed for the study of these institutions). The theory of property rights is at the core of the analysis made at level 2. The exchange through the market can only happen if the rights on the exchanged goods are clearly defined. However, a good definition of these rights does not remove the existence of potential problems. Therefore, institutions are needed to govern the exchange of rights, that is, contracts are needed. This is the basis of the literature on transaction costs.

This preference for one specific kind of institution, and the kind of analysis proposed for these institutions, stems from the theoretical dissatisfaction mentioned above. This dissatisfaction is related to the problems of asymmetric information. The discovery of institutions allows this basic element of the hypothesis of perfect information to be relaxed, upgrading neoclassical analysis but without questioning the concept of equilibrium.

Where do these information asymmetries come from? Of course, there is not just one source. In some cases, there are asymmetries because agents have some degree of monopoly on certain information. This has been further explored by the information economy theorists. In other cases, the asymmetries exist because individuals have bounded rationality (Simon 1987), that is, they have computational limits to process the available information and, therefore, the difficulty of the problem they must solve exceeds the available cognitive capacities. This second way has mostly been explored by those authors who try to place institutions at the core of neoclassical theory.

Building a solid link between the concepts of bounded rationality and the Neoclassical concept of efficiency has always been an objective of neoclassical theory. Until the surge of the NIE, which tried to solve the problem by incorporating institutions, the way used to build that link was the individual's learning capacity. Since the thresholds of satisfaction proposed by Simon tend to adjust themselves according to experience, they could gradually approximate a kind of Neoclassical optimal threshold. In this case, the notion of the satisfaction of needs would equal the neoclassical optimization criterion. The general equilibrium models would be long-run models, whilst the models of bounded rationality would be short-term models that would converge in the long term towards the economic equilibrium models.

However, Simon rejected that interpretation, arguing that such a convergence could not exist, because the individuals' speed of learning was lower than the speed of change of the environment. Therefore, by revealing the non-stationarity of the economic process, Simon rejected the assimilation attempted by Neoclassical thought. Nonetheless, Simon's concept of satisfaction of needs is an individualistic rational calculation approach, similar to that of the Neoclassical models. This approach is further explored by the NIE. Through the institutions, individuals can get the information they need and find the (institutional) procedures to solve their computational limits. The main theoretical problem would be the minimization of the costs generated by the lack of information. The best institutions would be those that allow this objective to be reached. Therefore, as relevant as the definition of property rights is the institutional framework that determines the governance of economic relations. The setting of the institutions located at levels 2 and 3 (property rights and contracts) is shown as a technical problem: all the institutions must favor the efficient allocation of resources through the market under the implicit assumption that individuals make rational calculations when they make optimal decisions.

Therefore, the institutional design is still considered as an exogenous variable (as a constraint) that can be rationalized according to some presumed technical requirements arising from the laws that rule the working of markets. The causal logic always goes from the market to the institutional framework.

Our dissatisfaction with this modern institutional analysis is twofold. First, from the microeconomic perspective, this New Institutionalism underestimates the relevance of the normative content of the institutional framework. That is, it underestimates the nature of the information codified and supplied by the institutional framework, information that for the institutionalist tradition (Rutherford 1994, Hodgson 1998) is the basis of individuals' behavior. Individuals are not isolated beings that make rational individual calculations when they are confronted with a choice. They are social beings that make decisions based on what they have learned. Dominant values in a certain society at a certain time, and the norms and customs arising from these values, are the basic elements that explain the behavior of individuals.

The social determination of individual behavior is a central issue in recent works of the 'Old Institutionalism'. But this is not the issue on which we will focus. We will concentrate on our second dissatisfaction with the NIE: its static dimension. In strictly theoretical terms, we could say that the NIE helps to show the different situations of structural economic stability by showing the links that may exist at any moment between the market requirements (in terms of some information constraints) and some components of the institutional framework. However, its conclusions remain in the field of static analysis, and, therefore, there are relevant methodological problems that arise from the compromise with economic equilibrium when trying to study the changes in the institutional framework.

The achievement of equilibrium means that the information that agents need to make their decisions must be available. Only under this assumption can the hypothesis of perfect information be defended. However, in the New Neoclassical models there is no loosening of that constraint. They assume that this problem of information does not exist. It is accepted that individuals do not know how to process the necessary information or that there exists an asymmetric distribution of information, but the assumption of the existence of perfect information still remains. Agents as a whole, do not face a problem of lacking information, that is, the existence of uncertainty as proposed by Post-Keynesian thought and the Old Institutionalism is rejected. Time is always identified with logical time.

The analysis of institutional change, however, cannot ignore the relevance of historical time for economics, a relevance that arises from the problems generated by the existence of uncertainty. In order to introduce the concept of historical time into the core of theoretical analysis, it is not sufficient to bear in mind historical facts when we want to place the design of and changes in institutions in their context. The institutions existing in a society are the outcome of its own idiosyncrasies. But this does not mean that the problem of historical time is considered. A static analysis of institutions is fully compatible with taking historical events into account. For instance, the regulation of property rights can be different between countries due to historical circumstances. But in any case, what is really relevant for economic theory is the fact that the regulation of these rights is needed for an efficient working of markets.

Taking into account historical time gives a dynamic and evolutionary nature to the social and economic process (Nelson and Winter 1982, 2002). The analysis of institutions is more complicated because the lack of predetermined directions in which they move makes it necessary to take into account the different normative approaches about how to organize social relations in the setting of possible future scenarios.

7.3.   THE IMPORTANCE OF HISTORICAL TIME

Paul Davidson defines uncertainty as follows:

> an environment of true uncertainty (that is, one which is nonergodic) occurs whenever an individual cannot specify and/or order a complete set of prospects regarding the future, because the decision maker cannot conceive of a complete list of consequences that will occur in the future or cannot assign probabilities to all consequences because the evidence is insufficient to establish a probability so that possible consequences are not orderable. (Davidson 1991, p. 134)

Therefore, uncertainty arises from the impossibility of using past frequencies as sources of information to forecast the future. This impossibility is due to the non-stationary nature of the economic process.

The existence of uncertainty removes the possibility of working with the notion of logical time and leads to putting the notion of historical time at the center of the analysis. For Joan Robinson,

> in an historical model, causal relations have to be specified. Today is a break in time between an unknown future and an irrevocable past. What happens next will result from the interactions of the behavior of human beings within the economy. Movement can only be forward. (Robinson 1962, p. 26)

Placing history at the heart of economic analysis means accepting, from a theoretical perspective, that events are not predetermined but contingent. That is, their probabilities are directly influenced by past events. A possible theoretical outcome can only happen if events take place according to the hypothesis on which the model is based. If these events do not happen, the outcome will not take place. In sum, the future does not exist. It is made in the present from the current decisions that agents make.

Let us assume that we can represent the economy, in a long-run time horizon, and from a strictly theoretical perspective, as presented in Figure 7.1. Then, let us assume that point A is a historical point in which the economy starts a period of change (the reasons for this change are not important now). Let us also assume that, from a theoretical perspective, two paths of change are possible: those represented by the points B and C. If the economy moves towards B it is not due to the existence of a kind of predetermination or a historical law that leads the economy to that point in an irreversible manner. On the contrary, the choice of this path is the outcome of the events that may have happened during the period of change. If the events had been different, the final outcome would also have been different, for instance, C.

A point like B_{11} informs us that the economy has moved through different events, and that this specific point is the outcome of the path followed (from

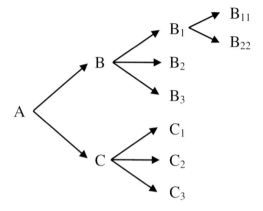

Figure 7.1   Path dependence

A to B, from B to B_1, and from B_1 to B_{11}). We cannot understand how that point has been reached from its specific features if we do not consider the whole chain of events. This point has specific features different from other potential points that we could imagine according to the hypothesis made about possible changes in the structural elements of the economy. The state of the economy, represented for instance in B_3, will provide different information from that provided by B_{11}, since the latter is the result of different past events.

Nonetheless, this is only a purely theoretical speculation, because the economy can only be located in one point at a time. However, this speculation helps us to understand that this state is not the only one possible, since it is the outcome of a specific combination, historically determined, of economic and social forces. A different combination would have produced a different outcome. Therefore, the process is irrevocable. The notion of irrevocability posed by Robinson when she stated that 'the movement can only be forward' stresses that it is impossible to move back from B_{11} to B. Any event that creates a new situation of change will lead the economy to a new and different point. Events are irreversible. Any change will lead to a different point. The 'arrow of time' only moves in one direction, forward, though we can imagine different possibilities.

Any economic process is an unstable and evolving one. It is not a stable and predetermined process, as shown in the models of economic equilibrium. The decisions of individuals are at the origin of this instability. The interaction among agents changes the historical forms used in these relations, helping to change the economic scenes where these relationships take place. In this world, uncertainty about the future plays a key role. Past events provide poor information about what we can expect to happen in the future, mainly if we try to foresee the very long-run future and/or if we use information from the very far past. We can always imagine different alternative states using alternative hypotheses. However, we cannot attach a true probability to all these alternatives.

The dynamic and evolutionary nature of social processes opens up a number of analytical questions about different fields: technology, specific institutions, individual behavior and so on. We will pay attention to one specific question: can we make analyses with logical time in the presence of uncertainty, that is, can we keep using the concept of economic equilibrium in a process with those characteristics? Would all the points of the graph be different points of equilibrium?

7.4.   EXPECTATIONS AND INSTITUTIONS

The answer to these questions depends on the concept of equilibrium we use. If by economic equilibrium we understand a point where all markets clear, the answer is no. For all markets to clear, and not only the markets that provide goods in the present but also those that will provide them in the future (this is the notion of equilibrium with intertemporal resource allocation), we should know at every moment the path that the economy will follow, something impossible for the reasons pointed out before. If we identify the equilibrium with the outcome of an optimizing strategy for individuals, the answer will also be negative: in the absence of perfect information, agents cannot make optimal decisions, no matter how 'rational' they may be.

However, the use of a notion of equilibrium must not be removed. When we talk of equilibrium, we mean the stability of the complex relations among economic and institutional elements and of the results of these relations. The notion of equilibrium as a synonym of order among complex relations leads, again automatically, to the problem of logical time, that is, to a discussion about the existence of laws that regulate the working of market economies. The problem is to know whether the different states of the economy can be studied through logical causal relations that help us to understand the interrelations among economic variables. That is to say, is it possible to develop an economic analysis that simultaneously combines the concepts of logical time and historical time?

Kregel (1976) states that, in an initial draft of the General Theory, Keynes incorporated into the consumption and investment functions an explicit variable, E, to represent the state of long-term expectations. This variable was independent of the system, and therefore a stochastic change in that variable could change the causal relations included in the consumption and investment functions. Finally, Keynes opted for building his argument on the presumption that those expectations were constant, though being aware of the fact that their change could change the relations among the variables. As Kregel stated,

> the assumption of constant expectations is obviously something quite different from the assumptions of perfect foresight and certainty. (Kregel 1976, p. 212)

Therefore, it can be said that the General Theory defines causal relations among variables starting from the assumption that the institutional framework, broadly defined, works to stabilize long-term expectations. The room for implementing stabilization policies derives from the self-contradictions generated in the short-term: because short-term expectations may be disappointed or because an equilibrium with full employment is not generated. For Dow, therefore, there exists a link between logical time and historical time: logical time provides a general analysis of the causal forces; historical time changes the causal relations of the processes in historical contexts, stressing the relevance of institutions and uncertainty and of their consequences (Dow 1998).

With institutions we can build economic states, that is, we can temporarily stabilize the causal relations among economic variables and, consequently, we can work with logical time. The word 'build' can lead to an excessively functional interpretation of the origin and evolution of the institutions that is far from our perspective. The typology of institutions in modern societies is very wide, and the interactions among individuals or between individuals and society are very different (Scott 2001). The evolution of institutions does not happen at similar speeds. Some institutions remain for a very long time and their change is slow and evolutionary. On the contrary, other institutions change faster as a result of a change in the economic paradigm. These latter institutions are those that best fit the idea of building economic states. According to Scott's typology they are the regulative institutions, that is, the institutions that arise from public intervention and whose objective is to set new 'rules of the game' (Williamson's level 2).

The stability of these relations gives us the capacity to forecast, and therefore the study of the future by probabilities becomes a feasible option. However, this does not mean that we are re-establishing the conditions for efficient outcomes as neoclassical economics proposes. Logical time is not synonymous with economic equilibrium, as Neoclassical economics states. The economy is not always in equilibrium, that is, the causal relations among variables are not always stable. Besides, the stability, when reached, is not permanent: it lasts whilst long-term expectations are constant.

Furthermore, not all the equilibrium states are socially acceptable. Some states can offer acceptable outcomes at a specific time but they can be differently valued at other times. Whether the final outcome is efficient or not, is a problem related to the notion of efficiency we use. Economic efficiency must be defined in the normative field. Williamson's level 1 should be the field where the criterion of economic efficiency used at any time must be defined.

7.5. THE CONFLICTING NATURE OF SOCIAL RELATIONSHIPS

As Joan Robinson stated, the future is the outcome of the interactions among individuals. The future is built in the present, that is, all economic states are the outcome of certain decisions, some of them intended, some others unintended. Institutions are also the outcome of the interactions among individuals. This interaction is made through the structure of incentives generated in the institutional framework. However, can this interaction be considered as a cooperative game or, on the contrary, is it the outcome of conflicting relations?

For the New Institutional economy, the institutions are the logical outcome of a cooperative game among the individuals of the society. Benefits from these institutions are symmetrically distributed among the members of the society. Furthermore, the use of a cooperative game is the direct result of the very concept of Neoclassical efficiency. The exchanges in the market generate efficient and beneficial outcomes for all the participants. Therefore, the institutions that promote this outcome cannot be the result of some kind of imposition that biases the outcome in favor of some individuals and allows them to reap extraordinary benefits above those that could be achieved with different rules of the game.

This method means an explicit rejection of one of the main features of any society: the conflicting dimension of social relations. On the contrary, an alternative approach to that of the new institutional economy must stress that the creation of institutions and institutional change is deeply influenced by the asymmetric distribution of power resulting from the asymmetric distribution of wealth. Therefore, the institutional framework is not the logical outcome of a cooperative game but the result of a conflict of interests. This does not mean that the rules of the game provided by the institutions do not generate the needed structure of incentives that markets need to work as mechanisms to satisfy needs. What we mean is that, in a given institutional framework, the market outcomes are the result of a certain equilibrium among agents with conflicting interests.

Society is not a harmonious world. Social relations conceal differences of power among agents. Some agents have the capacity to invest and create employment, but others do not. But even among those with that capacity, the power is not equally distributed. The objectives of all these agents can be, and very often are, in opposition to one another. Higher wages for some workers can involve lower benefits for other agents or higher prices for everyone. High interest rates may allocate resources in one direction but not in another. Some income redistribution policies may involve lower power for some agents and a relative improvement for others. Every political decision changes, with higher or lower intensity, the current distribution of power. Any analysis of the elaboration of economic policy, both in the design of new rules of the game and/or institutions and in the implementation of measures of macroeconomic policies, must accept that any decision is the result of an equilibrium of interests that can change the current distribution of power.

The analysis of the institutional design made by the government (and the orientation of stabilization policy) involves taking into account complicated issues like, for instance, the analysis of the interests of different agents. These interests can mean the maintenance of the current degree of power or the change of that degree to their own benefit or for the benefit of third parties. The ethical, or even ideological, considerations of this analysis are evident.

The analysis of institutional design in a democratic society now becomes a different perspective. The institutions cannot *only* be described as the result of a claimed scientific analysis of the kind of institutions that best fit for a 'neutral' right working of the economy. The analysis of institutional design cannot be separated from the particular interests to create a reality according to these interests. There can be as many different versions of that institutional design, some coincident, some conflicting, as there are groups with particular interests. At best, the only constraint that should be accepted is that there must be the chance to confront opposite options, that is, a bet for institutions generated by democratic decision-making processes.

The diversity of interests must not prevent us from talking of socially desirable interests or of interests accepted by the majority of agents. If we did not consider these interests, it would be difficult or impossible to define full employment or an egalitarian income distribution, for instance, as desirable objectives of economic policy. In every society, in each period of time, the existence of socially accepted values that inform the behavior of agents, both in the private and the public sphere can be assumed. However, despite the existence of shared objectives, differences remain because there can be different ways to reach these objectives.

We can return now to an issue already mentioned: the criteria of efficiency used to evaluate the institutions. In opposition to the notion of neoclassical efficiency, we can talk of an objective of social efficiency based on the values shared in a society in each historical period. We understand by social efficiency a historical situation in which the desirable economic objectives and the procedures to reach these objectives are neatly determined and shared by the majority: that is, a certain distribution of competences between the state and the market; certain institutions working as sources of information in the generation of expectations; or even certain public and private actions to correct undesired outcomes of the economic process. Some authors (De Bernis 1983) also refer to this idea under the generic notion of mode of regulation as an alternative concept to that of neoclassical equilibrium.[2]

In the above terms, equilibrium might be reached, at least as a theoretical solution. This can be relevant for the theory but not for the individuals of a society. What is relevant is to know that the economic outcomes are always the result of our decisions and that, therefore, there is no natural order to which we are moving in an irreversible way.

7.6. ECONOMIC POLICY AND INSTITUTIONS NOWADAYS

How can we make the importance of the normative content of the analysis of the 'rules of the game' compatible with the positive analysis of the economic process? In our view, the answer must be found in the definition of the priority objectives, that is, in the definition of social efficiency. In other words, (regulative) institutions are set according to the dominant vision about what is thought to be desirable.

The mainstream has changed the criteria used to evaluate economic outcomes and the nature of economic policy itself, not only in the definition and hierarchy of objectives but also in the instruments. Thus, full employment is identified with the non-accelerating inflation rate of unemployment, economic growth is identified with a non-accelerating inflation rate of economic growth, and the optimum rate of inflation is identified with zero inflation. The objective of an egalitarian income distribution has nearly disappeared from the objectives of economic policy, and full employment is subordinated to price stability.

In the case of the instruments of economic policy, there is an explicit refusal to use fiscal policy as stabilization policy. Monetary policy is exclusively focused on price stability, setting a specific target for the inflation rate. Sectoral policies are given up, being incorporated into a generic competition policy. Economic stability is identified with a 'right' working of the markets. And when it is recognized that there may exist economic disequilibria, there is a bet for the advantages of market solutions against political solutions. As Friedman stated,

> Speaking for myself, I do not believe that I have more faith in the equilibrating tendencies of market forces than most Keynesians, but I have far less faith than most economists, whether Keynesians or monetarists, in the ability of government to offset market failures without making matters worse.[3]

The neoliberal institutional reforms that they propose (Arestis and Sawyer 2004) can be analyzed in terms of their contribution to the long-term expectations. All these reforms share a common aim: the flexibilization and deregulation of markets, mainly of inputs (labor and capital) markets. These reforms have come along with the creation of new regulative institutions and/or with changes in the current institutions with the aim of adapting them to the new objectives. The independence of central banks, balanced budgets, the downsizing of the public sector, the reforms in the social protection systems, the surge of independent regulating agencies, the fall of direct taxation and the rise of indirect taxation, all of them are signs of the wish to move the institutional framework closer to the working conditions of markets, as shown in the equilibrium models.

Are these institutional changes helping to stabilize the long-term expectations and, consequently, to reinforce the causal relations among the short-term and long-term variables? The past experiences accumulated during the period of institutional change do not allow optimism. These reforms are not stabilizing long-term expectations. The international monetary and financial system clearly shows this outcome, as indicated by the instability and volatility of exchange rates and capital flows (Davidson 2002). There is a strong uncertainty about the working and relevance of the transmission channels of monetary policy, and a break in the relationship between short-term and long-term rates of interest is clearly detected (Bank for International Settlements 2005). The counter-inflationary monetary policy, though it may have reduced expectations of inflation, is generating low levels of economic activity and higher output volatility (Arestis and Mouratidis 2004). Labour market reforms are generating models of competitiveness that are negative in terms of their long-term consequences (Ferreiro and Serrano 2001).

Past experience concerning the consequences of these reforms posits the need of a new reform: the reform of the reform (Arestis and Sawyer 1998). If these changes do not take place, the lack of constant long-term expectations may deepen the short-term problems, which, in turn, may generate negative effects in the long run. In sum, we can reach a perverse outcome combining higher economic volatility and 'low-level' economic outcomes.

These new reforms must be designed starting from the evidence that information about the future does not exist. The aim is to generate a (regulating) institutional framework that helps to mitigate the undesired consequences from the lack of information. A necessary condition is that the public sector again plays a key role. Public authorities must play an active role in the management of fiscal and monetary policy tools and in the change of the current regulating framework. These changes must lead to a new hierarchy of objectives, where full employment and economic growth must be the priority objectives.

The task is not easy because of the multiple resistances that can be found.[4] However, the accumulated experience and knowledge allow us to know both the variables that we must change to stabilize the long-term expectations and the negative consequences that the non-implementation of short-run discretionary policies will generate in the long term. We have also learned that market economies do not only face demand-side shocks, but also significant supply-side shocks, and, therefore, that public intervention must be developed for this side of the economy as well.

But the public sector itself needs a deep reform. More public sector activism is not enough if we do not accept at the same time that, in many cases, its working is not the right one. The Neoclassical criticism of 'government failure' is proof of the lack of good governance that must be addressed.

7.7.   FINAL COMMENTS

The analysis of institutions is closely related to the study of the information problems faced by agents. All the paradigms that focus their attention on institutional analysis share that view. However, this is the only consensus among them. The origin of the differences is of a methodological nature. At the root these differences lie both in the kind of institutions analyzed and in the kind of analysis developed. For the Neoclassical approach, the individual is a rational being that makes optimizing decisions. The main problem faced by institutions is to remove the problems of asymmetric information that agents face in the markets. Post-Keynesian thought stresses the significance of uncertainty, and puts the key issue of expectations at the heart of economic analysis. Institutions are instruments for stabilizing expectations and for changing historical time into logical time.

From a pragmatic perspective, that is, from the point of view of the decisions that policy makers must make, both information problems are relevant, since in the real world both kinds of problems co-exist.

The choice of the 'best institutions' to solve these information problems must not only be based on technical criteria. The stable articulation of causal relations, or the reduction of transaction costs, can be reached in different ways. Every way holds a different normative content. The analysis of this normative content leads to a study of the socially dominant values, or the values that try to become socially dominant.

NOTES

1. The perfect information hypothesis, joined to the rational-optimizing behavior of individuals and the assumption of the stability of the individual preferences, are the central pillars of the Neoclassical theory of economic equilibrium.
2. Though there are a number of methodological differences, the concept of mode of regulation is very close to the neoclassical concept of equilibrium. In discussing the dynamics of the economic process, harmonious relationships between opposing interests, though historically determined, are utopian, as are normative discourses to fight uncertainty, as proposed by the Regulationist school. Obviously these are as incredible as the equilibrium theory. But we are not trying to defend an alternative notion of economic equilibrium. We try to stress the complexity surrounding economic analysis when we incorporate the historical dimension and the existence of conflicting social relations.
3. Quotation taken from an interview of Milton Friedman included in Snowdon and Vane (2005, p. 212).
4. For an analysis of the resistance of institutions to changes, see Setterfield (1993).

REFERENCES

Arestis, P. and K. Mouratidis (2004), 'Is there a trade-off between inflation variability and output-gap variability in the EMU countries?' *Scottish Journal of Political Economy*, 51(5), 691–706.

Arestis, P. and M. Sawyer (1998), 'Keynesian economic policies for the new millennium', *Economic Journal*, 108, 181–95.

Arestis, P. and M. Sawyer (eds) (2004), *Neo-Liberal Economic Policies*, Cheltenham, UK and Northampton, MA, USA: Edward Elgar.

Bank for International Settlements (2005), *75th Annual Report*, Basel: Bank for International Settlements.

Coase, R. (1937), 'The nature of the firm', *Economica*, 4, 386–405.

Coase, R. (1960), 'The problem of social cost', *Journal of Law and Economics*, 2, 1–44.

Davidson, P. (1991), 'Is probability theory relevant for uncertainty? A post Keynesian perspective', *Journal of Economics Perspectives*, 1, 129–43.

Davidson, P. (2002), *Financial Markets: Money and the Real World*, Cheltenham, UK and Northampton, MA, USA: Edward Elgar.

De Bernis, G. (1983), 'De Quelques Questions Concernant la Théorie des Crises', *Economies et Sociétés*, 25, 1277–329.

Dow, S. (1998), *The Methodology of Macroeconomic Thought*, Cheltenham, UK and Lyme, USA: Edward Elgar.

Ferreiro, J. and F. Serrano (2001), 'The Spanish labour market: Reforms and consequences', *International Review of Applied Economics*, 15(1), 31–53.

Hodgson, G. (1998), 'The approach of institutional economics', *Journal of Economic Literature*, 36(March), 166–92.

Joskow, P. (2004), '*New Institutional Economics: A Report Card*', available at http://econ-www.mit.edu/faculty/download_pdf.php?id=766, 30 August 2006.

Kregel, J. (1976), 'Economic methodology in the face of uncertainty: The modelling methods of Keynes and the post-Keynesians', *Economic Journal*, 86(June), 209–25.

Matthews, R. (1986), 'The economics of institutions, and the sources of economic growth', *Economic Journal*, 96, 903–18.

Nelson, R.R. and S.G. Winter (1982), *An Evolutionary Theory of Economic Change*, Cambridge, MA: Harvard University Press.

Nelson, R.R. and S.G. Winter (2002), 'Evolutionary theorizing in economics', *Journal of Economics Perspectives*, 16(2), 23–46.

North, D. (1990), *Institutions, Institutional Change, and Economic Performance*, New York: Cambridge University Press.

Robinson, J. (1962), *Essays in the Theory of Economic Growth*, London: St. Martin's Press.

Rutherford, M. (1994), *Institutions in Economics: The Old and the New Institutionalism*, Cambridge: Cambridge University Press.

Rutherford, M. (2001), 'Institutional economics: Then and now', *Journal of Economic Perspectives*, 15(3), 173–94.

Scott, W.R. (2001), *Institutions and Organization*, London: Sage Publications.

Setterfield, M. (1993), 'A model of institutional hysteresis', *Journal of Economic Issues*, 27(3), 755–74.

Simon, H.A. (1987), 'Bounded rationality', in Eatwell, J., Milgate, M. and P. Newman (eds), *New Palgrave: A Dictionary of Economics*, Vol. 1, London: Macmillan.

Snowdon, B. and H. Vane (2005), *Modern Macroeconomics: Its Origins, Development and Current State*, Cheltenham, UK and Northampton, MA, USA: Edward Elgar.

Stiglitz, J. (1994), *Whither Socialism?* Cambridge, MA: MIT Press.

Stiglitz, J. (2002), 'Information and the change in the paradigm in economics', in Frangsmyr, T. (ed.), *The Nobel Prizes 2001*, Stockholm: The Nobel Foundation, pp. 472–540.

Williamson, O. (1985), *The Economic Institutions and Capitalism: Firms, Markets, Relational Contracting*, New York: The Free Press.

Williamson, O. (1993), 'Transactions cost economics and organization theory', *Industrial and Corporate Change*, 2, 107–56.

Williamson, O. (2000), 'The new institutional economics: Taking stock, looking ahead', *Journal of Economics Literature*, 38(3), 595–613.

8. Structural reforms and macroeconomic policy – the example of Germany*

Gustav A. Horn

8.1. INTRODUCTION

When growth fades, most economists tend to demand structural reforms to ensure a return to a stable growth pattern. The reason is that they argue in line with dominant theoretical approaches focusing mainly on the supply side of the economy (Bofinger 2005, Horn 2005). According to these approaches anything more than short-run decline of growth that affects trend growth must have been caused by supply side developments (Sinn 2003). In times of high unemployment, labor market rigidities are the main suspect for supply side problems. Therefore, structural reforms in this chapter are understood as changes of labor market institutions aimed at improving employment performance.

The economy presently most affected by this line of thought is Germany. There, growth rates show a marked decline since the buoyant unification boom at the beginning of the nineties. The growth trend therefore has become weaker year after year (SVR 2004). This was seen as a justification by international as well as national institutions to demand far-reaching structural labor market reforms to overcome this weakness (IMF 2006, SVR 2002). As a result, the economic policy debate in Germany focused more and more on labor market reforms. Almost every day a new reform was suggested, seemingly necessary for better growth perspectives. At some stage suggestions of longer working hours were the reform of the day. After that, lower non-wage costs for firms were preferred.

Many of these ideas have now been realized. The German government decided to put forward an agenda for higher employment called Agenda

---

* Enlarged and updated version of an earlier paper that has been published as Horn (2006). Both the paper and this chapter are based on a presentation at the ETUI Conference on Delivering the Lisbon Goals: The role of macroeconomic policy making, Brussels, February 2005.

2010 (Bundesregierung 2003). The major focus of that reform was an overhaul of parts of the social security system and a fundamental change of labor market institutions. With lower non-labor costs and a more flexible labor market, a change for higher growth and employment was expected (Bundesregierung 2003). Fundamental reform concepts for the labor market were submitted by a federal commission (the Hartz Kommission). They were duly implemented at the beginning of 2005 (Bundesregierung 2004). Additionally, reforms of the health care system and the pension scheme were implemented. Although structural reforms were seen as particularly necessary in Germany, other European countries have also entered a phase of structural reforms, but to a lesser extent and mainly focusing on pension reforms. They aim at reducing the financial burden of pension schemes in view of ageing societies. Notable exceptions are the UK, Denmark and Sweden, where, as in Germany, major labor market reforms have taken place (OECD 2006).

The basic hypothesis triggering all these efforts is that only structural reforms can raise the growth path of an economy. In particular, labor market reforms increasing the flexibility of labor supply are supposed to be appropriate to foster growth. In section 2 the connection between structural reforms and macroeconomic policy will be outlined. The conclusion will be drawn that both are interdependent rather than separate issues. In section 3 a simulation example will be run, further stressing this point. The simulation tries to map the structural reforms of the Agenda 2010 in Germany. Finally, the hypothesis will be stated that structural reforms should be embedded into a macroeconomic policy framework in order to avoid negative side effects. Otherwise these reforms may be self-destructive in terms of growth. In the light of these findings, the reform process in Germany is marred by macroeconomic neglect. And the dismal economic situation that followed the reform package is at least partly due to this neglect, even endangering all necessary reform steps.

8.2. STRUCTURAL REFORMS AND MACROECONOMICS

What is a structural reform? Usually one understands it as an institutional change that changes individual behavioral incentives in a growth-promoting manner. The reform of unemployment benefits in Germany is an example. In the past, unemployment benefits were granted in Germany for an unlimited time, albeit decreasing after one or at most two years by 10 per cent. With the labor market reforms of the Agenda 2010 in place, unemployment benefits will cease after one year. After that the unemployed are left with the much lower social benefit payments (Bundesregierung 2004). This significant reduction should increase the incentive for the unemployed to look for work within their first year of unemployment. As a consequence, people should find another employment earlier than without the reform and employers should also be able to fill their vacancies faster. As a result, production as well as incomes and employment should be higher. In addition to that, changes of behavior should be induced by an intensified counseling process and more restrictive conditions for turning down a job offer (Bundesregierung 2004).

Furthermore, it was expected that employment would be increased because people would accept lower paid jobs they previously used to turn down since by these measures the reserve wage has been lowered. Since all or at least most of the unemployed would change their behavior in this manner, a general wage reduction should occur. In turn, cheaper labor supply should further increase labor demand and thus employment. With higher employment, incomes should be higher, too. With all these measures taken and all the expected effects occurring, consumption and investment should grow stronger. In the end, the economy should be on a higher growth path.

This optimistic outlook of structural reform effects in Germany did not happen in reality, at least not until two years after its implementation. Some argue that these reforms need more time to be effective (IW 2005). The reason given is that job seekers may need time to adjust their behavior. But taking a closer look, there are reasons to doubt that view. Especially if unemployed people do not adjust quickly to such a changed environment, they face a loss of income after the reforms, since their unemployment benefits are reduced. Furthermore, even if wages – and these are in the first place nominal wages – decline, it remains doubtful for several reasons whether the expected increase in the number of jobs will occur at least in the short run.

The first and most important reason is that there may simply be no labor cost problem. If it is not excessive labor costs but rather a lack of income and demand which is the main cause of high unemployment, a reduction of labor cost will simply not help. On the contrary, incomes will be lower than before the reform. Wages may decline also for those already employed, but nevertheless, firms will not increase their staff. As a consequence incomes and demand will be even lower. The unemployment problem will be bigger than before. So, before expecting a positive impact from a supply side reform one should check whether labor costs are the real problem and whether demand problems can be ruled out. In the case of Germany, there are reasonable doubts as to the cost problem, since wage developments have been more moderate than in other major countries (Düthmann *et al.* 2006).

The second reason why only a limited impact should be expected is that a decline in nominal wages is not the same as a decline in real wages, which is the relevant wage variable for employment. While the former is likely to happen as a consequence of the reforms, the latter will happen only to a limited extent. Competition will urge firms that have lowered their wage costs to reduce their prices, too. Then real wages will not decline to the same extent as nominal wages. With perfect competition they would not even change at all.

A third argument is that the elasticity of employment may be too small to reach the desired employment effect. As long as it is smaller than one, a reduction in real wages will lead to a less than proportionate increase of employment. As a consequence, real incomes will fall and thus demand will also fall. The economy will face lower instead of higher growth.

These arguments change somewhat when applied to open economies. When prices decline, at least compared to a situation without reforms, international competitiveness increases via a real depreciation as long as no similar reforms are implemented in other countries. Hence, it can be expected that exports will increase and thus growth will also increase. If labor costs are at the root of the employment problems, this will enhance the employment-creating effects of wage moderation. If demand is the problem, the outcome depends on the relative size of the domestic and the export market. In a small open economy in which domestic demand is of minor importance compared to foreign markets, employment will nevertheless rise due to the real depreciation. But if the domestic market is relatively large the negative impact on domestic demand will prevail. Therefore, it also remains important for open economies to detect the causes of unemployment properly in order to assess the employment effects of structural reforms.

This example shows that the macroeconomic impact of a structural reform is not necessarily positive. Nevertheless, the reform may be desirable. If the change of incentives increases labor market flexibility, people may increase their job search efforts. In times of an economic upturn this may lead to a faster build up of employment. Moreover, the labor capacity constraint is shifted outwards, leaving more room for growth. But this only comes with an economic upturn and not at times of economic slackness. So one should not expect structural reforms to lead to a turnaround and incite an economic up-turn. This can only be done by an appropriate macroeconomic policy.

These considerations lead to an obvious relationship between structural reforms and macroeconomic policy. Firstly, macroeconomic policy has to be such that potential side effects of structural reforms are compensated for. If negative impacts on domestic demand are expected as outlined above, macroeconomic policy has to be appropriately more expansionary to stimulate demand in order to make up for the losses caused by reforms. Secondly, macroeconomic policy has to be such that the macroeconomic environment is stable. Only then can the structural reforms unfold their positive impacts.

In the past, countries in Europe could react by a more expansionary monetary policy. This could have two beneficial effects. First, with lower interest rates, domestic demand could be stimulated. Second, a devaluation of currencies could occur, increasing international competitiveness and thus exports. This effect should be particularly positive in smaller countries with a relatively large export share. Those countries will also not have to dread reactions by other countries' exchange rate policies due to their minor importance for international trade. Both effects together are perfectly well able to compensate for potential negative effects of structural reforms.

In a currency union like the Euro area, such a compensating monetary policy is not possible any more for a single country. Monetary policy would only have a chance to react if these reforms were to be a Euro area-wide phenomenon. However, it is highly unlikely that these reforms would take place at the same time in all countries, or at least in the most important ones.

Therefore, the problem must be dealt with on a national level, and that means by national fiscal policy. The recommendation is that structural reforms that are a burden for domestic demand should be accompanied by a correspondingly more expansionary fiscal policy. Only if demand is no problem can one refrain from making any macroeconomic policy considerations.

Some of the reforms in Germany were meant to cut social security spending and lay a greater burden on private households (Bundesregierung 2003). By these measures, not even an incentive to save money is created. It simply redirects money from the usual spending of households to, for example, healthcare spending. Again, this improves supply conditions and hampers demand. Thus, basically the same reasoning as above applies. But in contrast to an improvement of incentives these do not become more effective, even if an economic upturn occurs. So, this is redistribution at the expense of private households and in favor of firms.

8.3. THE GERMAN EXAMPLE – A SIMULATION

When the German government decided upon the Agenda 2010, a debate started about whether this program should be accompanied by a more expansionary fiscal policy stance. The two most important measures proposed will be outlined in two alternative scenarios in the following. The first was a cut in the income tax. It was part of a longer-term tax reform, primarily to reduce tax rates at the high and low ends of the income scale. Particularly, the income of low earners that spend their money almost completely on consumption was meant to be stabilized such that this income group would not be adversely affected by reforms. By doing this, consumption would be stabilized at the same time. The second measure was a public investment program about the same size as the tax reductions. This is the example of an expansionary fiscal policy to counteract potential adverse effects of reforms. In a currency union like the Euro area, this reaction may be appropriate. The different scenarios will be assessed econometrically with the use of an aggregate business cycle model in the following.

Using DIW's macroeconomic multi-country business cycle model of the Euro area (EBC) (Duong *et al.* 2005), the scenarios outlined above were simulated separately. The model includes demand- as well as supply-side variables. Hence, one should detect whether the expected positive supply side effect could compensate for the expected negative demand side effects.

For the structural reforms the measures of the Agenda 2010 were taken into account, as they had been planned during late spring 2003. Although some of them never passed the parliamentary process, all in all, the outlined simulations still give a fairly accurate picture of the structural reforms in Germany (Horn *et al.* 2003). They give an example of macroeconomic impacts of structural reforms and thus give information on the necessity of a compensatory macroeconomic policy. The results are shown in Table 8.1.

The results show that structural reforms as planned in the Agenda 2010 were indeed a macroeconomic burden. GDP would be below baseline up to almost one percentage point after two years, only gradually recovering thereafter. In particular, private consumption is well below its baseline all the time. Even in the third year after the start of the reform it only recovers slightly. The reason for this pattern is a significant reduction of available income, caused by the higher social security payments of private households, reducing the leeway for consumption spending. Available incomes do not recover until the end of the simulation period. Thus, the results show that there will be an adverse impact caused by a demand squeeze.

But there is also the expected completely positive impact of structural reforms on exports. The reason is increased competitiveness in foreign markets. By reducing social security spending for firms, unit labor costs decrease. Consequently, firms can offer their products at a lower price on

Table 8.1　　*Macroeconomic effects of structural reforms (deviations in per cent against the baseline)*

	Scenario I Tax reform			Scenario II Structural reform			Scenario III Higher investment		
	2004	2005	2006	2004	2005	2006	2004	2005	2006
Real GDP	0.3	0.4	0.0	−0.6	−0.9	−0.6	0.9	0.9	0.4
Real private consumption	0.4	0.7	0.1	−0.5	−1.1	−0.9	0.1	0.5	0.4
Real investment	0.3	0.5	−0.1	−0.6	−0.8	−0.3	6.0	1.5	1.0
Real exports	0.0	0.0	−0.1	0.0	0.1	0.4	0.0	0.0	−0.2
Unit labor costs	−0.2	0.1	0.5	−0.5	−1.2	−1.7	−0.4	0.4	0.9
Consumption deflator	0.0	0.0	0.1	0.0	−0.3	−0.7	−0.1	0.1	0.3
Available income	0.9	0.7	0.1	−1.1	−1.6	−1.8	0.3	0.6	0.7
Employees	0.0	0.1	0.1	−0.1	−0.3	−0.4	0.1	0.3	0.2
Public expenditure	0.1	0.2	0.2	−0.9	−0.9	−1.1	1.4	1.0	1.1
Public revenues	−1.6	−0.1	0.5	0.4	−0.4	−1.0	0.2	0.8	1.1
Add									
Employees[1]	10	40	20	−30	−90	−130	40	90	80
Public deficit ratio[2]	−0.7	−0.1	0.2	0.6	0.2	0.1	−0.6	−0.1	0.0

Notes:
1. In 1000 persons.
2. In percentage points of nominal GDP, + lower deficit, − higher deficit.

Source:　Simulation with the German module of DIW's EBC-model.

global markets, which increases their market share and fosters exports. It takes some time for these effects to feed into the market because firms reduce their prices only reluctantly and rather try to raise profits by keeping prices constant. But competition urges them in due time to transfer the cost reduction at least to some extent to their customers. This time pattern determines the development of GDP. Since exports show positive impacts only gradually, GDP also moves back only gradually in the direction of the baseline without reaching it.

　　Investment is influenced from both sides, the negative domestic demand and the positive exports. Since the domestic economy effect prevails it remains below baseline. The same applies to employment, although due to lower wage

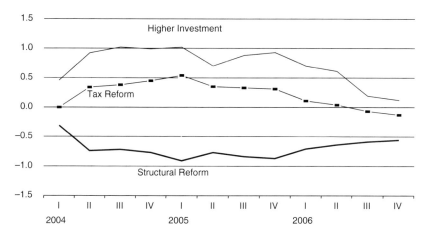

Figure 8.1   Real GDP (deviations in % against baseline)

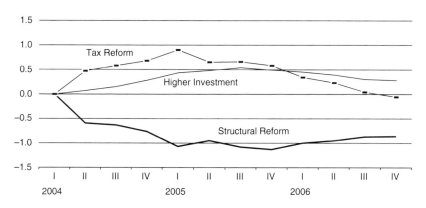

Figure 8.2   Real private consumption (deviations in % against baseline)

costs an increase was expected. But this is prevented by the significant lack of domestic demand and the resulting negative growth impact.

Looking at the simulation on potentially compensatory macroeconomic policies, one can state that the investment program is clearly superior in its effects to the tax reduction program. The reason for this is that investment spending affects production by 100 per cent of the amount spent. In contrast, tax reductions flow only partly into production via consumption and investment, since some of the money is saved. This applies especially to high income earners. But the amounts debated in 2003 were way too low to compensate for the relatively high negative impacts of the structural

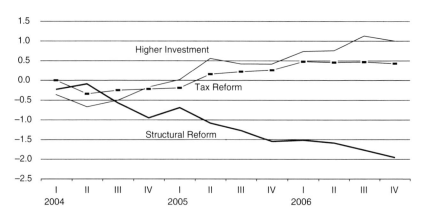

Figure 8.3   Unit labour cost (deviations in % against baseline)

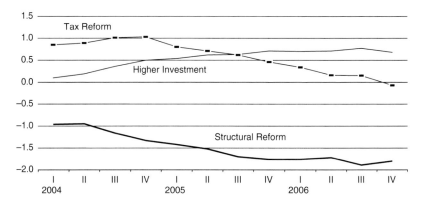

Figure 8.4   Available income (deviations in % against baseline)

reforms. This shows that a sufficiently expansionary fiscal policy would have been the appropriate response to the adverse macroeconomic effects of structural reforms.

8.4.   CONCLUSIONS

The simulation results presented in this chapter were obtained before structural reforms were put in place (Horn *et al.* 2003). Since then, reality has proven that the basic point of the simulation exercise was right. Structural reforms of the kind debated in Germany were a burden for domestic

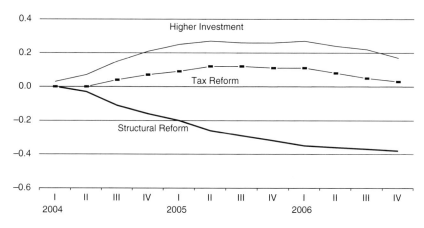

Figure 8.5   Employees (deviations in % against baseline)

demand that needed to be compensated for by an expansionary macroeconomic policy. In Germany that did not happen. The result was an ongoing
stagnation of domestic demand. Reality also demonstrated that the positive impacts on exports were also there. German firms achieved a remarkable export performance in relation to other major economies. That is
clearly the pattern indicated by the simulations. These findings reinforce the
point that structural reforms must be embedded into an appropriate macroeconomic environment. This point has been realized also by the OECD
(2006). In its reassessment of the 'Jobs Strategy', a sound macroeconomic
environment is named as one pillar of the suggested strategy. The simulation outlined above for the case of Germany shows that this is a promising
road to higher employment, indeed.

REFERENCES

Bofinger, P. (2005), *Wir sind besser als wir glauben: Wohlstand für alle*, München:
    Pearson.
Bundesregierung (2003), *Bulletin der Bundesregierung*, available as a free CD-Rom
    from bulletin@bpa.bund.de, 30 August 2006.
Bundesregierung (2004), *Bulletin der Bundesregierung*, available as a free CD-Rom
    from bulletin@bpa.bund.de, 30 August 2006.
Duong, M.H., Logeay, C., Stephan, S., Zwiener, R. and S. Yahnych (2005),
    *Modelling European Business Cycles (EBC Model): A Macroeconometric Model
    of Germany*, Version March 2005, Berlin: DIW (Data Documentation 5).
Düthmann, A., Hohlfeld, P., Horn, G.A., Logeay, C., Rietzler, K., Stephan, S. and
    R. Zwiener (2006), *Arbeitskosten in Deutschland bisher überschätzt: Auswertung
    der neuen Eurostat-Statistik*, IMK Report No. 11, Düsseldorf: IMK.

Horn, G.A. (2005), *Die deutsche Krankheit: Sparwut und Sozialabbau*, München: Hanser.

Horn, G.A. (2006), 'Structural reforms and macroeconomic policy', in Watt, A. and R. Janssen (eds), *Delivering the Lisbon Goals: The Role of Macroeconomic Policy*, Brussels: ETUI-REHS.

Horn, G.A., Meinhardt, V. and R. Zwiener (2003), *Konjunkturelle Effekte aktueller finanzpolitischer Massnahmen*, Manuscript.

IMF (2006), *Germany: Selected Issues*, Country Report, No. 06/17, available at http://www.imf.org/external/pubs/ft/scr/2006/cr0617.pdf, 30 August 2006.

IW – Institut der deutschen Wirtschaft Köln (2005), *Vision Deutschland: Was jetzt zu tun ist: Ein Reformkonzept für die neue Bundesregierung*, available at http://www.wiwo.de/wiworlzr/statics/pdf/merkelmeter/iw-reformkonzept.pdf, 30 August 2006.

OECD (1994), *The OECD Jobs Study: Facts, Analysis, Strategies*, available at http://www.oecd.org/dataoecd/42/51/1941679.pdf.

OECD (2006), *Boosting Jobs and Incomes: Policy Lessons from Reassessing the OECD Jobs Strategy*, available at http://www.oecd.org/dataoecd/47/53/36889821.pdf, 30 August 2006.

Sinn, H.W. (2003), *Ist Deutschland noch zu retten?* Berlin: Econ.

Sinn, H.W. (2005), *Basar Ökonomie Deutschland: Exportweltmeister oder Schlusslicht?* Berlin: Econ.

SVR (2002), *Zwanzig Punkte für Beschäftigung und Wachstum*, Jahresgutachten 2002/2003, available at http://www.sachverstaendigenrat-wirtschaft.de/download/gutachten/02_ges.pdf, 30 August 2006.

SVR (2004), *Erfolge im Ausland: Herausforderungen im Inland*, Jahresgutachten 2004/2005, available at http://www.sachverstaendigenrat-wirtschaft.de/download/gutachten/04_ges.pdf, 30 August 2006.

9. Theories of fiscal policies and fiscal policies in the EMU

Anthony J. Laramie and Douglas Mair

9.1. INTRODUCTION

Tax and fiscal policy rests on weak foundations if the possible or probable or actual effects of a tax or a tax system are unknown . . . our understanding of the complex [tax] shifting mechanism is still unsatisfactory and our knowledge is frequently uncertain or unproved. (Recktenwald 1971)

The theoretical framework that has been increasingly adopted in modern public finance is the competitive general equilibrium model set out definitively in Debreu's Theory of Value . . . this model . . . represents the most fully articulated view of the workings of the modern capitalist economy . . . the study of public policy can be no more firmly based than the economic theory on which it draws . . . the development of public economics is limited in crucial ways by the shortcomings of competitive equilibrium analysis. (Atkinson and Stiglitz 1980)

. . . many issues in public finance remain inherently controversial. (Musgrave 1985)

. . . tax incidence conclusions are critically dependent on which theory of economic equilibrium is chosen. We follow the main thrust of the literature in studying the effects of taxes in competitive economies where markets clear. This assumption has been adopted extensively not so much for its realism as because of the absence of widely accepted, fully articulated alternatives to the competitive paradigm. (Kotlikoff and Summers 1987)

The problem is that the aggregate or macro production function is a fictitious entity. (Felipe and Fisher 2003)

. . . the economics of Kalecki provides better foundations for a post-Keynesian or post-classical research programme than does the economics of Keynes. (Lavoie 1992)

The theme of this volume is alternatives to orthodox macroeconomics. In this chapter we present an alternative paradigm through which the macroeconomic effects and incidence of taxation may be analyzed. As a general rule, the dialogue (if any) in economics between the orthodoxy and the heterodoxy can be described as a dialogue of the deaf. Each side is convinced of the correctness of its own stance and the perversity, folly, stupidity or error of the other and each pursues its own separate path in search of the Truth. However, in the area of public finance, and of tax incidence in particular, economists whom we regard as leading exponents of the Neoclassical orthodoxy are prepared to concede weaknesses, if not yet downright errors, in their chosen approach. Several of our selected quotations at the beginning of this chapter are from respected public finance economists, including a recent Nobel prize winner, who are prepared to accept that there are limitations in their chosen Neoclassical paradigm which may affect the validity of the fiscal policy conclusions that follow therefrom. Economists of the calibre of Atkinson and Stiglitz, and Kotlikoff and Summers openly confess that is only *faute de mieux* that they have chosen the Neoclassical competitive market-clearing paradigm as the instrument for the analysis of the macroeconomic effects and incidence of taxation.

   Our purpose in this chapter is to present an alternative paradigm that identifies the effects of taxation on the long-run growth performance of the economy and to consider its implications for the operation of fiscal policy in the EMU. We have an immediate problem in finding an appropriate label for our paradigm. We have decided not to call it Post-Keynesian. Our approach contains nothing that can be identified as originating with Keynes. As practicing Post-Keynesians who 'came out' many years ago, we are somewhat dismayed by Davidson's (2003/4) claim that it is only those who are prepared to confess John Maynard Keynes as their lord and master who may properly consider themselves to be Post-Keynesians. Our intellectual inspiration is Kalecki and we agree with Lavoie (1992) that Kalecki provides better foundations than Keynes for the Post-Keynesian, or, perhaps we should say, post-classical research program. This is undoubtedly the case for the study of the macroeconomic effects and incidence of taxation. But this creates a dilemma for Post-Keynesians of a Keynesian or Davidsonian persuasion. Either they have to accept that on this issue at least Kalecki has the superior claim or they have to accept that as Post-Keynesians they have nothing to contribute to the development of an alternative paradigm for the study of the macroeconomic effects and incidence of taxation. To avoid any semantic confusion, we henceforward describe our approach as 'post-classical', leaving our fellow Post-Keynesians to make of that what they will.

9.2. WHY A NEW PARADIGM IS REQUIRED

The central problem of the Neoclassical approach to which Recktenwald and the others allude but have not been able to bring themselves to confront is the aggregate production function. In the Neoclassical paradigm, aggregate production functions of the general form $X = F(K, L)$ where X is output, K and L are the factor inputs of capital and labor and $F(.)$ is a well-defined function, are estimated for various purposes. One is to obtain measures of the elasticity of substitution between the factors and the factor-demand price elasticities which are then used to predict the effects on national income of changes in factor supplies. Another is to address policy issues.

The aggregate production function plays a central role in Neoclassical public finance, particularly in the analysis of tax incidence. There are a number of Neoclassical models of tax incidence – static one- and two-sector general equilibrium models, in both closed and open economies and dynamic life-cycle models with and without overlapping effects and inter-generational transfers (Harberger 1960, Mieszkowski 1969). The common feature of each is that it is predicated on an aggregate production function. The aggregate supply and demand elasticities of each factor play key roles in the analysis of the incidence of commodity and factor taxation in models in which all agents are assumed to have identical consumption preferences. The elasticities of substitution between taxed and untaxed commodities and taxed and untaxed factors are crucial to the determination of the incidence of taxation. Factor mobility, whether between sectors, regions or nations, is assumed to ensure ultimate equalization of after-tax returns to factors. The main thrust of Neoclassical analysis has been on identifying the price and substitution effects of tax changes and relatively little importance has been accorded to income effects. But the study of tax incidence is ultimately to do with the effect of tax shifting on the distribution of income and the ensuing macroeconomic consequences for the level of national income. The theory of income distribution that underpins the study of tax incidence is, therefore, of central importance.

The legitimacy of the concept of the aggregate production function and, consequently, of the marginal productivity theory of income distribution has been a subject of debate between neoclassical and Post-Keynesian economists since the Cambridge – Cambridge capital controversies of the 1950s and 1960s. As Felipe and Fisher (2003, p. 215) observe, ultimately the debates between the two Cambridges were about different theories of value, Cambridge (UK) espousing the Classical and Cambridge (MA) espousing the Neoclassical. The debates centered on a series of issues relating to the question whether it is legitimate to use an aggregate measure of capital in a macroeconomic production function without running into apparently paradoxical phenomena.

In the last decade or so Neoclassical models have recognized the possibility that fiscal policy may generate permanent growth effects. Earlier models, whether of the short-run comparative static macroeconomic variety or the dynamic variety such as Solow (1956), had denied the possibility of fiscal policy affecting the long-run performance of the economy. While fiscal policy might raise or lower income relative to some initial fiscal position, nevertheless, in the long run, the growth rate would return to its original position.

However, Gemmell and Kneller (2001, p. 101) observe that in recent years new endogenous growth models have identified a number of channels through which fiscal policy may have permanent growth effects. This has raised the possibility that there may indeed be a long-run role for fiscal policy in accelerating growth rates. The key characteristic of these models is that the processes of factor accumulation and/or technical progress are endogenously determined within the model and reproducible factors of production are not subject to diminishing returns. Faced with the long-run fiscal policy-ineffectiveness of the earlier Solow-type models, the newer endogenous growth models have responded by modifying the Neoclassical assumptions of the earlier models.

This is, however, a false dawn. Assessing the performance of Neoclassical endogenous growth models that have been used to analyze the effects of tax policy, Gemmell and Kneller (2001, p. 107) conclude:

> The empirical fiscal growth literature is of highly variable quality and has generally yielded non-robust results. To some extent, this appears to reflect changes in empirical methodologies over time and a tendency for many studies to test various ad hoc hypotheses or give insufficient attention to theoretical, as well as econometric, specifications.

Felipe and Fisher (2003, p. 209) pinpoint the source of difficulty for this family of endogenous growth models:

> The pillar of these [new neo-classical endogenous] growth models . . . is the neo-classical aggregate production function. The problem is that the aggregate or macro production function is a fictitious entity.

We do not propose to discuss further the difficulties associated with the definition or measurement of the aggregate production function and the implications this has for the practice of Neoclassical economics. These are dealt with at length by Felipe and Fisher (2003). For further discussion of the limitations of the Neoclassical paradigm see Arestis (1992, chapters 1–3) or Lavoie (1992, chapter 1).

9.3. WHERE DO WE GO FROM HERE?

At best, the Neoclassical approach to the study of the macroeconomic effects and incidence of taxation is problematic or, at worst, downright wrong. So where do we turn in search of an alternative paradigm? We propose Kalecki. At first sight this may sound surprising as Kalecki has no recognized reputation as a public finance economist. But, nearly seventy years ago, in an insight that came to him within a year of its publication, he recognized that an important consequence of the *General Theory* was that the macroeconomic theory of taxation would have to be rethought.

> Mr. Keynes' theory [*The General Theory*] gives us a new basis for the inquiry into the problems of taxation. The analysis of the influence of various types of taxes on effective demand leads, as we shall see, to quite unexpected results which may be of practical importance. (Kalecki 1937, p. 444)

In the correspondence between Kalecki and Keynes in his capacity as editor of the *Economic Journal* where Kalecki's paper was published, Keynes congratulated Kalecki on having worked out the conclusions of tax policy more rigorously than he (Keynes) had done. But apart from this brief pre-war paper in which he analyzed the short-period macroeconomic effects of taxes on commodities, income and capital, Kalecki never formally returned to the issue of taxation and its incidence in his subsequent writings. Nor, for that matter, did Keynes.

We have stated earlier our preference for making a clear distinction between Kalecki and Keynes on taxation. Partly, this is because Kalecki had appreciated earlier than Keynes the need for a rethink of the macroeconomic role of taxation and had set the process in motion as early as 1937. But principally, by adopting a Post-Classical approach we avoid the difficulties that have bedeviled the Neoclassical. Neoclassical economics has tied itself in knots as a consequence of its commitment to the concept of an aggregate production function. By adopting a Post-Classical approach, we cut the Gordian knot. Kalecki made virtually no use of those standard tools of Neoclassical economics – the utility function and the production function.

> Thus, in comparison with neo-classical economics, Kalecki rejected the notion of a technologically determined production function. (Sawyer 1985, pp. 10–11)

Also, despite his Marxist antecedents, Kalecki had no hang-ups over the theory of value.

> Kalecki did not deal with long-run equilibrium prices (specially relevant here would be prices of production) nor did he deal with the values of goods based on

> the socially necessary time of their production, both of which were used by Marx
> . . . whilst Marx had little interest in explaining market prices. (Junankar 1982)

> Kalecki was only interested in market prices; conversely whilst Marx was inter-
> ested in prices of production and values, Kalecki was not concerned with such
> concepts at all. (Sawyer 1985, p. 158)

By going down the Post-Classical route, we obviate the need for a macroeconomic production function or a theory of value. What we do need is a
theory of income distribution and this is where Kalecki's degree of monopoly theory (of which more below) comes into play.

9.4. FOUNDATIONS OF THE POST-CLASSICAL GROWTH MODEL

We now proceed to demonstrate that there is, we think, a credible post-
classical alternative to the Neoclassical orthodoxy by which to analyze the
effects of taxation on the long-run performance of the economy. We have
shown (Laramie and Mair 1996) how, from a Post-Classical perspective,
altering the *structure* but not the *level* of taxation within a balanced budget
framework can modify the amplitude of the business cycle around a zero
long-term growth rate. We do not propose to discuss this cyclical model
further in this chapter, and focus instead on considering how fiscal policy
may affect the economy's long-run growth rate.

In this section, we present the essential features of a Post-Classical long-
run tax model. The full derivation of the model with its attendant mathematical proofs can be found in Laramie and Mair (2003). We begin by
considering the role of taxation in an economy operating with a balanced
budget constraint. We assume that capitalists' consumption (Cc), workers'
savings (Ws), profit taxes (Tp) and wage taxes (Tw) can be simply written
as:

$$Cc = cc(\Pi - TP) \tag{9.1}$$

$$Ws = sw(V - Tw) \tag{9.2}$$

$$Tp = tp(\Pi) \tag{9.3}$$

$$w = tw(V) \tag{9.4}$$

where Π is pre-tax profits, cc is capitalists' propensity to consume, sw is
workers' propensity to save, V is pre-tax wages, tp is the rate of profits tax
and tw is the rate of wage tax.

The effects of taxation on national income, holding government expenditure, Ge, constant can be written as:

$$\Pi = [I + Ge + X - M](1 - \alpha)/\{(1 - \alpha)[1 - cc(1 - tp)] + \alpha[tx + sx(1 - tw)]\} \tag{9.5}$$

and

$$Y = [I + Ge + X - M]/\{(1 - \alpha)[1 - cc(1 - tp)] + \alpha[tw + sw(1 - tw)]\}$$

where I is investment, X is exports, M is imports and α is the wage share of value added.

The impact of taxation on the level of pre-tax profits and national income is explicitly reflected in the terms tp, tw and Ge. An increase in the profits tax rate, tp, holding government expenditures, Ge, constant, reduces capitalists' consumption, Cc, the levels of pre- and post-tax profits, Π and $P (= \Pi - Tp)$, the level of national income, Y, and the pre-tax wage bill, V. An increase in the wage tax rate, tw, holding government purchases, Ge, constant reduces workers' consumption, $Cw (= C - Cc)$ relative to the wage bill, W, reduces pre- and post-tax profits, Π and P, and the level of national income, Y.

As tax revenues change, the distribution factor, α, may also change, depending on the method of taxation that is used. For example, an increase in the wage tax, if shifted, will result in lower business mark-ups, causing α, the wage share, the Kaleckian income multiplier, $(1 - \alpha)$, and national income to increase, thereby dampening the negative impact of the rise in wage tax on national income. An increase in the taxation of profits, if shifted, will result in higher business mark-ups, reducing the wage share, α, the Kaleckian income multiplier, $(1 - \alpha)$, and national income, Y. Shifting of an increase in the profits tax heightens the negative impact that the profits tax has on national income.

In the Post-Classical approach, the macroeconomic impact of taxation on the economy depends on:

- the relative marginal propensities to consume out of wages and profits, cw and cc respectively,
- whether compensating changes in government expenditures, Ge, exist
- the degree to which a tax change is shifted through changes in business mark-ups.

A critical element, therefore, in the Post-Classical approach is the pricing behavior of firms because this determines whether or not changes in the taxes on wages or profits result in changes in prices.

Having demonstrated the basic process through which taxation can be introduced into Kalecki's theories of income determination and income distribution, the theory must be made dynamic. In order to do this, it is necessary to link taxation to Kalecki's theories of profits, national income, income distribution, investment and growth. For Kalecki, everything is driven by what happens to investment. Changes in the structure of taxation today can affect future investment and thus, future profits. The critical question, therefore, from a Post-Classical standpoint, is how do changes in the structure of taxation, achieved by balanced changes in taxation and government spending, affect investment?

In Kalecki's ([1968] 1971) theory of investment there are two channels through which taxation has an impact on investment:

- the rate of depreciation,
- the level of profits.

The rate of depreciation channel operates by altering the relative profitability after tax of new and existing plant and equipment. With technology continually improving through time, an increase in the tax on profits will lower the real profits generated by older plant and equipment relative to new plant and equipment, accelerating the obsolescence of the former and encouraging investment in the latter.

The effect of taxation on the level of profits also operates through two channels (ignoring the foreign sector):

- the impact on the government budget position,
- the effect on income distribution.

The effect via the government budget position is the balanced budget multiplier effect. The effect via income distribution depends on whether or not tax shifting occurs as a consequence of firms altering their mark-ups in response to changes in the structure of taxation. The extent to which this will occur will depend on the strength of the degree of monopoly. Quite different macroeconomic effects occur depending on whether or not tax shifting takes place.

We have explored the feasibility of influencing the growth path of the economy by varying tax rates within a balanced budget framework and now consider the effects of taxation on the trend component of fixed investment, on the trend rate of growth of capital stock and on the trend rate in capacity utilization. In order to do so, we use the version of Kalecki's growth theory that was corrected by Gomulka *et al.* (1990). This corrected version can be used to analyze the dynamic properties of Kalecki's investment theory to show that, depending on the parameters in the model, his approach can be used to explain both 'cautious capitalism', that is, capitalism with a dampening cycle, and 'rash' capitalism, that is, capitalism with an explosive cycle. Laramie and Mair (2003) show in detail how taxation can be introduced into this corrected version of Kalecki's growth theory and we present here only a summary of our results.

We consider how the economy's trend growth rate can be affected by changes in the structure of taxation when both the rate of capacity utilization and business balance sheets matter in making capital investment decisions. Our approach is structured as follows. First, we develop Kalecki's theory of fixed investment, modifying it to take account of the rate of capacity utilization, business balance sheets and the structure of taxation. Then, we reformulate Kalecki's theory of the trend level of investment, the trend capital stock and the trend rate of capacity utilization, accounting for the same factors, that is, businesses' balance sheets and the structure of taxation.

We modify Kalecki's expression for investment decisions by including the financial gearing ratio and the rate of capacity utilization as determinants. The reason for including the gearing ratio, the ratio of total liabilities to net worth, is to capture the effects of increasing risk associated with investment. An increase in the gearing ratio puts more of a business's capital at risk in the case of failure. Thus, an increase in the gearing ratio is likely to diminish businessmen's reactions to the stimulus provided by the situation where investment that yields the standard rate of profit, $I(\pi)$, is greater than actual investment, I. Likewise, an increase in the gearing ratio will accelerate the contraction of investment decisions when $I(\pi)$ is less than I.

The capacity utilization rate will also modify businessmen's reactions to the differences between $I(\pi)$ and I. Businessmen are assumed to desire a certain rate of capacity utilization. If the actual rate of capacity utilization rises above the desired rate, the increase will heighten businesses' reaction to the positive difference between $I(\pi)$ and I. When the difference between $I(\pi)$ and I is negative and businesses have an incentive to contract investment decisions, an increase in the rate of capacity utilization above the desired level will dampen such a contraction. A decrease in the rate of capacity utilization below the desired level will accelerate the contraction of investment decisions. In the long run, taxation has an impact on investment through three channels:

- the rate of depreciation,
- the level of profits,
- the rate of capacity utilization.

We now summarize the conditions under which changes in the rates of profits tax or wage tax will have an effect on the trend level of investment. We assume that the government maintains a balanced budget stance throughout and that the semi-autonomous component of capitalists' consumption remains unchanged.

The best way to consider the effects of an increase in the rate of profits is to consider the conditions sufficient for the relationship to be positive. A sufficient condition for an increase in the profits tax rate to have a positive effect on the trend level of investment is if the increase is not shifted, that is, businesses do not adjust their mark-ups in response to the tax change, and if workers do not alter their savings. An increase in the profits tax that is not shifted increases national income and workers' savings and reduces profits and the profit multiplier. However, if workers do not alter their savings, then the effect of a change in the profits tax on the profits multiplier is zero. An increase in the rate of profits tax that is not shifted increases the rate of depreciation and an increase in the rate of depreciation raises the investment coefficient.

However, these positive effects are dampened if the increase in profits tax is shifted, that is, businesses adjust their mark-ups to cover the increase in profits tax, and if workers alter their savings. These effects are subject to two further influences. If the gearing ratio reaction coefficient is non-zero negative, then the positive effect of the increase in the profits tax rate will be dampened. Offsetting that, however, if the capacity utilization rate reaction coefficient is non-zero positive, then the positive effects of the increase in profits tax rate will be heightened.

A sufficient condition for a change in the wage tax rate to have no effect on the trend level of investment is if the change is not shifted, that is, firms do not adjust their mark-ups, and workers do not alter their savings. With no tax shifting, a change in the wage tax rate has no effect on the profit multiplier, the rate of depreciation and the trend level of investment. If the increase in the wage tax rate is shifted and workers do alter their savings, then the profit multiplier decreases. The increase in the rate of depreciation increases the trend level of investment but the decrease in the profit multiplier reduces the trend level of investment, and the result is indeterminate.

Putting these two sets of conditions together, we find that a change in the structure of taxation, comprising an increase in the rate of profits tax offset by a reduction in the rate of wage tax so that the government budget remains unchanged, will have a positive effect on the rate of investment if:

- no tax shifting occurs,
- workers do not alter their savings,
- the capacity utilization rate reaction coefficient is non-zero positive.[1]

Thus, from a Post-Classical standpoint, fiscal policy, even with a balanced budget, can affect the long-run development of the capitalist economy. Given a balanced budget, the incidence and effects of taxation influence the course of capitalist development, depending on whether or not workers alter their savings and whether or not taxes are shifted.

One of the advantages of the Post-Classical approach is the compatibility of its micro- and macroeconomic elements. Kalecki's theory of profits is macroeconomic, while his theory of distribution is microeconomic, dependent on the degree of monopoly. The macroeconomic and microeconomic elements have different implications for tax shifting. For example, given an increase in the profits tax, if the government maintains a balanced budget and workers do not adjust their saving, then after-tax profits, P, are unaffected by the tax. However, the imposition of an increase in the profits tax can alter the microeconomic distribution of income, depending on the nature of the profits tax. This can result in changes in industry (sectoral) mark-ups, in the aggregate mark-up, in the wage share, α, and in national income, Y.

9.5. POST-CLASSICAL FISCAL POLICY AND THE EMU

The analysis we have presented above relates to a single closed economy. Elsewhere, we have demonstrated how an open economy multi-regional or multi-national variant can be developed (Laramie and Mair 2005). In this section we demonstrate what macroeconomic effects are likely to ensue if a member state of EMU, let us call it Evallonia,[2] makes a unilateral tax change while no other member state makes any tax adjustment. We assume that Evallonia's finance minister has been persuaded by our arguments and has raised profits tax and reduced income tax by equal amounts, keeping the Evallonian budget position unchanged. We identify three tax jurisdictions, Evallonia, EMU and Rest of EMU (REMU = EMU − Evallonia). The EMU is a single currency area with a single rate of interest and no internal trade barriers or impediments to factor mobility. Member states still retain discretion over domestic fiscal and budgetary policy subject to the constraints of the Stability and Growth Pact.

We present the analysis in a series of time periods, $t \ldots t_n$. A change in tax policy is introduced in Evallonia at the beginning of time period t. Evallonian businessmen review their investment decisions during time period t in the light of the change in tax policy but these decisions are not converted into new investment outlays until later time periods, $t_1 \, t_n$. We assume that Evallonia starts from an equilibrium position in period t in terms of the distribution of income between profits and employment income. Following Kalecki ([1954] 1971, p. 95),

> gross income [in the current time period] is pushed up to a point at which profits out of it, as determined by the 'distribution factors', correspond to the level of investment [in some previous time period]. The role of the 'distribution factors' is thus to determine [national] income or product on the basis of profits which are in turn determined by investment.[3]

In Evallonia, the effects of the tax change in period t will be as follows. Pre-tax profits at the beginning of time period t do not change as these have been determined by investment in a previous time period, t_{-1}. Critical to what happens is the behavior of capitalists' consumption, Cc. Here there are two possible scenarios. First, if Cc_t depends on post-tax profits, P_t, Cc_t will fall because of the rise in the rate of profits tax, tp_t. Workers' consumption, Cw_t, will rise because of the fall in income tax, tw_t and no change in workers' savings. The effect in this scenario will be to reduce both pre-tax profits, Π_t and post-tax profits, P_t by the end of time period t. By assumption, there is no tax shifting, that is, businesses do not adjust their markups in response to the changes in tp or tw. National income in Evallonia will increase and, to the extent that Evallonia is an open economy trading with REMU, imports into Evallonia from REMU increase and national income increases in REMU.

In the second scenario, Cc_t does not depend on P_t. Kalecki's ([1968] 1971, p. 167) view was that capitalists' consumption was a rather small fraction of post-tax profits, λP, and a slowly changing magnitude, A, dependent on past economic and social developments. In this situation, Cc_t depends on $P_{t-1} \ldots P_{t-n}$ and both Π_t and P_t remain unchanged. This is the scenario we consider to be the more likely. Again, national income in both Evallonia and REMU increase.

Although there has been no change in the factors determining degree of monopoly in Evallonia in time period t, the effect of the tax change has been to alter the distribution of post-tax income in such a way as to increase the wage share, α, at the expense of profits share, thereby disturbing the existing equilibrium. The tax change has been equivalent to an exogenous downward shift in the degree of monopoly. As a result, the level of national income in Evallonia in period t will rise to the point at which the lower relative share of profits in national income yields the same absolute level of profits.

However, this is not the end of the story. As we note above, the level of profits and/or the rate of depreciation are the two channels through which we expect taxation to have an impact on the long-run rate of growth. The economy now moves into periods $t_1 \ldots t_n$ in which Evallonian businessmen have had time to adjust their investment outlays in response to the tax change. As we have noted, the aggregate level of profits in Evallonia in period t has remained unchanged. But there are other influences at work. First, the rate of depreciation. As there has been an increase in the tax rate on profits in period t in Evallonia, this will affect the relative post-tax profitabilities of new and older plant and equipment, given the state of technology. The result will be an acceleration in the scrapping of older plant and equipment and an increase in investment in new plant and machinery of higher productivity and profitability. Thus, investment will increase in Evallonia in periods $t_1 \ldots t_n$, leading to a higher level of profits in periods $t_2 \, t_{n+1}$. Evallonia will experience a faster rate of growth and, because of its trading relations with REMU, this will have a positive effect on growth in REMU.

But there is a second influence on investment that also has to be taken into account. The effect of the period t tax change in Evallonia was to increase the wage share, α, so that the distribution of income changed from the 'equilibrium' level that was assumed to prevail prior to the tax change. Depending on the strength of the depreciation effect, it is possible that the increase in investment thereby generated in periods $t_1 \, t_n$ will result in a sufficient increase in the level of profits in periods $t_2 \, t_{n+1}$ to restore the profits share of national income to its pre-tax change 'equilibrium' level.

But what is meant by 'equilibrium' in this context? We are accustomed to thinking of the 'natural' rate of unemployment or of NAIRU (the non-accelerating inflation rate of unemployment). The 'equilibrium' we have in mind here is suggested by Kalecki (1943) in *Political Aspects of Full Employment*, in which he argues that businessmen will resist attempts to secure full employment by increased government borrowing and spending. The threat of full employment to business economic and political hegemony results in a prisoners' dilemma situation in which there is a conflict of interest between businessmen individually from reaping the higher profits of full employment against the collective threat to businessmen as a class from the loss of industrial discipline and political power consequent on full employment.

Interpreting Kalecki's argument in *Political Aspects of Full Employment* as an explanation of rent seeking rather than as an explanation of the political business cycle, Laramie and Mair (2002) argue that Kalecki's thesis finds a more modern expression in Olson's (1965) idea of 'selective incentives'. Olson's argument that the superior organizational ability of business will ensure that its interests prevail resonates with Kalecki's concept of the degree of monopoly. From a Kalecki–Olson perspective, the aggregate levels of national income and employment are determined by the outcome of the processes by which the distribution of income between profits and wages is determined. Thus, analogous to 'natural' rate of unemployment or NAIRU, there exists what we call the DNRU, the distribution-neutral rate of unemployment. At the DNRU, businessmen collectively are satisfied with the level of profits that the 'distribution factors' have carved out of national income, they do not feel economically or politically threatened and have no 'selective incentives' to seek to increase the degree of monopoly. We cannot specify a precise rate for the DNRU. All that we can say with confidence is that it will be less than 'full' employment.

The role of the DNRU is to place a ceiling on the level of national income that will be generated via the depreciation effect consequent on an increase in the profits tax and a reduction in the wage tax. As the ceiling is approached, businessmen collectively become more concerned over the distribution of income and act collectively to slow down, or even reverse, the growth in national income and employment.

Unlike its Neoclassical counterpart, Kalecki's degree of monopoly theory of income distribution is empirically testable. An early attempt was undertaken by Reynolds (1983). More recently, Laramie, Mair and Reynolds (2004) have estimated the determinants of the degree of monopoly for two separate samples of UK manufacturing industry in the 1980s and 1990s. Their results suggest that factors such as product differentiation, entry barriers and exposure to foreign competition influence the ability of businesses to determine the size of their mark-up of price over prime cost and, therefore, to influence the distribution of income. These are the factors that will determine the extent to which tax shifting will occur and will differ across Evallonia and REMU, making it difficult to generalize about the extent of tax shifting that may occur. The more competitive and flexible are factor and commodity markets in Evallonia and REMU, the lower the degree of monopoly is likely to be and the less likely the possibility of tax shifting.

9.6. CONCLUSION

In this chapter we have identified an alternative approach to the analysis of the effects of fiscal policy on the long-run rate of growth. Given the self-confessed limitations of existing approaches, we think this is an important issue for Post-Keynesians (or Post-Classicals) to pursue. We have sketched the skeleton of a Post-Classical approach and demonstrated how it may be adapted to fit the circumstances of the EMU. Given the generally poor economic performance of the EMU countries in recent years and the obvious irrelevance of monetary policy to deal with problems of growth, there is, we think, a strong case for a re-examination of the role of fiscal policy.

Arestis and Sawyer (2003), for example, demonstrate that many of the objections to fiscal policy raised by Monetarists and others do not stand up to scrutiny and conclude that fiscal policy remains a powerful tool for macroeconomic policy.

A similar concern is expressed by Mathieu and Sterdyniak (2005), who identify a strong new anti-Keynesian (NAK) view of public finances among European (particularly Italian) economists and policy makers (of all nationalities) at the European Commission. The emphasis of the NAK approach is on debt consolidation as the route to faster growth in Europe, while denying that fiscal expansion will have any positive effect. As with Arestis and Sawyer, Mathieu and Sterdyniak identify a number of scientific weaknesses with the NAK approach. For instance, they see it as being ideologically driven, denying as it does any usefulness from public spending. Second, the NAK view only applies in an economy working at full capacity (or being supply-constrained) where useless public expenditure could be cut. NAK cannot apply in a Keynesian unemployment regime where a rise in public spending will have expansionary effects. Finally, Mathieu and Sterdyniak question the reliability of the empirical results of tests of the so-called 'NAK effects'.

We strongly sympathize with the Arestis and Sawyer and Mathieu and Sterdyniak criticisms of the Monetarist/NAK approaches, but it seems to us that they are advocating a return to a 'golden age' of conventional Keynesian fiscal policy. As we have tried to argue in this chapter, there is a case for Post-Keynesians (or Post-Classicals) to abandon their commitment to Keynes and realign themselves with Kalecki on this issue. Too much emphasis, it appears to us, has been given to the stabilization role of fiscal policy and not enough to its potential to accelerate growth rates. If the Stability and Growth Pact is to make a meaningful contribution to enhancing economic performance among European economies, it surely must demonstrate a policy relevance to the issue of growth, rather than languish in the refrigerator, in the words of Dutch Finance Minister, Gerrit Zalm.

For fiscal policy to be successful it must avoid the theoretical pitfalls that render it irrelevant. It requires a change of mindset among public finance economists and policy makers and we have sought to identify the lines along which we think a new approach might develop. This does not necessarily mean abandoning all that has gone before. There are elements of conventional endogenous growth theory models that resonate with the Post-Classical approach we have developed here, for example, the effects of fiscal policy on productivity growth and factor accumulation. A Post-Classical approach underlines the critical importance of income distribution in determining the macroeconomic outcomes of fiscal policy. While some endogenous growth models have sought to incorporate distributional issues, we are by no means convinced that they have done so in a meaningful way.

NOTES

1. In our Post-Classical econometric analysis of the determinants of investment orders by UK manufacturing industry 1980–1996, we find the coefficient of the capacity utilisation variable to be positive and strongly significant (Laramie, Mair and Miller 2006).
2. Evallonia is an imaginary central European country that features in several of John Buchan's novels.
3. In our Post-Classical empirical analysis of the determinants of investment orders by UK manufacturing industry 1980–1996, we find that the coefficient of lagged profits is positive and strongly significant (Laramie *et al.* 2006).

REFERENCES

Arestis, P. (1992), *The Post Keynesian Approach to Economics*, Aldershot, UK and Brookfield, US: Edward Elgar.

Arestis, P. and M.C. Sawyer (2003), 'Reinventing fiscal policy', *Journal of Post Keynesian Economics*, 26(1), 3–25.

Atkinson, A. and J.E. Stiglitz (1980), *Lectures on Public Economics*, London: McGraw-Hill, pp. 12–13.

Davidson, P. (2003/4), 'Setting the record straight on a history of Post Keynesian economics', *Journal of Post Keynesian Economics*, 26(2), 245–72.

Felipe, J. and F.M. Fisher (2003), 'Aggregation in production functions: What applied economists should know', *Metroeconomica*, 54(2/3), 208–62.

Gemmell, N. and R. Kneller (2001), 'The impact of fiscal policies on long-run growth', *European Economy: Current Issues in Economic Growth*, 1, 97–129.

Gomulka, S., Ostaszewski, A. and R.O. Davies (1990), 'The innovation rate and Kalecki's theory of the trend, unemployment and the business cycle', *Economica*, 57, 525–40.

Harberger, A.C. (1960), 'The incidence of the corporation income tax', *Journal of Political Economy*, 93(2), 248–64.

Junankar, P. N. (1982), *Marx's Economics*, Deddington: Philip Allan.

Kalecki, M. (1937), 'A theory of commodity, income and capital taxation', *Economic Journal*, 47, 444–50.

Kalecki, M. (1943), 'Political aspects of full employment', *Political Quarterly*, 14, 322–31.

Kalecki, M. ([1954] 1971), 'Determination of national income and consumption', in Kalecki, M., *Selected Essays on the Dynamics of the Capitalist Economy*, Cambridge: Cambridge University Press, pp. 93–104.

Kalecki, M. ([1968] 1971), 'Trend and the business cycle reconsidered', *Economic Journal*, 78, 263–76 reprinted in Kalecki, M., *Selected Essays on the Dynamics of the Capitalist Economy, 1933–1970*, Cambridge: Cambridge University Press, pp. 165–83.

Kotlikoff, L. and L. Summers (1987), 'Tax incidence', in Auerbach, A.J. and M.J. Feldstein (eds), *Handbook of Public Economics*, Vol. II, Amsterdam: Elsevier, pp. 1043–4.

Laramie, A.J. and D. Mair (1996), 'Taxation and Kalecki's theory of the business cycle', *Cambridge Journal of Economics*, 20(4), 451–64.

Laramie, A.J. and D. Mair (2002), 'Full employment: Gift horse or Trojan horse?', *Review of Social Economy*, 60(4), 567–93.

Laramie, A.J. and D. Mair (2003), 'The effects of taxation in a Kaleckian growth model', *Metroeconomica*, 54(2/3), 326–45.

Laramie, A.J. and D. Mair (2005), 'Regional tax differentials: A Kaleckian approach', *Regional Studies*, 39(3), 345–55.

Laramie, A.J., Mair, D. and A.G. Miller (2006), 'Kalecki's investment theory: A critical realist approach', in Holt, R. and S. Pressman (eds), *Empirical Post Keynesian Economics: Looking at the Real World*, New York: M.E. Sharpe.

Laramie, A.J., Mair, D. and P.J. Reynolds (2004), 'Kalecki's theory of income distribution: The answer to a maiden's prayer?', in Wray, L.R. and M. Forstater (eds), *Contemporary Post Keynesian Analysis*, Cheltenham, UK and Northampton, MA, USA: Edward Elgar, pp. 227–46.

Lavoie, M. (1992), *Foundations of Post-Keynesian Economics*, Aldershot, UK and Brookfield, US: Edward Elgar.

Mathieu, C. and H. Sterdyniak (2005), *How to Improve the European Fiscal Framework*, Paris: OFCE.

Mieszkowski, P.M. (1969), 'Tax incidence theory: The effects of taxation on the distribution of income', *Journal of Economic Literature*, 7, 1103–24.

Musgrave, R.A. (1985), *Handbook of Public Economics*, Vol. 1, Amsterdam: Elsevier.

Olson, M. (1965), *The Logic of Collective Action*, Cambridge, MA: Harvard University Press.

Recktenwald, H.C. (1971), *Tax Incidence and Income Redistribution: An Introduction*, Detroit: Wayne State University Press.

Reynolds, P.J. (1983), 'An empirical analysis of the degree of monopoly theory of income distribution', *Bulletin of Economic Research*, 39, 59–84.

Sawyer, M.C. (1985), *The Economics of Michal Kalecki*, Basingstoke: Macmillan.

Solow, R.M. (1956), 'A contribution to the theory of economic growth', *Quarterly Journal of Economics*, 71, 65–94.

10. The link between fiscal and monetary policy – lessons for Germany from Japan

Richard A. Werner

10.1. INTRODUCTION

In December 2005, the European Central Bank (ECB) urged the EU to enforce the rules on budget deficits strictly in the case of Germany. In January 2006, the European Commission said it would launch disciplinary proceedings against Germany for breaking the EU's limit on budget deficits for four years in a row. For several years, the ECB had been adamant that the cause of German fiscal problems was to be found in government, not central bank policy.

How did the fiscal deficits and rising outstanding debt of Germany come about? Basic economic statistics for Germany suggest the German experience to be in line with the standard pattern of deficits during times of recession (Table 10.1).

Since about 2001, Germany's economy has grown at a disappointing rate, lagging behind other Eurozone economies. German industrial

Table 10.1 Data on German economic performance

	2000	2001	2002	2003
GDP per head ($ at PPP)	26 114	26 311	26 690	27 060
GDP (% real change pa)	2.86	0.85	0.18	−0.10
Government consumption (% of GDP)	18.99	19.01	19.16	19.70
Budget balance (% of GDP)	1.10	−2.80	−3.60	−4.00
Consumer prices (% change pa; av)	1.34	1.98	1.36	1.07
Public debt (% of GDP)	60.50	60.21	62.40	63.90
Recorded unemployment (%)	9.61	9.37	9.81	10.50

Source: Country Data, as compiled by the Economist Intelligence Unit, 25 May 2004; accessed on 2 January 2005 at www. http://www.economist.com/countries/Germany/profile. cfm?folder=Profile-Economic%20Data.

production declined during much of 2001, 2002 and 2003.[1] Real GDP growth slowed considerably, falling from almost 3 per cent in 2000 to less than 1 per cent in 2001. In 2002 and 2003, zero and negative growth rates were recorded. Unemployment rose to beyond 10 per cent in 2003, reaching 12.6 per cent in early 2005, the highest since 1932. As private demand fell, government consumption increased. The government budget deteriorated, moving from a surplus of 1.1 per cent of GDP in 2000 to a 3.6 per cent deficit in 2002, and a 4 per cent deficit in 2003.[2] Further, the outstanding national debt rose from 60.5 per cent of GDP in 2000 to 63.9 per cent in 2003, also in breach of the original Maastricht criteria for joining the euro.

The weakness of the German economy has become a worry for other European countries, whether as trading partners or recipients of German net contributions to the EU budget (in 2003 accounting for 40 per cent of all net contributions).

10.1.1 The Government's View

To stimulate the economy, demand-side policies (monetary and fiscal policy) and supply-side policies (structural reform) are discussed. Given the institutional design of the Eurozone, the German government has little influence on monetary policy. Attempts to influence the ECB – for instance by rational argument – could be considered illegal and a breach of the Maastricht Treaty or the statutes of the ECB.[3]

The deterioration of the fiscal balance indicates (if partly due to 'automatic stabilization') that the German government adopted or tolerated an expansionary fiscal stance, and thus has acted in a way economists would expect or recommend according to the textbooks. On several occasions, government ministers have also called on the ECB to loosen monetary policy (thereby technically breaching Article 107 of the Maastricht Treaty).[4] It seems accurate to conclude that the government has, at least for the first few years of the downturn, made notable attempts at using fiscal policy in order to engage in demand-side management, with the aim of stimulating growth.[5] In other words, it is difficult to contradict the argument that fiscal policy has been stimulatory and supportive of growth. The case concerning monetary policy is less straightforward.

10.1.2 The ECB's View

The sole and independent decision maker on monetary policy is the ECB. Its view has been that its monetary policy has already been supportive of the German economy, while structural problems have held growth back.

Thus the onus is on the German government to implement structural reform (deregulation, liberalization and privatization) and to reduce fiscal expenditure so as to meet the Maastricht deficit and debt criteria. According to the ECB the responsibility for fiscal deficits and debt also lies with the German government, while it has little to do with monetary policy.[6]

The ECB favors structural supply-side policies over anti-cyclical demand management. This view has become widespread among commentators and observers. If the ECB's structural argument is correct, any focus on demand-side policies would indeed be misguided and only of little academic interest. Thus, before proceeding to the main concern of this chapter, namely to analyze any link between the two main demand management policies, it is necessary to evaluate briefly the merits of the ECB's structural supply-side argument.[7]

10.2. A BRIEF EMPIRICAL EVALUATION OF THE SUPPLY-SIDE ARGUMENT

There are two theoretical foundations of the structural reform argument. The first is Neoclassical growth theory, and the second is Neoclassical welfare economics.

10.2.1 Neoclassical Growth Theory

Actual growth is due to the quantity of factor inputs employed (QFI), such as land, labor, capital and technology, and the total productivity of those factors (TFP). Thus:

$$\text{Actual growth} = f(QFI, TFP) \tag{10.1}$$

Neoclassical growth theory (see, for instance, Solow 1957, and subsequent work) is built on several important assumptions. These vary depending on the precise type of Neoclassical model, but usually include perfect information, complete markets, no transaction costs and perfectly flexible prices. Based on such assumptions, Neoclassical growth theory assumes that all markets are in equilibrium. Hence all factor inputs are fully utilized and actual growth is identical with potential growth.

By assumption, therefore:

$$\text{Actual growth} = \text{potential growth} \tag{10.2}$$

To explain weak economic performance in Germany in 2001–2004, this approach can only argue that the quantity of total factor inputs and/or their productivity have declined, thus restricting potential growth. Since actual growth is always at its potential, this also implies that actual growth is restricted.

It is therefore straightforward to put this first version of the structural reform argument to the empirical test. One merely needs to evaluate whether

- the productivity of the factors of production used has declined significantly (or their productivity growth has slowed sufficiently)
- the supply of available factor inputs has fallen significantly (or their growth slowed)
- and the combination of the above factors is sufficient to explain the decline in observed actual growth.

Alternatively, one can test whether the fundamental assumption of this approach actually holds, namely whether all available factors of production are actually employed (and thus equation (10.2) actually holds). Productivity refers to the factor inputs actually employed. It is invalid to include unused resources in a measurement of productivity. German labor productivity can only be measured for those working hours of those members of the workforce actually working. Unfortunately, the mistake of allowing unemployment to lower productivity estimates (or increased employment to boost them) is still widespread, so that often US productivity appears high, merely because US workers work longer hours than their European counterparts.[8]

Many careful studies on productivity found that German productivity was among the highest in the world and exceeded British productivity in the late 1990s and early 2000s.[9] *The Economist* (2003) concluded in its survey on the topic that the

> figures certainly show that when they are actually at their desks (or lathes) the Germans, French and Dutch (though not the British) are more productive than Americans.

According to the OECD (2005), in 2003 US labor productivity per hour worked was seventh highest among OECD members, while Germany was a close eighth. The UK, Spain, Switzerland, and in total 22 countries ranked below Germany. These facts indicate that productivity is not likely to be the reason why German economic growth was weak between 2001 and 2004.

As the structural reform argument is based on Neoclassical theory, it is valid to use an alternative and readily available measure of overall productivity and competitiveness: according to Neoclassical trade theory, German overall productivity is reflected in German trade performance, as represented by its trade or current account balance.[10] What is the evidence on German productivity during the 1990s and early 2000s on the basis of this measure?

Germany is often given low rankings in international so-called 'competitiveness' or 'productivity' surveys. These are often conducted by think tanks and based on subjective assessments or polls of businesses that may reflect other issues – such as costs – rather than productivity. Germany is the world's largest net exporting nation. During our observation period (2001–2005) we find that the surplus rose to record highs, reaching a level in 2005 that was more than twice as large as the previous record of 1990. The surplus in 2004 was approximately twice as large as the trade surplus of Japan, then the second largest exporter (approximately USD180bn versus USD 83bn in 2004).[11] There is no evidence that the weak German economic performance of the recent years has been due to a decline in productivity (or productivity growth).[12]

What about factor inputs? It can be mentioned that there is little evidence that the available factor inputs have declined (or their growth rate has declined) sufficiently to explain the weaker economic performance 2001–2004.[13]

The ultimate test of the hypothesis that structural reforms are necessary is to examine whether all factors of production were fully employed during the

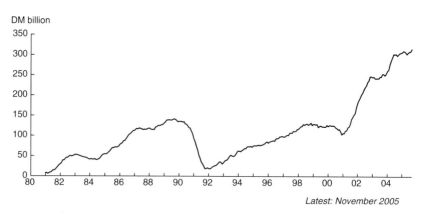

DM billion

Latest: November 2005

Source: Profit Research Center Ltd., Tokyo.

Figure 10.1   German trade balance (annual moving sum)

observation period. If unemployed resources are found, the Neoclassical growth theory, and hence any recommendation to reform the economic structure based on it, would have to be dismissed, as equation (10.2) would not hold. If actual growth is falling short of potential, increasing the potential growth rate will not have an impact on actual growth.[14]

The evidence concerning this point is straightforward. Not all factors of production were fully employed, as seen from the unemployment figures cited in section 10.1. The capacity utilization of the manufacturing sector had declined since 2001. According to the DIW, it fell from a peak of 87.1 in 2000, to 86.1 in 2001 and 83.9 in 2002.[15]

An empirical examination of the structural reform thesis as based on Neoclassical growth theory cannot find empirical support. The thesis that the German recession has been due to an under-utilization of available factor inputs is more compelling. It is not supply-side reforms that are required, but demand-management policy, such as fiscal and monetary policy.

10.2.2   Neoclassical Welfare Economics

The second possible argument why structural reform may be a suitable policy to stimulate growth is Neoclassical welfare economics. The fundamental theorem of welfare economics states the particular set of assumptions under which the competitive economy is Pareto-efficient (see Pareto [1906] 1971, Lange 1942, Allais 1943, Samuelson 1947, Bator 1957). These include perfect information, complete markets and so on, and define an economy where interventions, such as by the government in the form of regulations, cannot but reduce allocative efficiency. This theory is often interpreted to mean that the less an economy resembles the conditions for Pareto efficiency, the lower its efficiency and hence economic performance. As a result, it is often argued that structural reform should be implemented to deregulate, liberalize and privatize an economy, in order to increase its market orientation and help it to move closer to the Pareto-efficient ideal. The German economy does not appear to have met any of the necessary conditions for Pareto efficiency. Could this explain its weak economic performance?

Two testable hypotheses can be derived. The first concerns the link between economic structure and economic growth. The second concerns the link between structural reform (that is, changes in the economic structure) and economic growth. The first hypothesis based on Neoclassical welfare economics is that countries that are more market-oriented are more efficient and thus deliver higher growth than countries that are less market-oriented. It is common to regard the US and UK as countries that are more

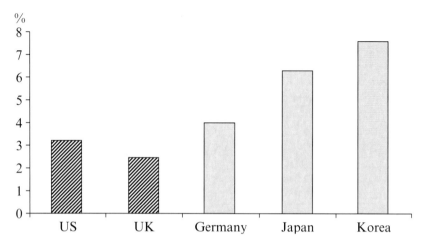

Source: Financial and Economics Statistics Monthly, Bank of Japan.

Figure 10.2   Average real GDP growth, per annum 1950–2000

market-oriented and focused on shareholder value, while Germany, Japan and Korea are examples of less market-oriented economies that are characterized more by government regulation, government intervention, cross-shareholdings, cartels, less reliance on equity markets for corporate finance, less influence of shareholders, lower dividends and so on (see Dore 2000, Werner 2003). If the Neoclassical welfare theory was empirically relevant in the way proclaimed, we would expect over longer time periods (thus abstracting from business cycles) that the more market- and shareholder-oriented economies would deliver higher economic growth.

Figure 10.2 shows the average real GDP growth per annum of the US, the UK, Germany, Japan and Korea in the half-century from 1950 to 2000. As can be seen, Germany has higher real GDP growth in these fifty years than the UK or the US. Meanwhile, the even less market-oriented economies of Japan and Korea recorded still higher long-term economic growth. The first hypothesis of Neoclassical welfare economics is rejected by the data.

The second testable hypothesis derived from Neoclassical welfare economics is that the reform of a non-market economy towards greater market orientation would increase economic growth. For the purposes of this chapter we restrict ourselves to the case of Japan, which after the Second World War showed an extreme case of a non-market economy, and which has experienced significant structural reform over the past half century to increase its market orientation (via deregulation, liberalization and privatization programs, begun in the early 1970s, accelerated in the 1980s and

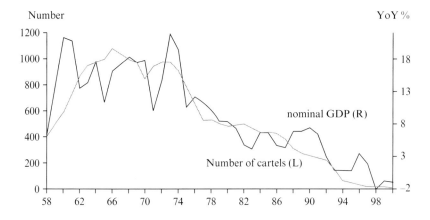

Source: Werner (2004).

Figure 10.3 Number of cartels and economic growth in Japan, 1958–2000

peaking under the Koizumi administration since 2001). Werner (2004) has argued that this structural change can be measured by the number of official cartels, as they represent direct non-market mechanisms to settle economic transactions that were pervasive in the early post-war era. The number of cartels reached over 1000 at their peak. As a result of decades of structural reform today there are none. The testable hypothesis is that an increase in the number of cartels should be associated with lower economic growth and a decrease with higher economic growth. Thus the two variables should be negatively correlated. Figure 10.3 shows the correlation between the number of cartels and economic growth over 42 years. As can be seen, it is positive. Over this long time period, more cartels have been associated with higher growth, and fewer cartels with lower growth.

While more detailed data on Germany awaits compilation, it can be stated that the literature so far cites no compelling empirical evidence in support of the asserted relationship between economic growth and structural reform. It would appear that the empirical record is not supportive of the claims by Neoclassical welfare economics concerning the link between economic structure and economic growth. This is not surprising, as, after all, Neoclassical welfare economics is based on a highly restricted set of assumptions that apply nowhere in the world we live in. Neoclassical welfare economics has demonstrated that the conditions for market efficiency are so stringent that we cannot expect them to apply to us, and hence we cannot expect markets to be efficient. That, in turn, provides a rationale for government intervention and non-market solutions.

10.2.3   Conclusion on the Structural Reform Argument

There is no empirical support for the structural reform view. The ECB's argument that supply-side structural reforms are the policy initiative that is most needed in order to stimulate the German economy is without merit. A far more plausible explanation of events in Germany (as well as Japan) is weak demand. We therefore now consider the role and impact of the two main demand management policies, monetary and fiscal policy.

10.3.   THE LINK BETWEEN FISCAL AND MONETARY POLICY

According to Keynesian, Post-Keynesian and fiscalist economists, fiscal policy is more effective than monetary policy. In contrast, Monetarist and Neoclassical economists argue (for different reasons) that fiscal policy is not likely to be effective. So far, the empirical record has been mixed. As the topic is vast, and it is the purpose of this contribution to identify the linkage between fiscal and monetary policy, some narrowing of focus is required. The subsequent discussion will focus on the government expenditure and investment policy aspect of fiscal policy.

A significant number of empirical studies have aimed at estimating the contribution of public expenditures to economic growth, using time-series or cross-country data. The IMF (1995) summarizes the findings as follows:

> Empirical studies have yielded conflicting results: some support the hypothesis that a rise in the share of public spending is associated with a decline in economic growth (Landau 1986, and Scully 1989); others have found that public spending is associated positively with economic growth (Ram 1986); and still other studies have found no significant relationship (Kormendi/Meguire 1985, and Diamond 1989).

One study found that public expenditures had no impact on growth in developed countries, but a positive impact in developing countries (Sattar 1993). The IMF (1995) concluded that the relationship between aggregate public expenditure and economic growth is not empirically well supported. The same conclusion applies to public investment as a component of public expenditure. Here, the IMF (1995) summarizes:

> While the contribution of public investment to economic growth has been invariably assumed theoretically, empirical studies based on aggregate public expenditure data have found only weak links between public investment and economic growth.

Barro (1991) found only a statistically insignificant relationship. Crowding out is found, among others, by Aschauer (1989), Munnell (1990) and Holtz-Eakin (1994). Cross-country studies have not produced robust statistical support for a link between public investment and growth (Levine and Renelt 1992).

Due to simultaneity and exogeneity problems it is advisable to begin an empirical examination of the issue of the efficacy of fiscal expenditure policy, and its link to monetary policy, with reference to a major economy that has experienced fiscal stimulation of fairly extreme proportions. We thus focus our attention on the Japanese case and the lessons that can be learnt from it for countries such as Germany.

Total government expenditures, as calculated by the national income accounts (aggregating government consumption, investment and inventories), are a consistent measure of the expenditure part of the fiscal stance. According to these data, Japanese government expenditure increased from a total of Y705 trillion in the 1980s to Y1136 trillion in the 1990s, amounting to Y113.6 trillion every year on average during the decade of the 1990s (up from Y70.5 trillion on average per year during the 1980s). As a percentage of nominal GDP, this represented an increase from 20.9 per cent on average in the 1980s to 22.7 per cent in the 1990s. During the 1990s, the share of government expenditure (*G*) rose from a low of 19.8 per cent in 1991 to a high of 23.9 per cent in 1999. The expansionary fiscal expenditure stance during the 1990s becomes more obvious on a growth basis. The increase in government expenditure amounted to Y32 trillion in the 1980s, and Y33 trillion in the 1990s. Table 10.2 shows the breakdown by contribution to growth of each GDP component. On average, government spending contributed

Table 10.2   *Contribution to nominal GDP growth in the 1980s and 1990s, Japan*

CY %	Cons. + Housing	Capex (+ Invent.)	Net Exports	Private Demand	Gov't Cons.	Gov't Invest- ment (+ Invent)	Total Gov't	Nominal GDP
1980s ave.	3.4	1.5	0.3	5.2	*0.8*	0.2	1.0	*6.2*
1990s ave.	1.0	−0.1	0.4	0.8	*0.6*	0.2	0.7	*1.5*

Note: Cons. = consumption; Capex = capital expenditure; CY = calendar year.

Source: National Income Accounts Statistics, Cabinet Office, Government of Japan.

almost half of growth in the 1990s, while it only contributed a sixth of growth in the 1980s.

Since nominal GDP grew by Y199 trillion in the 1980s, but only Y72 trillion in the 1990s, $\Delta G/\Delta nGDP$, the ratio of government expenditure growth to GDP growth, jumped from 16.3 per cent in the 1980s to 46.5 per cent in the 1990s. In the second half of the 1990s, there were years when this ratio was negative: in 1997 and 2000, government expenditure declined, but nominal GDP rose (in 2000, this amounted to a one-to-one relationship). In 1998 and 1999, government expenditure rose, but nominal GDP declined (with the 1999 increase in government expenditure being three quarters the size of the fall in nominal GDP). The simple period 'multiplier' ($\Delta nGDP/\Delta G$) fell from an aggregate of 6.1 in the 1980s to only 2.2 in the 1990s. However, for half of the 1990s, it was below 1, and for the last four years of the decade it was significantly negative. The apparent diminishing positive 'effect' of government expenditure was not predicted by contemporary observers, including the official government forecasts at the time.

Tanaka and Kitano (2002, p. 1) summarize a common view when they state that 'aggressive fiscal policy was implemented in Japan. . . . However, despite the aggressive fiscal mobilization, the economy remained in recession'. They also find that the Japanese experience was not an outlier: fiscal expenditure policy had virtually no impact in all the countries they examined. Such findings require an explanation that is consistent with the empirical facts and general enough to account for the experience in other countries, such as Germany.

10.3.1 Explanations of Fiscal Policy Ineffectiveness in the Literature

When fiscal expenditure rises, but total GDP fails to rise as much, other components of GDP must have operated to reduce GDP. In other words, consumption, capital expenditure, private sector housing investment or gross exports must have fallen and/or inventories or imports must have risen. The question why this should have happened repeatedly during the 1990s requires an answer.

The literature has focused on three answers. They will be discussed below. What they have in common is that they suggest that the simple first-round positive effects of fiscal expenditure policy may be partially or completely negated by negative effects that result from the need of the government to procure money in order to fund the fiscal expenditure.

Textbooks such as Dornbusch and Fischer (1987) point out that there are two options to fund the public sector borrowing requirement (PSBR): debt finance or money finance. In the former case, the government borrows from the private sector; in the latter, it either creates money directly, or borrows from the central bank, which pays by creating money.

In Japan's case, the government has funded the revenue shortfall virtually entirely from the private sector, mainly via bond and bill issuance.[16] As a result, new government borrowing increased by Y300.4 trillion during the 1990s (58.6 per cent of 2000 nominal GDP). This raised total outstanding debt to Y522.1 trillion by the end of 2000, amounting to 101.8 per cent of GDP. At the end of 2003 the government estimated that, with its budgeted new bond issuance of Y30 trillion in fiscal year 2004, the outstanding balance of government debt would reach over Y700 trillion by the end of March 2005.

10.3.1.1 Interest-rate-based crowding out

The first explanation focuses on interest-rate-based crowding out, resulting in lower capital expenditure and housing investment. Christ (1968), Blinder and Solow (1973), Hansen (1973) and others showed that for bond-financed deficit spending, the stimulatory effect of fiscal policy is smaller than that derived in traditional Keynesian models that do not take funding into consideration.[17] The crowding out effect of increased government expenditure via higher interest rates is reflected in standard Keynesian models and the IS-LM synthesis, but also the mainstream Monetarist models (such as Friedman 1956, Brunner and Meltzer 1976). The main problem with the interest-rate-based arguments for fiscal policy ineffectiveness is that it is not supported by the Japanese data.[18] Short-term and long-term interest rates (as measured by call rates and ten-year government bond yields, respectively) have trended down during the 1990s.

10.3.1.2 Ricardian equivalence

Krugman (1998) applied a model of intertemporally optimizing rational representative agents to Japan to demonstrate the possibility of Ricardian equivalence of the type Barro (1974) proposed: Japanese consumers believe that any fiscal spending funded by the issuance of government debt (as most of it has been) will require the debt to be fully paid off in the relevant future by raising taxes on individuals. In this setting, for every yen in government spending, rational consumers would increase savings by one yen – preparing the money to repay the government in the future.

Analytically, this approach suffers from a number of problems. The model does not allow for the possibility that the debt will be paid off by other means – such as money creation, higher corporate taxes, economic growth that boosts tax revenues without raising individual taxes, or asset sales to foreign investors. It is not clear why rational consumers would not consider these possibilities, especially in a deflationary economy operating below the full employment level. The assumption of full employment renders such models unsuitable for commenting on increased fiscal expenditure due to weak demand. Further, there is also no empirical evidence to support this theory.

10.3.1.3 Quantity-based crowding out and the link to monetary policy
The third major approach allows for direct crowding out of fiscal expenditure, without the need for interest rates to rise or without the need for the economy to operate at full employment. It is based on a modified credit view and emphasizes the link between fiscal and monetary policy.

So far, the debate about fiscal policy effectiveness has centered on bond-financed deficits. The possibility of money-financed fiscal expenditure remains neglected.[19] This is surprising, because the literature has always agreed unanimously that fiscal policy, if funded this way, will be effective. In the words of Blinder and Solow (1973, p. 323):

> There is no controversy over government spending financed by printing money. Both sides agree that it will be expansionary; but one group likes to call it fiscal policy, while the other prefers to call it monetary policy. Nothing much hinges on this distinction.

In the case of money-financed deficits, new money is issued. In the words of Dornbusch and Fischer (1987, pp. 605–6):

> While there is some argument about whether bonds are wealth, there is no question that money is wealth. . . . That, too, means that aggregate demand at any given price level will be higher with money than with debt financing.

The link between monetary and fiscal policy: standard quantity equation
According to monetary economics textbooks, the link between money and the economy is expressed by the 'quantity equation':

$$MV = PY \tag{10.3}$$

Handa (2000) writes that equation (10.3) 'is an identity since it is derived solely from identities. It is valid under any set of circumstances whatever . . .'. Considering changes, we can rewrite this to state that nominal GDP growth is proportional to money supply growth:

$$\Delta(PY) = V\Delta M \tag{10.4}$$

Any exogenous increase in a component of nominal GDP (such as in G) cannot affect total nominal GDP, if the money supply remains unaltered:

with $\Delta M = 0$, and breaking down nominal GDP (PY) into nominal consumption c, nominal government expenditure g, nominal investment i and nominal net exports nx, we obtain:

$$\Delta M = 0 \tag{10.5}$$

$$\Rightarrow \Delta(PY) = \Delta c + \Delta i + \Delta g + \Delta nx = 0 \tag{10.6}$$

Thus:

$$\Delta c + \Delta i + \Delta nx = -\Delta g \tag{10.7}$$

Under the condition expressed in equation (10.5) that the money supply is unaltered, each dollar of additional government spending must crowd out exactly one dollar of private spending, as shown in equation (10.7). Thus the level of aggregate income will be unchanged and the multiplier for bond-financed government spending (that is, government spending that does not affect the money supplied) is zero.

This conclusion is not dependent on the assumption of full employment. Instead of the employment constraint, the economy can be held back by a lack of money, at any level of employment. Fiscal policy not backed by monetary policy can thus crowd out private demand even with significant unemployment. It is also not dependent on any particular level of interest rates: the original quantity equation by Fisher, favored also by the early Keynes and later Friedman, does not include interest rates. Instead, there is a direct quantity crowding out effect: the money used by the government for its fiscal expenditure cannot at the same time be available for spending by the private sector. Thus equations (10.5–10.7) show that without an increase in the money supply, nominal GDP will remain unaltered and fiscal policy is completely ineffective.[20]

Could this theoretical argument be empirically applied to explain the lack of effectiveness of fiscal policy in countries such as Japan or Germany? Unfortunately, it faces an empirical obstacle: macroeconomic models based on the quantity equation and predicated on the assumption of constant velocity have broken down (Goldfeld and Sichel 1990): substantial declines in velocity (and hence a 'breakdown' in the money demand function) have been observed in a large number of countries since the 1980s, including the UK, the US, Scandinavian countries and Japan. The previously stable relationship between M and PY 'increasingly came apart at the seams during the course of the 1980s' (Goodhart 1989). As a result, the usefulness of the quantity equation has declined in the case of most countries, including Japan and Germany.

The link between monetary and fiscal policy: modified quantity equation   A suggestion has been made to render the standard quantity equation effective and relevant again for our purposes. Werner (1992, 1997) suggested firstly that the breakdown in the relationship between M and nominal GDP may have been due to the neglect of financial transactions.[21] A disaggregated quantity equation, which relates changes in nominal GDP to the change in money used for transactions that enter GDP (that is, excluding real estate and financial transactions), was shown to be consistent over long time periods and reliable for forecasting (Werner, 1992, 1994, 1997, 2003, 2005). This disaggregated quantity equation is shown below:

$$\Delta(P_R Y) = V\Delta M_R \tag{10.8}$$

where P_R stands for the GDP deflator and M_R for money used for GDP transactions.

Secondly, concerning the measure of the 'money supply' M, Werner (1992, 1997) pointed out that the Fisher equation originally referred to money used for transactions. As deposit aggregates measure money that is not used for transactions, Werner suggested replacing deposit aggregates with credit counterparts, based on theoretical and empirical reasons.[22] Thus equation (10.8) is rewritten as follows:

$$\Delta(P_R Y) = V\Delta C_R \tag{10.8'}$$

A further advantage of this model is that it is simpler than other explanations (it does not require restrictive assumptions such as perfect information, market clearing and so on), while at the same time reflecting advances in the 'credit view' approach.

Equation (10.8') suggests that lowering interest rates may not be useful to stimulate an economy, as there may be reasons why lower or falling interest rates do not result in an increase in credit. Further, the equation suggests that 'pure' fiscal stimulation cannot on its own stimulate overall nominal GDP growth: as seen from the above quantity formulations, if there is no increase in credit used for GDP transactions C_R, there cannot be an increase in nominal GDP. Under such circumstances, increased fiscal expenditure must crowd out private demand:

if

$$\Delta C_R = 0 \tag{10.5'}$$

then

$$\Delta(P_R Y) = \Delta c + \Delta i + \Delta g + \Delta nx \qquad (10.6')$$

$$(\Delta c + \Delta i + \Delta nx) = -\Delta g \qquad (10.7')$$

Fiscal policy can only affect nominal GDP growth, if it is linked to the monetary side of the economy, via an expansion in credit. This proposition suggests that fiscal and monetary policy should not be analyzed or operated independently – as Lerner (1943) argued earlier.[23] In general, with non-zero credit growth, by substituting (10.6') and (10.7') into (10.8') we get:

$$\Delta(c + i + nx) = V\Delta C_R - \Delta g \qquad (10.9)$$

whereby in a regression of private demand $\Delta(c + i + nx)$ on credit and government expenditure, the coefficient of Δg is expected to be approximately -1. Equation (10.9) shows that, given the amount of credit creation produced by the banking system, an autonomous increase in government expenditure must result in an equal reduction in private demand. As the government issues bonds to fund increased fiscal stimulation, private sector investors (such as life insurance companies) that purchase the bonds must withdraw purchasing power elsewhere from the economy.

We observe a different kind of crowding out than postulated by standard Keynesian or Neoclassical Ricardian models: it is quantity-based and does not require any particular movement in interest rates; it does not depend on restrictive assumptions about unobservable expectations and their formation and it does not operate via a change in household savings. Crowding out occurs due to increased claims by the government on limited credit, together with a lack of new purchasing power supplied by the financial system (credit creation).

The policy advice is uncontroversial. There 'is no controversy over government spending financed by printing money. Both sides agree that it will be expansionary', in the words of Blinder and Solow (1973, p. 323). Of course, 'printing money' is, in a modern economy, a metaphor for creating credit. In terms of the modified 'early Keynesian' model this means that the Japanese or German authorities would need to increase credit creation, in order to stimulate growth. This can, for instance, be done via fiscal policy that is funded by credit creation, as will be discussed briefly after putting the above framework to the empirical test.

Empirical evaluation   Starting with a general model of GDP growth which includes a number of competing potential explanatory variables (including short-term and long-term interest rates, M1, M2+ CD and other

variables) a downward reduction yields the following parsimonious model
(of seasonally differenced quarterly logs):

$$\Delta GDP_t = \alpha + \beta_1 \Delta GDP_{t-1} + \gamma_0 \Delta C_{Rt} + \gamma_3 \Delta C_{Rt-3} + \varepsilon_t \qquad (10.10)$$

Substituting equation (10.10) into equation (10.9) and solving for non-
government demand, we obtain:

$$\Delta(c_t + i_t + nx_t) = \alpha + \beta \Delta g_t + \beta_1 \Delta GDP_{t-1} + \gamma_0 \Delta C_{Rt}$$
$$+ \gamma_3 \Delta C_{Rt-3} + \varepsilon_t \qquad (10.11)$$

The proposition of complete fiscal policy ineffectiveness advanced by the
early Keynesian, proto-Monetarist and early Post-Keynesian economists
can now be tested. In this case the regression would yield the following
coefficient for government expenditure:

$$\beta_0 = -1 \qquad (10.12)$$

For accurate tests, seasonally differenced absolute changes of the variables
must be used. Figure 10.4 shows the original data for Japan during the 1990s,
namely changes in government spending and private demand. Visual inspection indicates that a negative correlation is likely, although there are periods
when both variables fell or rose together. According to the present approach,

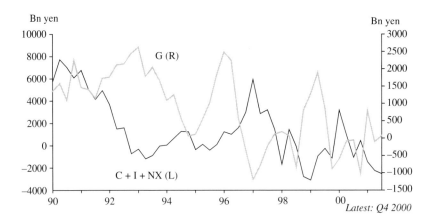

Note: Nominal private demand and government expenditure, absolute changes.

Source: Cabinet Office, Government of Japan.

Figure 10.4   Private and government demand: Japan

such episodes should be explained by the presence of the monetary (credit) variable. The results of the regression, using the longer time period including most of the 1980s, are shown in Table 10.3, with D480CINX denoting private demand, D480G denoting government expenditure and D4CR denoting

Table 10.3   Estimation results of private demand model

Modelling D480CINX by OLS; sample 1983 (1) to 2001 (1)					
	Coeff	Std.Err	t-val	t-prob	Part.R^2
Constant	440.268	224.6	1.80	0.076	0.046
D480nGDP_1	0.476	0.098	4.85	0.000	0.257
D4CR	0.085	0.031	2075	0.008	0.100
D4CR_3	0.059	0.036	1.64	0.105	0.038
D480G	−0.974	0.140	−6.94	0.000	0.415
Sigma	1231.87		RSS		103190221
R^2	0.832		F(4.68)	=	83.97
					[0.000]***
log-likelihood	−620.482		DW		2.03
no. of obs.	73		no. of param		5
mean	2441.51		var(D480CINX)		8.39605e+006
(D480CINX)					
AR 1-5 test:	F(5, 63)	=	1.214	[0.313]	
ARCH 1-4 test:	F(4, 60)	=	0.605	[0.661]	
Normality test	Chi^2(2)	=	5.672	[0.059]	
hetero test	F(8059)	=	1.990	[0.064]	
hetero-X test:	F(14, 53)	=	1.772	[0.068]	
RESET test:	F(1, 67)	=	0.199	[0.657]	
Solved static long-run equation for D480CINX					
Constant	440.286	244.6	1.80	0.076	
D480nGDP	0.476	0.098	4.85	0.000	
D4CR	0.144	0.029	4.93	0.000	
D480G	−0.974	0.140	−6.94	0.000	
Long-run sigma = 1231.87					

ECM = D480CINX − 440.286 − 0.476*D480nGDP − 0.144*D4CR +0.974*D480G;
WALD test: Chi^2(3) = 334.98 [0.000] **

Tests on the significance of each variable				
Variable	F-test		Value	[Prob]
Constant	F(1, 68)	=	0.239	[0.076]
D480nGDP	F(1, 68)	=	23.512	[0.000]**
C4CR	F(2, 68)	=	13.189	[0.000]**
D480G	F(1, 68)	=	48.223	[0.000]**

Note: From the 1980 GDP series.

Source: Cabinet Office, Government of Japan.

credit in the 'real circulation'. Figure 10.5 presents the graph of the dependent variable and the fitted model.

Evaluation of the empirical tests   The model of private demand has a good fit and no obvious mis-specification problems. It is found that the coefficient for government expenditure is –0.974. Rounding to one digit, we obtain:

$$\beta_0 = -1$$

More formal linear restriction tests are conducted to see if the null hypothesis that $\beta_0 = -1.0$ can be rejected (Table 10.4).

As can be seen, the linear restriction F-test fails to reject the null hypothesis that $\beta_0 = -1.0$ (probability: 85.5 per cent). These findings suggest that for every yen in government spending that is not monetized (that is, not supported by credit creation), private demand shrank by one yen. The empirical evidence supports the contention of the pre- and early Keynesian economists that an economic recovery and fiscal stimulation require monetary expansion.

This finding holds not only for the 1990s. The above tests were conducted for the longer time period, including much of the 1980s. This finding strengthens confidence in the credit model, as it appears to be a general model that can account for a variety of economic circumstances, including the more extreme 1990s. Testing separately only for the 1990s, the same result of complete fiscal policy ineffectiveness was found ($\beta_0 = -1.0$), as well as when the long-run static equilibrium formulation was used. The credit quantity model appears to fit the Japanese experience of the 1980s and 1990s, in preference to alternative explanations.

10.3.2   Policy Implications for Japan and Germany

Fiscal policy can only be effective if it is supported by monetary policy. The early Keynesian and proto-Monetarist quantity equation view of fiscal policy has been confirmed in a credit-based model. The policy implication is that the coordination of fiscal and monetary policy is crucial. With economists as diverse as Lerner (1943), Wray (2001) or Schabert (2004) calling for such coordination, this is not controversial.[24] However, there is little debate about the political implications concerning the independence of central banks.

10.3.2.1   Japan
Some of the ways in which the central bank could have rendered the government's significant fiscal expenditure efforts effective are open market

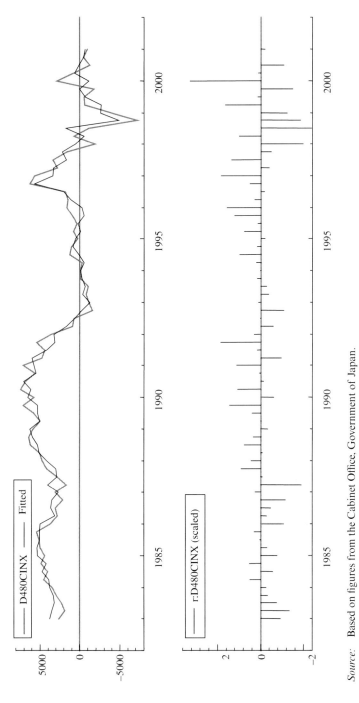

Source: Based on figures from the Cabinet Office, Government of Japan.

Figure 10.5   Private demand and fitted model: Japan

Table 10.4   Linear restriction test of ineffectiveness hypothesis

Test for linear restrictions (Rb=r): R matrix

Const	D480nGDP_1	D4CR	D4CR_3	D480G	r vector
0.000	0.000	0.000	0.000	1.000	−1.000

LinRes $F(1, 68) = 0.0335743$ [0.8552]

purchase operations. Policies to stimulate bank credit creation could also have been adopted. The central bank could have been more helpful, for instance by utilizing its unique status to solve the bad debt problem (as it did after 1945, when it moved the banks' non-performing assets on to its own balance sheet, where they could do no harm). None of these policies were implemented. The Japanese central bank failed to support fiscal policy specifically and economic growth generally during the 1990s. From this it would appear that the lack of incentives to coordinate monetary policy with the government's fiscal policy is one of the disadvantages of central bank independence.[25]

10.3.2.2   Germany

The ECB is in error if it blames the German government for failing to meet the Maastricht criteria. According to equation (10.8'), growth is a function of credit creation; a decline in credit creation results in a recession, which in turn produces fiscal deficits and debt. This appears also to be the chain of causation in Germany: bank lending declined in Germany from 2000 onwards (Figure 10.6). As can be seen, bank lending decelerated precipitously in 2000. In 2002 and 2003 bank lending contracted temporarily. If we recognize imperfect information and hence rationed markets (which are determined by the 'short side') we can deduce that a credit crunch occurred in Germany. The credit-induced recession resulted in greater fiscal expenditure, higher deficits and aggregate debt. As equation (10.8') also shows, the recession could have been ended through suitable policy that expanded credit creation. Stimulatory monetary policy could have included monetization of the fiscal stance. Thus the rise in the German fiscal deficit and debt have been largely the result of actions or lack of action by the ECB.

Without the cooperation of the central bank, money-financed fiscal expenditure policy is not an option. Yet there is a way for governments to monetize fiscal policy even without cooperation from the central bank. Werner (1998, 2000a, 2000b, 2000c, 2002, 2003, 2005) pointed out that credit-financed fiscal policy can be implemented by the government alone, if the Ministry of Finance chooses to cover the public sector borrowing

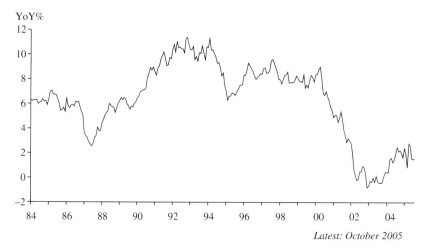

Latest: October 2005

Source: Bundesbank.

Figure 10.6   Bank lending in Germany

requirement by borrowing from commercial banks. This would increase credit creation and stimulate the economy.

That is the policy adopted by Germany in the early 1930s. From 1933 to 1937, the Reichsbank, under President Hjalmar Schacht, stepped up its own credit creation (by purchasing various forms of assets, including government bonds and bonds of other government institutions); Schacht also guided the establishment of semi-public institutions that implemented fiscal spending and were funded by the issuance of bills of exchange that were purchased by the banks and the central bank.

During the high-growth 'economic miracle' period of the 1950s and 1960s, fiscal policy in Germany continued to be effective, with little crowding out. Monetized fiscal policy appears to have been important: In 1968, under finance minister Karl Schiller, long-term bank credit accounted for about 70 per cent of the PSBR in Germany (amounting to DM13bn). Today this proportion is zero: in 1999, Germany funded its public sector borrowing requirement (amounting to E35bn, approximately DM70bn) entirely through the issuance of government bonds, and, additionally, reduced its borrowing from financial institutions (by a net E10bn, approximately DM20bn).[26] The differing impact is apparent.

The proposal to fund the PSBR through bank credit was also discussed in the UK in the 1930s, but Hawtrey, before the Macmillan Committee of 1930, raised objections.[27] However, Hawtrey's objections were predicated on the assumptions that (a) the market for credit is in equilibrium, so that interest rates respond proportionately to an increase in the demand for credit; and/or (b) that banks are merely financial intermediaries that cannot create new credit, so that any extension of bank loans to the government must be at the expense of bank lending to alternative uses. The theoretical literature has provided for the case of a rationed credit market, whereby interest rates do not respond proportionately to changes in the demand for money. The institutional reality of banking systems allows banks to create new purchasing power without withdrawing existing purchasing power from other parts of the economy (Werner 2005, 2006).

Thus funding fiscal expenditure by borrowing from banks would increase credit creation and hence the total amount of purchasing power in the economy. As a result, C_R in equation (10.8') above would rise, which would, in turn, boost nominal GDP. By shifting government funding away from bond finance and replacing it with borrowing from the commercial banks via simple loan contracts, credit creation will be stimulated. Unlike bond markets, banks create new purchasing power when they lend. This means that overall economic activity can be boosted (via fiscal policy), without any quantity crowding out that rendered fiscal policy ineffective during the 1990s.[28]

Figures 10.7 and 10.8 are used to illustrate the difference between stimulatory fiscal policy funded via bond issuance and stimulatory fiscal policy that is backed by credit creation. The example of a fiscal spending package amounting to E50bn illustrates that this can have, in the extreme case, zero effect (when not backed by credit creation) or boost demand by E50bn (when backed by credit creation). As most countries, including Japan and

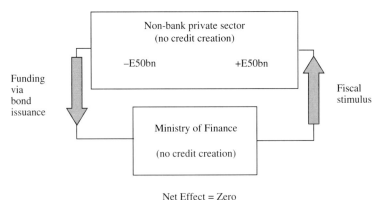

Net Effect = Zero

Note: Government spending of E50bn is used as an example.

Figure 10.7   Bond-funded fiscal expenditure with credit rationing

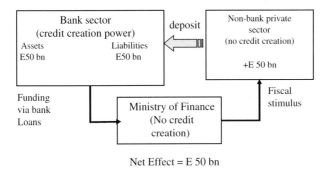

Note: Government spending of E50bn is used as an example.

Figure 10.8   Net effect of credit-funded fiscal expenditure

Germany, nowadays fund the bulk of fiscal expenditure via the issuance of bonds, there may be substantial, if not complete crowding out of private activity.

10.4.   CONCLUSION AND FURTHER RESEARCH

The proposed alternative model has provided an answer to the question why fiscal expenditure policy has appeared ineffective during the 1990s in major economies, including Germany. Empirical tests on the extreme case of Japan, which otherwise had not been explained by the literature, were strongly supportive.

The framework indicates that the cause of the German recession since 2000 was a lack of credit creation. This problem could have been addressed through policies to stimulate bank credit, including coordination of fiscal and monetary policy. Even without bank lending, the central bank could have created a recovery, by increasing its own credit creation. The government could also have stimulated the economy by funding fiscal expenditure through borrowing from banks. None of these policies were implemented.

There is much that members of the ECB, but also governments and policy makers, can learn from the Japanese experience in general and these findings in particular. They also highlight the need for future research on whether the ECB may have political reasons for downplaying its role and influence over the economy, and instead advancing a predetermined political agenda (structural reform) through misguided monetary policy. Again, Japan may have lessons for us, as evidence for such a link was found and detailed in Werner (2003). Implications are discussed further in Werner (2005, 2006).

NOTES

* This chapter draws heavily on earlier work by the author. Reproduction of selected figures from Werner (2003, 2005) with permission from M.E. Sharpe and Palgrave Macmillan.
1. Data compiled by the Profit Research Center Ltd., Tokyo, from official sources.
2. The surplus of 2000 includes the revenue from Universal Mobile Telecommunications System (UMTS) auctions. Correcting for this, a deficit of approximately 1.2 per cent of GDP can be estimated. I am grateful to the editors for pointing this out.
3. Article 107 in the original Maastricht Treaty.
4. For example, German finance ministers Oskar Lafontaine and Hans Eichel and economy minister Wolfgang Clement.
5. While cyclically adjusted deficit estimates are likely to show a less stimulatory, if not restrictive fiscal policy, the main concern of this analysis is fiscal policy over the business cycle (that is, cyclically unadjusted).
6. See, for instance, Issing (2001).
7. Unfortunately, media coverage of central banks has become reduced to an unquestioning and uncritical regurgitation of assertions made without empirical backing by central bank spokesmen.
8. Hayashi and Prescott (2002) confidently proclaimed that Japan's weak economic performance was due to an exogenous productivity shock and not demand-side factors. However, Fukao *et al.* (2003) and Jorgenson and Motohashi (2003) have shown that Hayashi and Prescott had assumed that all factors are fully employed and thus erroneously counted unemployed factors as not being productive. Jorgenson and Motohashi (2003) in their more careful study found that Japanese productivity actually increased in the second half of the 1990s.
9. Gordon (1999) found that 'after adjusting for the effects of the economic cycle, all of the increase in labour productivity was concentrated in the manufacturing of computers, with no net gain in the rest of the economy'. Other issues are whether to count IT spending as investment or expenditure, or whether higher prices in the IT sector are productivity rises (due to better quality) or inflation.
10. In the 1980s, the US Congress held sessions about 'Japanese productivity – Lessons for America', as it was widely argued that superior Japanese productivity explained the Japanese trade surplus. When China overtook Japan in 2004 as the world's third largest gross exporter (behind Germany and the US), the WTO explained this surge in China's exports with its 'surplus productivity'.
11. In 2005, China overtook Japan as the world's third largest gross and net exporter, with its trade surplus (annual moving sum) reaching USD94bn in November 2005.
12. Other measures of productivity or efficiency also did not appear to deteriorate noticeably. Germany did not appear to record a decline in the efficiency of its energy use, for instance. Final energy consumption in Germany only rose by 2.6 per cent between 1993 and 2003, while that in the UK and US rose by 5.8 per cent and 17.4 per cent over the same time period, respectively. As for environmental efficiency, German sulphur oxide emissions stood at 7 kg per capita in 2003, while they were as high as 17 and 48 in the UK and US, respectively (OECD 2005).
13. A few readily available statistics concerning land and labour can be cited here: land has remained unchanged in Germany over the observation period. According to the OECD (2005), the German fertility rate rose from 1.28 in 1993 to 1.34 in 2003, while that of the UK and US fell (from 1.75 and 2.05 in 1993 to 1.71 and 2.04, respectively). The female participation rate rose from 61.4 in 1994 to 66.6 in 2004 in Germany, while remaining unchanged in the US during the same time period at 69.8.

14. Instead, it may merely increase deflationary pressures, if inflation and deflation are thought of as functions of the output gap or the gap between actual and potential growth.
15. Accessed on 2 January 2006 at http://www.diw.de/english/produkte/datensammlungen/kapaziauslastung/kapatab.html, 30 August 2006.
16. Indeed, the government's borrowing is another measure of the stance of fiscal policy.
17. Their work was preceded by Lerner (1943) who rejected debt-financed deficits entirely.
18. Examples of empirical studies of the link between fiscal policy and interest rates in the US are Hutchison and Pyle (1984) and Hoelscher (1986). For examples and reviews of empirical work on the influence of fiscal policy on aggregate demand, see, for instance, Aschauer (1985) and Tatom (1985).
19. Ludvigson (1996) seems representative in the neglect of this possibility. A recent exception is Schabert (2004).
20. See also Werner (2005). As Milton Friedman put it in his entry under 'Money: Quantity Theory' in the Encyclopaedia Britannica: 'The quantity theory implies that the effect of government deficits or surpluses depends critically on how they are financed. If a deficit is financed by borrowing from the public without an increase in the quantity of money, the direct expansionary effect of the excess of government spending over receipts will be offset to some extent, and possibly to a very great extent, by the indirect contractionary effect of the transfer of funds to the government through borrowing' (Vol. 24, p. 476).
21. Such a disaggregation into 'real' and 'financial' transactions was also suggested, among others, by Spindt (1985), Allen (1989, 1994) and Howells and Biefang-Frisancho Mariscal (1992). Keynes (1930) made a similar suggestion.
22. See Werner (2005, 2006). The original equation of exchange, as cited by Fisher (1911) and others, attempted to express what could in words be formulated as follows: 'The amount of money changing hands to pay for transactions during a given time period must be equal to the nominal value of these transactions'. Only then is Handa (2000) right in calling it true by definition. Deposit aggregates (such as M0, M1, M2, M3 and so on) are inadmissible as a measure of money that is changing hands to pay for transactions. Credit aggregates measure this and, unlike deposit measures, can also be disaggregated by the use money is put to.
23. This means that the theory also has sound post-Keynesian credentials. See Bell (1999).
24. Wray (2001) frames his argument in terms of high-powered money, which however does not necessarily translate to greater effective spending.
25. Independence is not necessarily an obstacle, since a central bank can voluntarily cooperate to support the government's policy. As Bernanke (2000, p. 163) pointed out, 'Cooperation with the fiscal authorities in pursuit of a common goal is not the same as subservience'. Unfortunately, there are few examples of such cooperation.
26. I am grateful to Mr Wolfgang Eichmann, Head of Section III of the German Federal Statistical Office, for kindly writing to me, upon reading some of my work, and pointing out these supportive facts from Germany to me. See also Eichmann's (2002) relevant article on the velocity of money, which, among others, cites Werner (1997).
27. Klein (1968), as quoted by Spencer and Yohe (1970, p. 15). It is not made explicit who had launched this 'radical idea' in the UK. However, there is some evidence that it emerged from the German credit school of economists, who had been advancing it at least since the early 1920s.
28. This proposal has subsequently been endorsed by Congdon (2001), Smithers (2001) and Martin Wolf of the Financial Times (2002).

REFERENCES

Allais, M. [1943] (1952), *Traité d'Economie Pure*, 1952 edition of *A la Recherche d'une Discipline Economique*, Paris: Impremerie Internationale.

Allen, R.E. (1989), 'Globalization of the U. S. financial markets: The new structure for monetary policy', in O'Brian, R. and T. Datta (eds), *International Economics and Financial Markets,* Oxford: Oxford University Press, pp. 266–86.

Allen, R.E. (1994), *Financial Crises and Recession in the Global Economy,* Aldershot, UK and Brookfield, US: Edward Elgar.

Aschauer, D. (1985), 'Fiscal policy and aggregate demand', *American Economic Review,* 75(1), 117–27.

Aschauer, D.A. (1989), 'Does public capital crowd out private capital?', *Journal of Monetary Economics,* 24, 171–88.

Barro, R.J. (1974), 'Are government bonds net wealth?', *Journal of Political Economy,* 82, 1095–117.

Barro, R.J. (1991), 'Economic growth in a cross section of countries', *Quarterly Journal of Economics,* 106, 407–43.

Bator, F.M. (1957), 'The simple analytics of welfare maximization', *American Economic Review,* 47, 22–59.

Bell, S. (1999), *Functional Finance: What, Why, and How?,* Working Paper No. 287, Annandale-on-Hudson: The Levy Economics Institute of Bard College.

Bernanke, B.S. (2000), 'Japanese monetary policy: A case of self-induced paralysis?', in Mikitani, R. and A.S. Posen (2000), *Japan's Financial Crisis and its Parallels to US Experience,* Special Report 13, September, Washington DC: Institute for International Economics.

Blinder, A.S. and R.M. Solow (1973), 'Does fiscal policy matter?', *Journal of Public Economics,* 2, 319–37.

Brunner, K. and A. Meltzer (1976), 'An aggregate theory for a closed economy', in Stein, J. (ed.), *Monetarism,* Amsterdam: North-Holland Publishing, pp. 69–103.

Christ, C.F. (1968), 'A simple macroeconomic model with a government budget restraint', *Journal of Political Economy,* 76, 53–67.

Congdon, T. (2001), 'Money and the Japanese economic crisis', *Lombard Street Research Monthly Economic Review,* August.

Diamond, J. (1989), *Government Expenditures and Economic Growth: An Empirical Investigation,* IMF Working Paper, WP/89/45, Washington, DC: International Monetary Fund.

Dore, R. (2000), *Stock Market Capitalism: Welfare Capitalism, Japan and Germany versus the Anglo-Saxons,* Oxford: Oxford University Press.

Dornbusch, R. and S. Fischer (1987), *Macroeconomics,* New York: McGraw-Hill.

Economist (2003), *Special report: American productivity,* 13 September.

Eichmann, W. (2002), 'Sinkt die Geldumlaufgeschwindigkeit?', *Wirtschaftsdienst,* 82(2), 99–101.

Fisher, I. (1911), *The Purchasing Power of Money, its Determination and Relation to Credit, Interest and Crises,* New York: Macmillan.

Friedman, M. (1956), 'The quantity theory of money: A restatement', in Friedman, M. (ed.), *Studies in the Quantity Theory of Money,* Chicago: University of Chicago Press, pp. 3–21.

Fukao, K.T.I., Kawai, H. and T. Miyagawa (2003), *Sectoral Productivity and Economic Growth in Japan, 1970–98: An Empirical Analysis Based on the JIP Database,* paper presented at the NBER Thirteenth Annual East Asian Seminar on Economics: Productivity, 20–22 June 2002, Melbourne.

Goldfeld, S.M. and D.E. Sichel (1990), 'The demand for money', in Friedman, B.M. and F.H. Hahn (eds), *Handbook of Monetary Economics,* Vol. I, Amsterdam: Elsevier Science Publishers, pp. 300–356.

Goodhart, C.A.E. (1989), 'The conduct of monetary policy', *Economic Journal*, 99, 293–346.

Gordon, R.J. (1999), *Has the* 'New Economy' *Rendered the Productivity Slowdown Obsolete?*, mimeograph, Evanston, IL: Northwestern University.

Handa, J. (2000), *Monetary Economics*, London and New York: Routledge.

Hansen, B. (1973), 'On the effects of fiscal and monetary policy: A taxonomic discussion', *American Economic Review*, 63(4), 546–71.

Hayashi, F. and E.C. Prescott (2002), 'The 1990s in Japan: A lost decade', *Review of Economic Dynamics*, 5(1), 206–35.

Hoelscher, G. (1986), 'New evidence on deficits and interest rates', *Journal of Money, Credit and Banking*, 18(1), 1–17.

Holtz-Eakin, D. (1994), 'Public sector capital and productivity puzzle', *Review of Economics and Statistics*, 76(1), 574–82.

Howells, P. and I. Biefang-Frisancho Mariscal (1992), 'An explanation for the recent behavior of income and transaction velocities in the United Kingdom', *Journal of Post Keynesian Economics*, 14(3), 367–88.

Hutchison, M. and D. Pyle (1984), 'The real interest rate/budget deficit link', *Federal Reserve Bank of San Francisco Review*, Fall, 26–35.

IMF (1995), *Unproductive Public Expenditures*, Fiscal Affairs Department Pamphlet Series, 48, Washington DC: International Monetary Fund.

Issing, O. (2001), 'Euro reflections: Interview with Otmar Issing', *The International Economy*, May, 24–7.

Jorgenson, D.W. and K. Motohashi (2003), *The Role of Information Technology in Economy: Comparison between Japan and the United States,* prepared for RIETI/KEIO Conference on Japanese Economy: Leading East Asia in the 21st Century? Keio University, 30 May 2003.

Keynes, J.M. (1930), *A Treatise on Money*, Vol. 1, London: Macmillan.

Klein, L.R. (1968), *The Keynesian Revolution*, London: Macmillan.

Kormendi, R.C. and P.G. Meguire (1985), 'Macroeconomic determinants of growth: cross-country evidence', *Journal of Monetary Economics*, 16, 141–63.

Krugman, P. (1998), 'It's Baaack: Japan's slump and the return of the liquidity trap', *Brookings Papers on Economic Activity*, 2, 137–205.

Landau, D. (1986), 'Government and economic growth in the less-developed countries: An empirical study for 1960–80', *Economic Development and Cultural Change*, 35, 35–75.

Lange, O. (1942), 'The foundations of welfare economics', *Econometrica*, 10(3), 215–28.

Lerner, A.P. (1943), 'Functional finance and the federal debt', *Social Research*, 10(1), 38–52.

Levine, R. and D. Renelt (1992), 'A sensitivity analysis of cross-country growth regressions', *American Economic Review*, 82(4), 942–63.

Ludvigson, S. (1996), 'The macroeconomic effects of government debt in a stochastic growth model', *Journal of Monetary Economics*, 38, 25–45.

Munnell, A.H. (1990), 'Why has productivity declined? Productivity and public investment', *New England Economic Review*, January–February, 3–22.

OECD (2005): *OECD in Figures,* OECD Observer Supplement 1, Paris: OECD.

Pareto, V. [1906] (1971), *Manual of Political Economy*, 1971 translation of 1927 edition, New York: Augustus M. Kelley.

Ram, R. (1986), 'Government size and economic growth: A new framework and some evidence from cross-section and time-series data', *American Economic Review*, 76, 191–203.

Samuelson, P.A. (1947), *Foundations of Economic Analysis*, Cambridge, MA: Harvard University Press.

Sattar, Z. (1993), 'Public expenditure and economic performance: A comparison of developed and low-income developing economies, *Journal of International Development*, 5(1), 27–49.

Schabert, A. (2004), 'Interactions of monetary and fiscal policy via open market operations', *The Economic Journal*, 114, C186–C206.

Scully, G.W. (1989), 'Size of the state, economic growth, and the efficient utilization of national resources', *Public Choice*, 63, 149–64.

Smithers, A. (2001), *The Importance of Funding Policy for Japan's Recovery*, Smithers & Co., 29 September (commercial report).

Solow, R.M. (1957), 'Technical change and the aggregate production function', *Review of Economics and Statistics*, 39, 312–20.

Spencer, R.W. and W.P. Yohe (1970), 'The "crowding out" of private expenditures by fiscal policy actions', *Federal Reserve Bank of St. Louis Review*, 52, 12–24.

Spindt, P.A. (1985), 'Money is what money does: Monetary aggregation and the equation of exchange', *Journal of Political Economy*, 93, 175–204.

Tanaka, H. and Y. Kitano (2002), 'Obei shokoku ni okeru zaisei seisaku no makurokeizaiteki kōka', ('Macro-economic effects of fiscal policy in OECD countries', in Japanese), *Financial Review*, 63, Tokyo: Ministry of Finance.

Tatom, J.A. (1985), 'Two views of the effects of government budget deficits in the 1980s', *Federal Reserve Bank of St. Louis Review*, 67, 6–16.

Werner, R.A. (1992), *Towards a Quantity Theorem of Disaggregated Credit and International Capital Flows*, paper presented at the Royal Economic Society Annual Conference, York, April 1993, and at the 5th Annual PACAP Conference on Pacific–Asian Capital Markets in Kuala Lumpur, June 1993.

Werner, R.A. (1994), 'Japanese foreign investment and the "land bubble"', *Review of International Economics*, 2(2), 166–78.

Werner, R.A. (1997), 'Towards a new monetary paradigm: A quantity theorem of disaggregated credit, with evidence from Japan', *Kredit und Kapital*, 30(2), 276–309.

Werner, R.A. (1998), 'Minkan ginkō kara no kariire de, keikitaisaku wo okonaeba "issekinichō"', *Shukan Economist*, 8 December, Tokyo: Mainichi Shinbunsha.

Werner, R.A. (2000a), 'Indian macroeconomic management: At the crossroads between government and markets', in Rhee, S.G. (ed.), *Rising to the Challenge in Asia: A Study of Financial Markets, Vol. 5: India*, Manila: Asian Development Bank.

Werner, R.A. (2000b), 'Macroeconomic management in Thailand: The policy-induced crisis', in Rhee, S.G. (ed.), *Rising to the Challenge in Asia: A Study of Financial Markets, Vol. 11: Thailand*, Manila: Asian Development Bank.

Werner, R.A. (2000c), 'Japan's plan to borrow from banks deserves praise', *Financial Times*, 9 February.

Werner, R.A. (2002), 'How to get growth in Japan', *Central Banking*, 13(2), 48–54.

Werner, R.A. (2003), *Princes of the Yen: Japan's Central Bankers and the Transformation of the Economy*, Armonk, New York: M. E. Sharpe.

Werner, R.A. (2004), 'No recovery without reform? An empirical evaluation of the structural reform argument in Japan', *Asian Business and Management*, 3(1), 7–38.

Werner, R.A. (2005), *New Paradigm in Macroeconomics: Solving the Riddle of Japanese Macroeconomic Performance*, Basingstoke: Palgrave Macmillan.

Werner, R.A. (2007), *Neue Wirtschaftspolitik für Europa*, München: Vahlen.

Wolf, M. (2002), 'How to avert a ratings disaster', *Financial Times*, 27 March.

Wray, R. (2001), *The Endogenous Money Approach*, Working Paper, 17, August, Kansas City: Center for Full Employment and Price Stability.

11. Monetary policy, macroeconomic policy mix and economic performance in the Euro area*

Eckhard Hein and Achim Truger

11.1. INTRODUCTION

Since the growth slowdown in 2000–01, the Euro area has had a difficult time to recover and macroeconomic performance has been worse than in the USA. There the economy returned rather quickly to its late 1990s growth path. On average over the period 2001–2005, annual real GDP growth in the Euro area has remained more than 1 percentage point below US growth (Table 11.1). The growth differential between these two large currency areas already found since the mid-1990s (Hein and Niechoj 2006),

Table 11.1 Real GDP growth, growth contributions of demand aggregates, unemployment rate and inflation rate in the Euro area and in the USA, average values 2001–2005*

	Germany	France	Italy	Spain	Austria
Real GDP, annual growth rate, %	0.7	1.6	0.8	3.1	1.5
Growth contribution of domestic demand including stocks, %	−0.3	2.1	1.1	4.2	0.7
Growth contribution of private consumption, %	0.2	1.2	0.6	2.0	0.5
Growth contribution of public consumption, %	0.0	0.5	0.3	0.8	0.1
Growth contribution of gross fixed capital formation, %	−0.4	0.3	0.1	1.3	0.0
Growth contribution of balance of goods and services, %	1.0	−0.4	−0.4	−1.0	0.8
Employment, annual growth, %	−0.1	0.5	1.2	3.1	0.2
Unemployment rate, %	8.7	9.2	8.4	10.8	4.4
Inflation rate (HICP), %	1.6	2.0	2.4	3.2	1.9

Table 11.1   (continued)

	Belgium	Finland	Greece	Ireland
Real GDP, annual growth rate, %	1.5	2.2	4.2	5.1
Growth contribution of domestic demand including stocks, %	1.3	2.0	4.3	3.9
Growth contribution of private consumption, %	0.6	1.4	2.5	1.9
Growth contribution of public consumption, %	0.5	0.5	0.3	0.8
Growth contribution of gross fixed capital formation, %	0.3	0.2	1.6	1.1
Growth contribution of balance of goods and services, %	0.2	0.2	−0.1	1.3
Employment, annual growth, %	0.5	0.8	1.0	2.7
Unemployment rate, %	7.6	8.9	10.3	4.3
Inflation rate (HICP), %	2.0	1.4	3.5	3.5
	Netherlands	Portugal	Euro area	USA
Real GDP, annual growth rate, %	0.7	0.6	1.4	2.6
Growth contribution of domestic demand including stocks, %	0.4	0.3	1.3	3.0
Growth contribution of private consumption, %	0.2	0.8	0.8	2.2
Growth contribution of public consumption, %	0.5	0.4	0.3	0.5
Growth contribution of gross fixed capital formation, %	−0.1	−0.9	0.1	0.4
Growth contribution of balance of goods and services, %	0.3	0.3	0.1	−0.5
Employment, annual growth, %	0.0	0.4	0.8	0.7
Unemployment rate, %	3.7	5.9	8.5	5.4
Inflation rate (HICP), %	2.9	3.2	2.2	2.5

Note: *Forecast values for 2005.

Source: European Commission (2005), OECD (2005), authors' calculations.

which was the start of the convergence process towards the European Monetary Union (EMU), seems to have become persistent. Whereas the USA relies heavily on prosperous domestic demand and accepts a negative growth contribution from external balances, the Euro area as a whole displays a more balanced picture, albeit on a lower level: the lower growth relies on domestic demand with a positive but small growth contribution from foreign balances. Although employment has been growing at a similar rate as in the USA – due to lower productivity growth in the Euro area – the unemployment rate in the Euro area is still considerably above the US level. Between 2001 and 2005, inflation in the Euro area has on average slightly exceeded the inflation target of the European Central Bank (ECB) of 'below, but close to, 2 percent in the medium term' (ECB 2003, p. 79). But the deviation from the US inflation rate is quite small. Taken together, in the recent years the US economy has once more managed to combine reasonable growth, low unemployment and low inflation in a far better manner than the Euro area, as in the 1990s.

Slow growth and high unemployment are by no means equally distributed across the Euro area. Whereas during the period 2001–2005 in particular the large economies Germany and Italy, together with the Netherlands and Portugal, were suffering from real GDP growth rates well below the Euro area average, Spain, Finland, Greece and Ireland experienced growth considerably above this average. Spain, Ireland and Greece had even higher growth rates than the USA. France, Austria and Belgium grew with Euro area average rates. And the unemployment rates also display a wide dispersion across Euro area countries, with particularly low rates in Austria, Ireland, the Netherlands and Portugal and well above Euro area average rates in France, Spain and Greece. Unemployment in Austria, Ireland and the Netherlands was even below the US level. And finally we find that inflation rates also show major differences between Euro area countries, with rates well below the ECB's target in Germany and Finland, rates close to this target in France, Belgium and Austria, and inflation rates well above the ECB's target rate in Spain, Greece, Ireland, the Netherlands and Portugal.

In order to explain the long-run growth and employment differences between the Euro area and the USA, we have put forward a macroeconomic policy view focusing on the more restrictive stance of monetary, fiscal and wage policies in the Euro area compared to the macroeconomic policy regime in the USA.[1] In this chapter we will focus on the particular role of monetary policy. Interaction with wage policies and fiscal policies will be taken into account at the outset, but then the determinants of ECB policies will be assessed in detail.

As is well known, whereas monetary policy has been centralized within the Euro area and has now been run by the ECB since 1999, fiscal and wage policies have not been centralized. Regarding wage policies, the Maastricht regime and in particular the 'Employment Guidelines' and the 'Broad Economic Policy Guidelines' exert strong pressure towards further decentralization of wage bargaining and deregulation of the labor market, exacerbating the general tendencies in this field and making it increasingly difficult to coordinate wage policies across the Euro area with an eye to its macroeconomic effects.[2] Fiscal policy remains essentially a matter of national responsibility and is coordinated through the Treaty of Maastricht and the Amsterdam Stability and Growth Pact (SGP). As conditions of entry to the monetary union, the Maastricht Treaty has set a maximum deficit ratio (proportion of current budget deficit in relation to GDP) of 3 per cent and a maximum debt ratio (proportion of public debt in relation to GDP) of 60 per cent. The SGP makes this regulation even tougher by prescribing for the medium term, that is, a time span which stretches across economic cycles, balanced budgets or even budget surpluses in order to reduce the level of debt.[3] During the low growth, high unemployment period 2001–2005, more and more countries failed to comply with the regulations of the SGP. This led to at least some modifications in the application of the SGP in 2005. In our view, however, these do not go far enough to allow fiscal policies to stabilize economic development in the Euro area.[4]

The chapter is organized as follows. We address the macroeconomic policy mix in the Euro area in the period 2001–2005 in Section 2. In Section 3 we take a closer look at monetary policies since 1999. We try to identify the determinants of the ECB's monetary policy decisions by means of estimating 'naïve' and expanded Taylor rules. In Section 4 we apply and interpret our estimation results against the background of the course of ECB policies since 1999, and Section 5 draws some brief economic policy conclusions.

11.2.   THE STANCE OF MONETARY, FISCAL AND WAGE POLICIES 2001–2005

Monetary policy can be assessed by the development of the short-term real interest rate. It is now widely accepted that modern central banks use the short-term nominal interest rate as an economic policy instrument. But if central banks target inflation, they have to set nominal interest rates with an eye to the ensuing real rate, as proposed in the famous Taylor rule for example (Taylor 1993).[5] In this section we refrain from applying predetermined Taylor rules in order to assess the monetary policy stance,[6] because we doubt that the 'equilibrium real interest rate' underlying Taylor rules is independent of monetary policies. The same problem of endogeneity arises with respect to potential output, which is required to calculate the output gap as one of the determinants of monetary policy. In Section 3 we will estimate *ex-post* monetary policy rules for the ECB since 1999 and will address these problems in more detail.

In order to discuss the macroeconomic effects of monetary policy's real interest rate variations in a compact way, we consult the differences between

Table 11.2   Indicators for monetary, wage and fiscal policies in the Euro area and in the USA, average values, 2001–2005*

	Germany	France	Italy	Spain	Austria
Monetary Policy					
Short-term real interest rate, %	1.2	0.8	0.4	−0.4	0.9
Long-term real interest rate, %	2.6	2.3	2.0	1.1	2.5
Short-term real interest rate minus real GDP growth, percentage points	0.5	−0.8	−0.4	−3.5	−0.5
Long-term real interest rate minus real GDP growth, percentage points	1.9	0.7	1.3	−2.0	1.0
Wage Policy					
Nominal compensation per employee, annual growth, %	1.7	2.7	3.1	3.3	2.0
Nominal unit labor costs, annual growth, %	0.3	1.7	3.2	2.9	0.8
Labour income share[#], %	58.1	57.4	55.6	57.1	62.5
Change in labor income share from previous year, perentage points	−0.5	0.0	0.2	−0.5	−0.6
Fiscal Policy					
Cyclically adjusted budget balance (% of cyclically adjusted GDP), annual change	−0.1	−0.1	−0.3	0.3	0.4
Output gap, (% of cyclically adjusted GDP), annual change	−0.8	−0.5	−0.5	−0.1	−1.0
Number of years with pro-cyclical fiscal policy during an economic slowdown	3 (2003–2005)	1 (2005)	3 (2002–2004)	2 (2002–2003)	3 (2001–2002, 2004)
Negative fiscal stimulus in economic slowdown, cumulated (% of potential GDP)	1.1	0.5	0.8	0.9	3.0

the short-term real interest rate and real GDP growth and also the difference between the long-term real interest rate and real GDP growth. We expect a negative influence of real interest rates on economic growth working through different transmission channels (money, credit, asset prices, exchange rates) (Bernanke and Gertler 1995, Cecchetti 1995).

Whereas the Euro area short-term real interest rate was positive on average over the period after the 2000–01 growth slowdown, the Federal Reserve (Fed) managed to establish a negative short-term real interest rate of −0.2 per cent in the USA (Table 11.2). These expansionary monetary policies

Table 11.2   (continued)

	Belgium	Finland	Greece	Ireland
Monetary Policy				
Short-term real interest rate, %	0.8	1.4	−0.7	−0.6
Long-term real interest rate, %	2.3	2.9	1.0	0.9
Short-term real interest rate minus real GDP growth, percentage points	−0.7	−0.8	−4.9	−5.7
Long-term real interest rate minus real GDP growth, percentage points	0.8	0.7	−3.3	−4.3
Wage Policy				
Nominal compensation per employee, annual growth, %	2.8	3.2	6.5	5.7
Nominal unit labor costs, annual growth, %	1.8	1.8	3.3	3.3
Labour income share[#], %	61.7	55.6	58.0	47.8
Change in labor income share from previous year, percentage points	−0.2	0.5	−0.2	−0.2
Fiscal Policy				
Cyclically adjusted budget balance (% of cyclically adjusted GDP), annual change	0.3	−0.8	−0.2	−0.8
Output gap, (% of cyclically adjusted GDP), annual change	−0.5	−0.5	0.4	−0.8
Number of years with pro-cyclical fiscal policy during an economic slowdown	4 (2001–2003, 2005)	1 (2005)	1 (2005)	2 (2003–2004)
Negative fiscal stimulus in economic slowdown, cumulated (% of potential GDP)	1.9	0.5	2.2	2.8

contributed to the quick recovery of the US economy. In 2002 the USA had already seen again – as in the years before 2001 – a negative difference between the short-term real interest rate and the real GDP growth rate, whereas in the Euro area this difference only became negative in 2003 (Figure 11.1). On average over the period 2001–2005, the Fed established a favorable difference between the short-term real interest rate and the real GDP growth (−2.7 percentage points), and also a growth-friendly long-term real interest rate and real GDP growth constellation (−0.7 percentage points). The ECB was much more reluctant to stimulate the economy by means of cutting interest rates in the face of the 2000–01 slowdown and thereby contributed to weak growth in the Euro area. Whereas on average over the period

Table 11.2   (continued)

	Netherlands	Portugal	Euro area	USA
Monetary Policy				
Short-term real interest rate, %	0.0	−0.4	0.6	−0.2
Long-term real interest rate, %	1.4	1.2	2.1	1.9
Short-term real interest rate minus real GDP growth, percentage points	−0.8	−1.0	−0.8	−2.7
Long-term real interest rate minus real GDP growth, percentage points	0.7	0.6	0.7	−0.7
Wage Policy				
Nominal compensation per employee, annual growth, %	3.9	2.3	2.5	4.0
Nominal unit labor costs, annual growth, %	2.7	2.1	1.7	1.7
Labour income share[#], %	59.2	63.0	58.0	62.6
Change in labor income share from previous year, percentage points	0.0	−0.6	−0.2	−0.4
Fiscal Policy				
Cyclically adjusted budget balance (% of cyclically adjusted GDP), annual change	0.1	0.1	−0.1	−0.9
Output gap, (% of cyclically adjusted GDP), annual change	−1.4	−1.4	−0.6	−0.3
Number of years with pro-cyclical fiscal policy during an economic slowdown	2 (2003, 2005)	3 (2002– 2004)	3 (2003– 2005)	0
Negative fiscal stimulus in economic slowdown, cumulated (% of potential GDP)	1.2	3.8	0.5	–

Notes: *Forecast values for 2005, #compensation per employee divided by GDP at current market prices per person employed.

Sources: European Commission (2005), OECD (2005), authors' calculations.

2001–2005 in the Euro area as a whole the difference between the short-term real interest rate and the real GDP growth was at least slightly negative (−0.8 percentage point), the difference between the long-term real interest rate and the real GDP growth remained positive (0.7 percentage points).

The ECB policy was particularly harmful for the largest member country, Germany (Table 11.2). As the German inflation rate has been lower than the EMU average and the nominal interest rates have almost

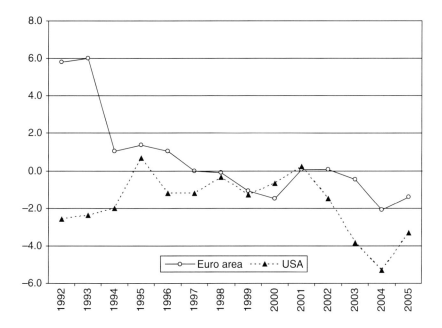

Sources: European Commission (2005), OECD (2005), author's calculations.

Figure 11.1   *Short-term real interest rate minus real GDP growth in the Euro area and the USA, 1992–2005, percentage points*

completely converged since 1999, Germany's real interest rates have been even higher than the Euro area average since then. This has contributed to an unfavorable difference between the short-term real interest rate and the real GDP growth, which among the Euro area countries remained on average positive only in Germany over the period 2001–2005. On the other hand, the high inflation countries Spain, Greece, Ireland, and to a lesser extent even Portugal, had negative short-term real interest rates and a very growth-conducive constellation with negative differences between the short-term real interest rate and real GDP growth and also negative differences between the long-term real interest rate and real GDP growth (except Portugal).

Therefore, the ECB's 'anti-growth-bias', that is, a too restrictive definition of price stability for the heterogeneous currency area and an asymmetric response to the expected deviation of actual from target inflation,[7] contributed to the weak growth and employment performance of the Euro area as a whole and to the economic problems of the largest Euro area member, Germany, in particular. However, it has to be conceded that the ECB cannot react in relation to the inflation differences between Euro area member countries. This is where wage policies become relevant.

Wage policies can be assessed by nominal wage growth (compensation per employee), unit labor cost growth and the labor income share. Nominal wage setting affects unit labor cost growth and inflation. If nominal wages increase at a faster pace than productivity plus the price level, unit labor cost growth and inflation will speed up. This will cause real interest rates to fall and may make monetary policies intervene in order to stabilize inflation at some target rate. If nominal wages increase at a rate below the sum of productivity growth and inflation, unit labor cost growth will slow down and cause disinflation. Finally, deflation may be the result. Deflation causes increasing real interest rates and rising real debts with potentially negative effects on investment and growth.[8] If deflationary processes have started, monetary policies lowering nominal interest rates will be ineffective.

Wage policies, however, may not only affect prices, but also change distribution if firms do not completely pass unit labor cost variations on to prices or if prices of other inputs do not change in step with unit labor costs (Hein *et al.* 2006). Under these conditions, nominal wage moderation causes the labor income share to fall. Hypothetically, the effects of income shares on GDP growth are ambiguous (Bhaduri and Marglin 1990). With the propensity to save out of wages falling short of the savings propensity out of profits, a falling labor income share means a cutback in consumption demand and capacity utilization with directly contractive effects on investment and GDP growth. On the other hand, a fall in labor income shares that is associated with nominal wage restraint will improve international competitiveness and therefore, stimulate demand for exports, investment and growth. With a slowdown in inflation, the central bank may also cut interest rates and stimulate investment and growth. Finally, a falling labor income share is associated with rising unit profits, which may also improve investment and growth.

Since the stimulating effects of wage moderation and declining labor income shares for investment and growth are rather indirect and uncertain, in particular in large and quite closed economies such as the Euro area and the USA, the direct and contractive effects will presumably dominate. And since nominal wage increases, which will shift distribution in favor of labor income, will also trigger inflation and concomitant restrictive central bank interventions, nominal wage growth according to the sum of long-run productivity growth and the central bank's inflation target, and hence roughly constant labor income shares, should be generally favorable conditions for growth and employment in large and quite closed currency areas.

On average over the period 2001–2005, nominal wage growth in the Euro area was lagging behind the USA (Table 11.2). But taking into account pro-

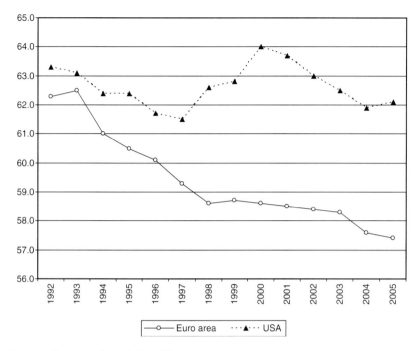

Source: European Commission (2005).

Figure 11.2 Labour income share in the Euro area and the USA, 1992–2005, percent of GDP at market prices

ductivity growth, nominal wage increases in both currency areas were stability oriented: nominal unit labor costs grew by 1.7 per cent and have hence not caused any inflationary pressures. Moderate wage increases were accompanied by a decline in the labor income share, both in the Euro area and in the USA. Whereas in the USA this decline compensated for the increase in the previous years, generating a stationary trend since the early 1990s, in the Euro area the recent decline has continued the decreasing trend since the early 1990s (Figure 11.2). Although labor income shares were similar in the early 1990s, the Euro area value has plunged 4 percentage points below the US value so far and has contributed to domestic demand problems.

Below the surface of Euro area aggregate values we see a wide dispersion of wage and nominal unit labor cost developments (Table 11.2). In Italy, Spain, Greece, Ireland and the Netherlands, nominal unit labor costs grew at rates around 3 per cent, which interfered with the ECB's inflation target. Nominal unit labor costs in Germany, however, and to a lesser

Table 11.3   Current account balances as a percentage of GDP, 2001–2005

	2001	2002	2003	2004	2005
Germany	0.2	2.3	2.2	3.8	4.1
France	1.6	0.9	0.4	−0.4	−1.6
Italy	−0.1	−0.8	−1.3	−0.9	−1.5
Spain	−3.9	−3.3	−3.6	−5.3	−7.7
Austria	−1.9	0.3	−0.5	0.3	−0.4
Belgium	3.4	4.6	4.1	3.3	1.4
Finland	7.2	7.6	3.8	5.3	3.5
Greece	−8.1	−7.5	−7.2	−6.3	−7.0
Ireland	−0.6	−1.0	0.0	−0.8	−1.5
Netherlands	2.4	2.9	2.8	3.3	5.8
Portugal	−8.4	−8.0	−0.9	−3.6	−6.7
Euro area	0.1	0.7	0.3	0.5	−0.2
UK	−2.2	−1.6	−1.5	−2.0	−1.8
Sweden	4.4	5.3	7.5	8.2	7.1
Japan	2.1	2.8	3.2	3.7	3.4
USA	−3.8	−4.5	−4.7	−5.7	−6.5

Source: OECD (2005).

extent in Austria, increased at especially low rates, causing deflationary risks, which were accompanied by a rapid decline in labor income shares, contributing to domestic demand problems. In particular, the German wage development was completely inappropriate for the largest economy in a currency union:[9] overly moderate wage policies improved the price competitiveness and profitability of German firms and made German export surpluses almost quadruple between 2001 and 2005. And since around 44 per cent of German exports go to the Euro area, increasing German export surpluses have caused major problems for the other Euro area countries. Whereas Germany continually increased its current account surplus, amounting to 4.1 per cent of GDP in 2005, the other larger Euro area countries (France, Italy, Spain) were driven into current account deficits (Table 11.3). Some of the smaller countries also either saw their surpluses shrink (Belgium, Finland) or they were not been able to decrease their huge deficits (Greece, Portugal). This constellation will inevitably push the other Euro area countries to introduce deflationary wage policies as well, and hence the risk of deflation will spread across the Euro area.

We assess the extent to which fiscal policy exerts a stabilizing or destabilizing influence on the business cycle by comparing changes in the output gap and the cyclically adjusted budget balance-potential GDP ratio (CBR) (Table 11.2).[10] The output gap serves as an indicator of the current state of economic activity. If it is positive, capacity is outstripped; if it is negative, capacity is not fully utilized. Consequently, a positive change in the output gap indicates a cyclical upturn, whereas a negative change points to a cyclical downturn. If there is a positive (negative) change in the CBR, then structural deficits fall (rise) or structural surpluses rise (fall), and fiscal policy exerts a restrictive (expansive) stimulus on demand. If the CBR remains constant when there is a change in the output gap, fiscal policy is neither expansive nor restrictive and the automatic stabilizers are simply left to take effect.

Measured this way, in the face of an average annual fall in the output gap of 0.6 per cent of GDP, Euro area fiscal policy was only slightly expansive with an average annual increase in the cyclically adjusted budget deficit of 0.1 per cent of GDP from 2001 to 2005. Furthermore, almost all of the expansive, counter-cyclical reaction occurred in 2001, when the fall in the output gap was small. In 2002 the expansion was hardly measurable and since 2003, fiscal policy has even been slightly pro-cyclically restrictive. The cumulated negative fiscal stimulus over the last three years amounted to 0.5 per cent of GDP. In striking contrast to the European experience, US fiscal policy from 2001 to 2005 was very expansive, with an average annual increase of the cyclically adjusted budget deficit of 0.9 per cent of GDP. There was not a single year with pro-cyclical fiscal restriction during the economic downturn. Since 2005, the second year with an improving output gap, US fiscal policy has returned smoothly to careful restriction.

For the individual Euro area countries, the picture is quite diverse (Table 11.2). The high-growth countries Finland and Ireland both reacted in a strongly counter-cyclical way to the slowdown. Italy, France and Germany saw a slightly expansive fiscal policy over the whole period. However, in these countries the expansion almost exclusively occurred in the first years of the slowdown. After the countries faced excessive deficit problems, they all had to switch to pro-cyclical restriction despite the ongoing crisis. In the five remaining countries, Spain, Austria, Belgium, the Netherlands and Portugal, fiscal policy was pro-cyclically restrictive over the whole period from 2001 to 2005. With the exception of Spain, both the drop in the output gap as well as the negative pro-cyclical fiscal stimulus were substantial in the countries concerned.

Thus, the SGP led to destabilizing, pro-cyclical fiscal policy reactions to the post-2000 crisis in several countries. Almost all countries with excessive deficit problems stopped their initially expansive fiscal policy and were driven into pro-cyclical, restrictive measures as soon as their deficit had reached the 3 per cent of GDP level. Without doubt, the resulting negative fiscal stance has contributed to the ongoing stagnation tendencies after 2000 within these countries and in the Euro area as a whole. Moreover, the growth divergences between the countries seem to have been reinforced.

Summing up so far, the Euro area suffered from a too restrictive monetary policy which especially hurt the slowly growing low inflation countries, in particular Germany. Wage development was stability oriented on average over the whole currency union and would have allowed for a more growth-oriented ECB policy. But there have developed serious imbalances below the surface with wage developments in Germany putting increasing deflationary pressure on the Euro area. The SGP prevented fiscal policy in many countries from reacting in a counter-cyclical way and aggravated the crisis even further. This macroeconomic policy constellation contributed to slow growth and high unemployment, in particular in Germany and some other countries mentioned above. The major obstacle for improved growth and higher employment seems to have been the ECB. That is the reason why we analyze ECB policies in more detail in the following section.

11.3. WHY HAS THE ECB BEEN SO UNFRIENDLY TO GROWTH?

In what follows we try to assess the determinants of ECB policies since 1999 in order to get a deeper understanding of the reasons that drive the ECB to act – or not to act. We use quarterly data from the ECB (2006), except for the output gap, which is taken from the OECD (2005), and the Federal funds rate, which is from the Federal Reserve Bank of New York (2006).[11] The data cover the period between the first quarter of 1999 and the fourth quarter of 2005, if available. This means that we have only 28 observations at the maximum for each time series, which prevents the application of time series econometrics. Instead, we have to rely on simple OLS regressions, which is why the results below should be interpreted with great care.[12]

11.3.1. 'Naïve' Taylor Rule

In the first step we estimate a 'naïve' Taylor rule for the ECB since 1999, in which the ECB key interest rate (i^{ECB}) is determined by the output gap and the inflation gap, calculated as the difference between the increase in the HICP and the ECB inflation target, which is assumed to be 1.9 per cent ('below, but close to, 2 percent', ECB 2003, p. 79). According to Taylor (1993), the Fed's interest rate (i) policy between 1987 and 1993 was determined by the 'equilibrium real interest rate' (i^r), current inflation ($\hat{p}$), the deviation of actual output (Y) from potential output (Y^p), that is, the output gap, and by the deviation of actual inflation ($\hat{p}$) from target inflation ($\hat{p}^T$), that is, the inflation gap:

$$i_t = i_t^r + \hat{p}_t + \alpha_1(Y_t - Y^p) + \alpha_2(\hat{p}_t - \hat{p}^T) \qquad (11.1)$$

Taylor (1993) assumed that the equilibrium real interest rate and the inflation target were 2 per cent each, and the values of α_1 and α_2 were 0.5 each, that is, the Fed placed equal weight on the output gap and the inflation gap. Here, the output gap is the deviation of actual output from trend output, which increased by 2.2 per cent per year. Taylor then showed that the Federal funds rate indeed followed the rate of interest calculated according to equation (11.1). Reviewing the rich amount of literature on monetary policy rules which emerged during the 1990s, Taylor (1999) confirmed the robustness of simple rules like the one he had proposed originally and also recommended such a rule for the ECB.[13]

Our estimation results of a 'naïve' Taylor rule for the ECB are shown in Table 11.4. We find that the current output gap (OG) has affected the ECB's policies in the expected way, whereas the current inflation gap ($INFG$) has not (Table 11.4, estimation (1)). However, it is by now well known that central banks respond to expected inflation and output gaps (Clarida *et al.* 1998, 2000). If we assume that the ECB policies are 'forward looking' and that they respond to rationally expected future inflation and future output gaps one quarter ahead, also the inflation gap has a positive impact on the ECB key interest rate, albeit statistically less significant than the output gap (Table 11.4, estimation (2)):

$$i_{t-1}^{ECB} = f(OG_t, INFG_t) \qquad (11.2)$$

From the estimated constants we can also calculate the underlying 'equilibrium real interest rate', which is slightly below 1 per cent given that actual inflation has been slightly above 2 per cent on average since 1999. This value is considerably below what is usually assumed to be the 'equilibrium real interest rate' in Taylor rules, but similar to what Arestis and Chortareas (2006), applying Taylor rules to the ECB since 1999, have assumed to be the 'equilibrium real interest rate' perceived by the ECB.

Our estimations, however, suffer from the omitted variable problem, which is indicated by the Durbin–Watson statistics in Table 11.4. Therefore, we follow the common strategy in the literature and add interest rate smoothing to the estimated equations. We assume that the ECB does not respond violently to deviations of inflation and output from target values,

Table 11.4   The ECB's Taylor rule

	(1)	(2)	(3)
ECB key interest rate	i_t^{ECB}	i_{t-1}^{ECB}	i_{t-1}^{ECB}
C	2.90***	2.84***	1.27*
t-statistics	35.30	21.32	6.44
OG_t	0.75***	0.69***	0.39***
t-statistics	11.52	7.53	6.93
$INFG_t$	0.20	0.51*	0.44***
t-statistics	1.04	1.74	3.57
i_{t-2}^{ECB}			0.52***
t-statistics			8.02
Adj. R-squared	0.90	0.81	0.96
Durbin-Watson	0.71	0.88	1.77
N	28	27	26

Notes:
i^{ECB}: ECB key interest rate at the end of quarter, per cent; C: constant; OG: output gap, percentage points; *INFG*: inflation gap, HICP growth minus 1.9 % as ECB inflation target, percentage points.
Significance: *** 1%, ** 5% level, * 10% level, Newey-West heteroskedasticity consistent coefficient covariance.
Software: EViews 5.1.

Data sources: ECB (2006), OECD (2005) (ecowin), authors' calculations.

but that it acts in a gradual way in order to smooth out real as well as expectation effects:

$$i_{t-1}^{ECB} = \mathrm{f}(OG_t, INFG_t, i_{t-2}^{ECB}) \qquad (11.3)$$

As estimation (3) in Table 11.4 shows, interest rate smoothing improves our results remarkably. The present ECB key interest rate is significantly affected by the rate of the previous quarter. The output gap and the inflation gap are highly significant and have a similar quantitative impact on ECB policies.

11.3.2.   Expanded Taylor Rule

Interest rate smoothing is only one statistical alternative to improve regression results in the face of the omitted variable problem. A theoretically more interesting alternative is to introduce further variables into the equation which might explain monetary policy action, in particular those variables which are under the control of the other macroeconomic policy actors. We add unit labor cost growth (*ULC*) as an indicator for the effects of wage bargaining, cyclically adjusted fiscal balances as percentage of potential GDP (*CBR*) as an indicator for the fiscal policy stance, the US-dollar-euro-exchange rate (*ER*) and the Federal funds rate (i^{FED}) in order to cover the effects of financial markets and US monetary policies. With the exception of the Federal funds rate, these variables can be found in what the ECB (2003, pp. 87–89) in the 'two-pillar approach' calls 'economic analysis', which is relevant for the ECB's assessment of the short- to medium-term risks for price stability.

We refrain from introducing monetary aggregates into our estimations because we consider the quantity of money to be an endogenous variable with respect to economic activity, following the Post-Keynesian endogenous money view, which has also been accepted by now in the New Consensus model.[14] The growth rate of a monetary aggregate will be highly collinear with the development of real GDP growth and hence the output gap. In the reformulated monetary policy strategy, the ECB (2003, pp. 89–92) has also downgraded the relevance of 'monetary analysis'. Having formerly been the first pillar, it is now only the second pillar within the ECB's 'two pillar approach', serving as a means of 'cross checking'. A long-term relationship between monetary aggregates and inflation is still assumed, but the ECB has no monetary target, and also the reference value for M3 is no longer reviewed on an annual basis. The ECB (2003, p. 91) stresses that there is no direct link between the development of M3 and monetary policy decisions. The relation between M3 and the interest rate decisions is hence rather vague, from the ECB's point of view, although the ECB still believes that inflation is a monetary phenomenon in the long run (see also Issing 2005).[15]

We apply a general to specific method and add all the additional variables to the equation. Then we drop those variables which are not significant at the 10 per cent level and re-estimate the equation. We start with the following equation:[16]

$$i_{t-1}^{ECB} = f(OG_t, INFG_t, ULC_t, CBR_t, ER_t, i_t^{FED}) \qquad (11.4)$$

As can be seen from estimation (4) in Table 11.5, rationally expected unit labor cost growth as a major determinant of inflation and the Federal funds rate have also affected ECB policies in the expected positive way. The significance of the Federal funds rate improves, if we assume that the ECB does not react in a forward looking manner with respect to this variable, but rather responds to actual Fed policies (estimation (5)).[17] But neither the

Table 11.5   *Determinants of the ECB's key interest rate: the Taylor rule expanded*

ECB key interest rate	(4) i_{t-1}^{ECB}	(5) i_{t-1}^{ECB}	(6) i_{t-1}^{ECB}	(7) i_{t-1}^{ECB}	(8) i_{t-1}^{ECB}
C	2.09	1.50***	0.02	−1.85**	−4.38***
t-statistics	1.10	4.94	0.04	−2.13	−3.87
OG_t	0.48**	0.40***		0.31**	
t-statistics	2.32	4.74		2.80	
GDP_t			0.29*		0.10
t-statistics			1.77		0.70
$INFG_t$	0.43***	0.53***	0.80***	0.67***	0.88***
t-statistics	3.03	4.90	8.61	3.36	4.67
ULC_t	0.46**	0.51***	0.92***		
t-statistics	2.50	5.00	5.61		
NW_t				1.71***	2.54***
t-statistics				5.78	5.74
i_t^{FED}	0.13**				
t-statistics	2.43				
i_{t-1}^{FED}		0.19***	0.28***	0.21***	0.33***
t-statistics		3.72	3.84	3.71	4.60
CBR	−0.05				
t-statistics	−0.63				
ER	−0.39				
t-statistics	−0.24				
Adj. R-squared	0.88	0.91	0.86	0.90	0.87
DW	1.59	1.62	1.83	1.72	1.69
N	26	26	26	27	27

Notes:
i^{ECB}: ECB key interest rate at the end of quarter, per cent; C: constant; OG: output gap, percentage points; GDP: real GDP growth rate, %; $INFG$: inflation gap, HICP growth minus 1.9% as ECB inflation target, percentage points; ULC: nominal unit labor cost, annual increase in %; NW: negotiated wages, index, annual increase in %; i^{FED}: Federal funds rate at the end of quarter, %; CBR: cyclically adjusted government financial balances in % of potential GDP; ER: exchange rate, US-$/€.
Significance: *** 1%, ** 5%, * 10% level, Newey-West heteroskedasticity consistent coefficient covariance.
Software: EViews 5.1.

Data sources: ECB (2006), OECD (2005) (ecowin), authors' calculations.

rationally-expected structural fiscal balances nor the US-dollar-euro-exchange rate have had a significant impact on ECB policies.[18] The ECB does not seem to have responded to fiscal policies in the Euro area. And although the ECB has been affected by the Fed policy, we have no direct impact of the US-dollar-euro-exchange rate on ECB policies.

$$i_{t-1}^{ECB} = f(OG_t, INFG_t, ULC_t, i_{t-1}^{FED}) \qquad (11.5)$$

Taken together, from our 'best fit' estimation (5) in Table 11.5, we conclude that the ECB's interest rate policy is mainly determined by the rationally-expected values of the output gap, the inflation gap and unit labor cost growth with similar weight, and that there is also a smaller impact of the current Federal funds rate. Note that in the specifications shown in Table 11.5 the constant can no longer be interpreted as the 'equilibrium rate of interest'.

11.3.3. Some Problems with (Expanded) Taylor Rules

Finally, we modify our 'best fit' estimation (5) in order to address some problems related to Taylor rules. The first problem is the endogeneity problem with respect to the output gap as an indicator for real economic activity. Potential output is determined by capital stock and productivity, and past investment affects present capital stock and present productivity. The latter requires that technical progress is embodied in capital stock. Therefore, past investment determines present potential output.[19] If overly restrictive monetary policies have driven down investment in the past, this will reduce current potential output and, with present output given, the output gap. Current monetary policy may therefore seem to be more responsive to output than would have been the case if past monetary policies had been more expansive. The estimated coefficient for the output gap may therefore depend on past monetary policies in an inverse way: expansive monetary policies in the past increasing present potential output and the output gap make present monetary policies look less responsive to output, and vice versa. Instead of the output gap we therefore insert real GDP growth into the equation to be estimated, because real GDP growth (or the deviation of real GDP growth from an exogenous real GDP growth trend) does not suffer from the above endogeneity problem:

$$i_{t-1}^{ECB} = f(GDP_t, INFG_t, ULC_t, i_{t-1}^{FED}) \qquad (11.6)$$

The results of estimation (6) in Table 11.5 show that real GDP growth as a determinant of the ECB key interest rate is statistically less significant than the output gap in the previous estimations. Therefore, using the output gap as a 'real economy' determinant of ECB policies may be misleading.

Unit labour cost growth as an indicator for inflationary pressure of wage setting may also suffer from a similar endogeneity problem as the output gap. Unit labour cost growth is affected by labour productivity growth, and with technical progress embodied in capital stock, productivity is affected by investment in capital stock. Therefore, restrictive monetary policies in the past, depressing investment, may cause current unit labour costs to rise without any change in the tendency of labour unions' wage setting. Therefore, we replace unit labour cost growth as a determinant of ECB policies by the annual increase in negotiated wages (NW) as a direct outcome of wage bargaining.[20]

$$i_{t-1}^{ECB} = f(OG_t, INFG_t, NW_t, i_{t-1}^{FED}) \qquad (11.7)$$

As can be seen from estimation (7) in Table 11.5, the increase in negotiated wages is a highly significant determinant of the ECB key interest rate. The ECB seems to put high emphasis on wage bargaining when setting the key interest rate. The inflation gap still has a major impact, and the output gap again has the expected effect, but is statistically less significant. The influence of the Fed's interest rate policy remains significant as well.

$$i_{t-1}^{ECB} = f(GDP_t, INFG_t, NW_t, i_{t-1}^{FED}) \qquad (11.8)$$

Replacing the output gap in estimation (7) by real GDP growth in order to circumvent the endogeneity problem with respect to this variable renders the real variable in the reaction function statistically insignificant (Table 11.5, estimation (8)). This underlines our previous result that the output gap may be a misleading indicator for the responsiveness of monetary policy to real economic activity.

11.4. ESTIMATION RESULTS AND THE COURSE OF ECB POLICIES SINCE 1999

Our estimation results can now be applied to the course of ECB policies since 1999. According to our estimations the ECB has placed a heavy weight on expected inflation (HICP growth) and on the inflation gap. The ECB raised interest rates when inflation exceeded its target of below, but close to, 2 per cent. Since HICP growth has exceeded the ECB's target for considerable periods of time since 1999 (Figure 11.3), this has given monetary policies a restrictive stance which has mainly contributed to the

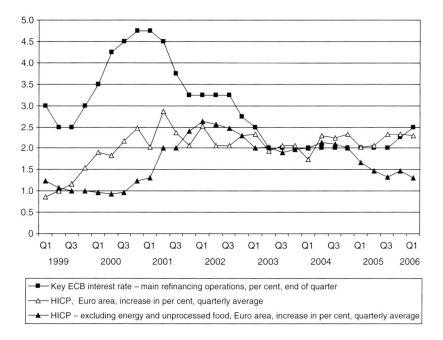

Source: ECB (2006), authors' calculation.

Figure 11.3   ECB key interest rate and inflation in the Euro area

2000–2001 growth slowdown and the slow recovery since then. Note, however, that core inflation (HICP excluding energy and unprocessed food) has been well below 2 per cent since the first quarter of 2005 and that the ECB started to increase interest rates in the third quarter of 2005 despite core inflation remaining low.

We have found that the ECB has also put high emphasis on unit labor cost growth and on the development of negotiated wages. In particular, unit labor cost growth has indeed been a problem for the inflation target in 2001–2002 and in 2003 (Figure 11.4). The main reason for this, however, has been the drop in productivity growth during the economic downswing since late 2000 and the weak recovery since then, both caused by ECB policies (Figure 11.5). Since early 2004 neither negotiated wages nor unit labor cost growth rates have been a challenge for the ECB inflation target.

According to our results, the ECB has also responded to the expected output gap. If we take into account the endogenous nature of potential output and hence the output gap, and consider the impact of actual real economic activity on ECB policies, we have found that real GDP growth

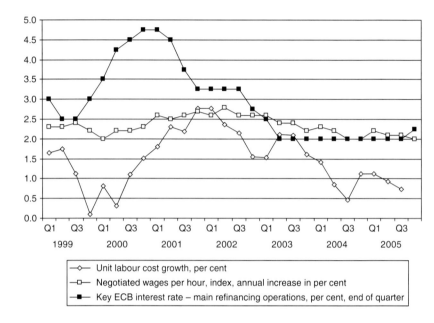

Source: ECB (2006), authors' calculation.

Figure 11.4   *ECB key interest rate, unit labor costs and negotiated hourly*
wages in the Euro area

has been of low significance or even insignificant. Indeed, the ECB has responded very slowly and very little to the recession in 2000–2001 and has also not taken action in the face of the recent slow growth and even persistent underutilization of productive capacity since early 2003 (Figure 11.6). On the contrary, in late 2005 the ECB started to raise interest rates in the face of imperiled growth and a persistent negative output gap, which is only slowly improving.

Finally, we have found that the ECB has been influenced by the Fed's interest rate policy. The ECB followed the Fed raising interest rates in 1999–2000 (Figure 11.7). When the Fed cut rates in 2000–2001, the ECB was initially reluctant to follow but finally also reduced the ECB key rate, albeit to a much lesser extent. Currently, the ECB seems to be following the Fed again, which had already started to raise interest rates in 2004. From our analysis, however, it is not clear why the ECB has been affected by the Fed's monetary policy. Some authors have speculated that the ECB has used its interest rate tool in order to defend the euro-dollar exchange rate (Bibow 2002, Heine and Herr 2004, pp. 188–196). However, we have not

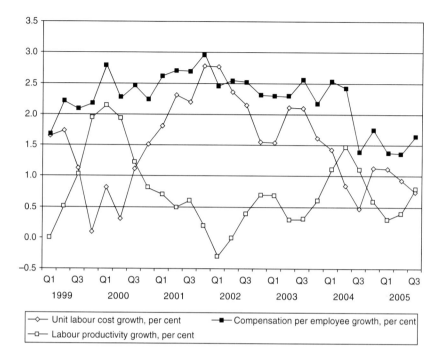

Source: ECB (2006).

*Figure 11.5   Unit labor costs, compensation per employee and labor
productivity in the Euro area, annual growth rate*

found any direct impact of the exchange rate on ECB policies. Other
authors have envisaged that in an environment of global uncertainty the
ECB follows the Fed, because the Fed is more effective in dealing with
macroeconomic shocks (Belke and Gros 2003). In a sense, the ECB tries to
take advantage of the 'option value of waiting', it is argued. This, however,
is not easy to reconcile with the results of a meta-analysis of empirical
studies on monetary policies by De Grauwe and Costa Storti (2004), who
find that the long-run output effects of monetary policies have been larger
in the Euro area than in the USA. But here is not the place to pursue this
problem any further.

Considering the ECB policies against the background of our estimation
results, neither the development of the output gap, nor the development of
unit labor costs or negotiated wages can explain the most recent interest
rate hikes. In the most recent past, it seems that the ECB has been driven
particularly by the failure to achieve its overly ambitious inflation target
and by the Fed's interest rate policy.

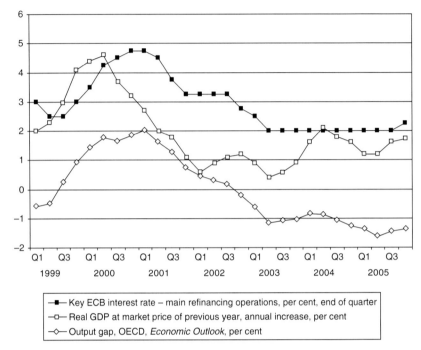

Source: ECB (2006), OECD (2005).

Figure 11.6   ECB key interest rate, real GDP growth and output gap in the Euro area

11.5.   CONCLUSIONS

Our analysis has confirmed that it is the policy of the ECB in attaching too much importance to low inflation which is a major problem for growth and employment in the Euro area. This has two aspects. First, the ECB's inflation target is too ambitious for a heterogeneous monetary union with divergent unit labor cost growth and hence persistent inflation differentials. Second, the ECB is too exclusively occupied with inflation and wage developments and puts too low an emphasis on the development of real variables. Since further progress with the coordination of wage bargaining in the Euro area along the formula 'national long-run productivity growth plus ECB inflation target' cannot be expected for the near future, it will be impossible to reduce average unit labor cost growth and inflation further in line with the ECB's target without increasing deflation risks in major parts of the Euro area. In order to improve growth and employment the ECB should therefore raise its inflation target. And the ECB should also place

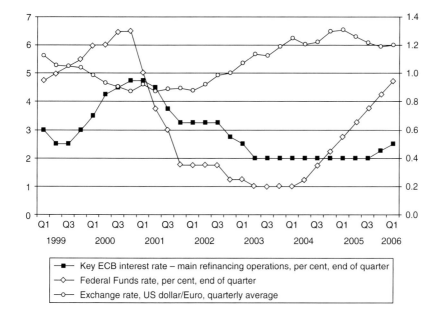

Sources: ECB (2006), Federal Reserve Bank of New York (2006), authors' calculation.

Figure 11.7 *ECB key interest rate, Federal Funds rate and Euro exchange rate*

higher emphasis on the development of real variables, thereby taking into account that the development of the output gap might be misleading as an indicator. Given the experience gained during the last seven years, however, this might require major institutional reforms in the Euro area macroeconomic policy framework determined by the European Treaty, in particular a change in the ECB's hierarchical mandate and the ECB's independence in defining what price stability means.

NOTES

* We are grateful to Sabine Stephan for helpful comments on the econometrics. Remaining errors are, of course, ours.

1. See Hein and Truger (2005a, 2005b) on the Maastricht regime, Hein and Truger (2005c, 2005d) on the special situation of the German economy, and Hein and Truger (2006a), and Hein *et al.* (2006) on the risks of deflation in Germany and Europe associated with this constellation. Also Fritsche *et al.* (2005), Palley (1998) and Solow (2000) have argued that a favorable coordination between monetary and fiscal policies rather than deregulated labor markets can be held responsible for the superior development of the US economy during the 1990s compared to Germany or the EU.

2. See Hein and Niechoj (2006) on the Broad Economic Policy Guidelines and Hein and Schulten (2004) on wage bargaining and wage developments in the European Union.
3. See Allsopp and Vines (1998), Eichengreen (1998) and Arestis *et al.* (2001), for a critical assessment of the SGP.
4. See Hein and Truger (2006b) for a detailed analysis of fiscal policies in the EMU.
5. This is the way monetary policy is introduced in the now prevalent New Consensus models. See Goodfried and King (1997), Clarida *et al.* (1999), Romer (2000), Taylor (2000), and Carlin and Soskice (2006).
6. See Arestis and Chortareas (2006) for such an exercise and a discussion of some of the related problems.
7. The ECB has tended to tighten whenever inflation increased above the target without relaxing when inflation expectations came down. For a general critique of the ECB's 'anti-growth bias' see Bibow (2002, 2005a, 2005b) and Hein (2002).
8. See Arestis and Sawyer (2005) and Sawyer (2002) for recent post-Keynesian models of distribution conflict and inflation, and Hein (2006a, 2006b) for the integration of real debt effects into Kaleckian models of distribution and growth with conflict inflation.
9. See Hein and Truger (2006a) for a more extensive discussion.
10. See Hein and Truger (2006b) for a more extensive discussion. It should be noted that the cyclically adjusted measures can be criticized for a number of theoretical and empirical reasons (implicit acceptance of some medium-term stable equilibrium, endogeneity of potential output and budget balances, sensitivity to different methods) so that they should be interpreted with great care.
11. We are well aware of Orphanides's (2001, 2003) convincing suggestion of using 'real time data' in order to assess monetary policies. However, since the ECB always stresses the medium-term orientation of its policies and since our data only cover 28 quarters, we feel that our procedure is appropriate. It goes without saying that we will not interpret our results in an exactly quantitative way but rather qualitatively.
12. The variables we use are either growth rates or shares which should not have a unit root from an economic theory point of view. However, the Augmented Dickey Fuller (ADF) test does not confirm this presumption for each time series under consideration. However, since the ADF test is known to have only low power when applied to small samples, this is another reason for interpreting our results carefully.
13. For estimation results of monetary policy rules for the Federal Reserve and other central banks see for example Clarida *et al.* (1998, 2000). These rules are of the 'forward looking' type. For a detailed analysis of the monetary policy of the Federal Reserve see Weller (2002) and Thorbecke (2002). For the Bank of England see Mihailov (2006).
14. On Post-Keynesian monetary theory see Lavoie (1984, 1992, pp. 149–216), Moore (1988) and Fontana (2003). On the New Consensus model see Goodfried and King (1997), Clarida *et al.* (1999), Romer (2000) and Carlin and Soskice (2006).
15. The 'two pillar approach' may therefore send different and contradicting signals to market participants. This questions the credibility of the ECB's monetary strategy (see Arestis and Chortareas 2006).
16. We also tried equation (11.4) with interest rate smoothing, but did not find any significant impact of the additional variables, so we essentially returned to equation (11.3). Note that our estimations only indicate the qualitative impact of other economic variables on ECB policies, because there seem to be some non-linearities in the estimations.
17. Applying a Granger causality test, Belke and Gros (2003) find that after 11 September 2001, the Federal funds rate has Granger caused the ECB interest rate but the ECB interest rate has not Granger caused the Federal funds rate. Before 11 September 2001, there was mutual Granger causality.
18. We also tried different lags without getting a statistically significant relationship.
19. On the endogeneity of potential output or 'natural growth' see Arestis and Sawyer (2004, 2005), Lavoie (2004) and Leon-Ledesma and Thirlwall (2002).
20. We also tried the increase in compensation per employee, which, however was not statistically significant and made our estimation considerably worse.

REFERENCES

Allsopp, C. and D. Vines (1998), 'The assessment: Macroeconomic policy after EMU', *Oxford Review of Economic Policy*, 14(3), 1–23.

Arestis, P. and G. Chortareas (2006), 'Monetary policy in the euro area', *Journal of Post Keynesian Economics*, 28, 371–94.

Arestis, P., McCauley, K. and M. Sawyer (2001), 'An alternative stability pact for the European Union', *Cambridge Journal of Economics*, 25, 113–30.

Arestis, P. and M. Sawyer (2004), *Re-examining Monetary and Fiscal Policy for the 21st Century*, Cheltenham, UK and Northampton, MA, USA: Edward Elgar.

Arestis, P. and M. Sawyer (2005), 'Aggregate demand, conflict and capacity in the inflationary process', *Cambridge Journal of Economics*, 29, 959–74.

Belke, A. and D. Gros (2003), 'Does the ECB follow the Fed?', *Applied Economics Quarterly*, 49, 195–212.

Bernanke, B. and M. Gertler (1995), 'Inside the black box: The credit channel of monetary policy transmission', *Journal of Economic Perspectives*, 9, 27–48.

Bhaduri, A. and S. Marglin (1990), 'Unemployment and the real wage: The economic basis for contesting political ideologies', *Cambridge Journal of Economics*, 14, 375–93.

Bibow, J. (2002), 'The monetary policies of the European Central Bank and the euro's (mal)performance: A stability-oriented assessment', *International Review of Applied Economics*, 16, 31–50.

Bibow, J. (2005a), *Europe's Quest for Monetary Stability: Central Banking Gone Astray*, Working Paper No. 428, Annandale-on-Hudson: The Levy Economics Institute of Bard College.

Bibow, J. (2005b), *Bad for Euroland, Worse for Germany – the ECB's Record*, Working Paper No. 429, Annandale-on-Hudson: The Levy Economics Institute of Bard College.

Carlin, W. and D. Soskice (2006), *Macroeconomics: Imperfections, Institutions and Policies*, Oxford: Oxford University Press.

Cecchetti, S.G. (1995), 'Distinguishing theories of the monetary transmission mechanism', *Federal Reserve Bank of St. Louis Review*, 77(3), 83–97.

Clarida, R., Gali, J. and M. Gertler (1998), 'Monetary policy rules in practice: Some international evidence', *European Economic Review*, 42, 1033–67.

Clarida, R., Gali, J. and M. Gertler (1999), 'The science of monetary policy: A New Keynesian perspective', *Journal of Economic Literature*, 37, 1661–707.

Clarida, R., Gali, J. and M. Gertler (2000), 'Monetary policy rules and macroeconomic stability: Evidence and some theory', *The Quarterly Journal of Economics*, 115, 147–80.

De Grauwe, P. and C. Costa Storti (2004), *The Effects of Monetary Policy: A Meta-analysis*, CESifo Working Paper No. 1224, Munich: CESifo.

ECB (2003), 'The outcome of the ECB's evaluation of its monetary strategy', *Monthly Bulletin*, June, 79–92.

ECB (2006), *Monthly Bulletin Data*, available at http://www.ecb.int/stats/services/downloads/html/index.en.html, 30 August 2006.

Eichengreen, B. (1998), 'European monetary unification: A tour d'horizon', *Oxford Review of Economic Policy*, 14(3), 24–40.

European Commission (2005), *Annual Macro-Economic Database* (AMECO), December, available at http://ec.europa.eu/economy_finance/indicators/annual_macro_economic_database/ameco_en.htm, 30 August 2006.

Federal Reserve Bank of New York (2006), *Historical Changes of the Target Federal Funds and Discount Rates*, available at http://www.newyorkfed.org/markets/statistics/dlyrates/fedrate.html, 30 August 2006.

Fontana, G. (2003), 'Post Keynesian approaches to endogenous money: A time framework explanation', *Review of Political Economy*, 15, 291–314.

Fritsche, U., Herr, H., Heine, M., Horn, G. and C. Kaiser (2005), 'Macroeconomic regime and economic development: The case of the USA', in Hein, E., Niechoj, T., Schulten, T. and A. Truger (eds), *Macroeconomic Policy Coordination in Europe and the Role of the Trade Unions*, Brussels: ETUI.

Goodfried, M. and R. King (1997), *The New Neoclassical Synthesis and the Role of Monetary Policy*, NBER Macroeconomic Annual, Cambridge, MA: MIT Press, 231–83.

Hein, E. (2002), 'Monetary policy and wage bargaining in the EMU: Restrictive ECB policies, high unemployment, nominal wage restraint and inflation above the target', *Banca Nazionale del Lavoro Quarterly Review*, 55, 299–337.

Hein, E. (2006a), 'Wage bargaining and monetary policy in a Kaleckian monetary distribution and growth model: Trying to make sense of the NAIRU', *Intervention. Journal of Economics*, 3, 305–29.

Hein, E. (2006b), 'On the (in-)stability and the endogeneity of the "normal" rate of capacity utilisation in a Post-Keynesian/Kaleckian "monetary" distribution and growth model', *Indian Development Review*, 4, 129–50.

Hein, E. and T. Niechoj (2006), 'Guidelines for sustained growth in the EU? The concept and the consequences of the Broad Economic Policy Guidelines', in McCombie, J. and C. Rodriguez (eds), *The European Union: Current Problems and Prospects*, Basingstoke: Palgrave/Macmillan, forthcoming.

Hein, E. and T. Schulten (2004), 'Unemployment, wages and collective bargaining in the European Union', *Transfer. European Review of Labour and Research*, 10, 532–51.

Hein, E., Schulten, T. and A. Truger (2006), 'Deflation risks in Germany and the EMU: The role of wages and wage bargaining', in Hein, E., Heise, A. and A. Truger (eds), *Wages, Employment, Distribution and Growth: International Perspectives*, Basingstoke: Palgrave/Macmillan.

Hein, E. and A. Truger (2005a), 'European Monetary Union: Nominal convergence, real divergence and slow growth?', *Structural Change and Economic Dynamics*, 16, 7–33.

Hein, E. and A. Truger (2005b), 'Macroeconomic coordination as an economic policy concept: Opportunities and obstacles in the EMU', in Hein, E., Niechoj, T., Schulten, T. and A. Truger (eds), *Macroeconomic Policy Coordination in Europe and the Role of the Trade Unions*, Brussels: ETUI.

Hein, E. and A. Truger (2005c), 'What ever happened to Germany? Is the decline of the former European key currency country caused by structural sclerosis or by macroeconomic mismanagement?', *International Review of Applied Economics*, 19, 3–28.

Hein, E. and A. Truger (2005d), 'A different view of Germany's stagnation', *Challenge: The Magazine of Economic Affairs*, 48(6), 64–94.

Hein, E. and A. Truger (2006a), *Germany's Post-2000 Stagnation in the European Context: A Lesson in Macroeconomic Mismanagement*, IMK Working Paper, 3/2006, Duesseldorf: Macroeconomic Policy Institute (IMK) in the Hans Boeckler Foundation.

Hein, E. and A. Truger (2006b), *Fiscal Policy and Macroeconomic Performance in the Euro Area: Lessons for the Future*, IMK Working Paper, 6/2006, Duesseldorf: Macroeconomic Policy Institute (IMK) in the Hans Boeckler Foundation.

Heine, M. and H. Herr (2004), *Die Europäische Zentralbank: Eine kritische Einführung in die Strategie und Politik der EZB*, Marburg: Metropolis.

Issing, O. (2005), 'The ECB and the euro – the first 6 years: A view from the ECB', *Journal of Policy Modeling*, 27, 405–20.

Lavoie, M. (1984), 'The endogenous flow of credit and the Post-Keynesian theory of money', *Journal of Economic Issues*, 18, 771–97.

Lavoie, M. (1992), *Foundations of Post Keynesian Economic Analysis*, Aldershot, UK and Brookfield, US: Edward Elgar.

Lavoie, M. (2004), 'The New Consensus on monetary policy seen from a Post-Keynesian perspective', in Lavoie, M. and M. Seccareccia (eds), *Central Banking in the Modern World: Alternative Perspectives*, Cheltenham, UK and Northampton, MA, USA: Edward Elgar.

Leon-Ledesma, M.A. and A.P. Thirlwall (2002), 'The endogeneity of the natural rate of growth', *Cambridge Journal of Economics*, 26, 441–59.

Mihailov, A. (2006), 'Operational independence, inflation targeting, and UK monetary policy', *Journal of Post Keynesian Economics*, 28, 395–422.

Moore, B.J. (1988), *Horizontalists and Verticalists: The Macroeconomics of Credit Money*, Cambridge: Cambridge University Press.

OECD (2005), *Economic Outlook*, No. 78, Paris: OECD.

Orphanides, A. (2001), 'Monetary policy rules based on real-time data', *American Economic Review*, 91, 964–85.

Orphanides, A. (2003), 'Historical monetary policy analysis and the Taylor rule', *Journal of Monetary Economics*, 50, 983–1022.

Palley, T. (1998), 'Restoring prosperity: Why the U.S. model is not the answer for the United States or Europe', *Journal of Post Keynesian Economics*, 20, 337–52.

Romer, D. (2000), 'Keynesian macroeconomics without the LM curve', *Journal of Economic Perspectives*, 14(2), 149–69.

Sawyer, M. (2002), 'The NAIRU, aggregate demand and investment', *Metroeconomica*, 53, 66–94.

Solow, R.M. (2000), 'Unemployment in the United States and in Europe: A contrast and the reasons', *Ifo-Studien*, 46, 1–12.

Taylor, J.B. (1993), 'Discretion versus policy rules in practice', *Carnegie Rochester Conference Series on Public Policy*, 39, 195–214.

Taylor, J.B. (1999), 'The robustness and efficiency of monetary policy rules as guidelines for interest rate setting by the European Central Bank', *Journal of Monetary Economics*, 43, 655–79.

Taylor, J.B. (2000), 'Teaching modern macroeconomics at the principles level', *American Economic Review*, 90(2), 90–4.

Thorbecke, W. (2002), 'A dual mandate for the Federal Reserve System: The pursuit of price stability and full employment', *Eastern Economic Journal*, 28, 255–68.

Weller, C. (2002), 'What drives the Fed to act?', *Journal of Post Keynesian Economics*, 24, 391–417.

Index

Accoce, Jean-Vincent 3
ADF test, aggregate demand and
    wages, France 124, 125, 129,
    137–8
Agenda 2010 (Germany) 158–9, 162,
    163
agents 141, 142, 143, 144, 146
    see also individuals
aggregate demand
    production and employment and
        55–6
    wages and, France 4, 119–20, 134–5
        consumption 124–6
        data definitions 136–7
        econometric tests 137–8
        exports 128–31
        imports 131–2
        investment 127–8
        method 123–4
        theoretical background 120–23
        total results 132–4
    see also demand
aggregate production function,
    neoclassical economics and 171
aggregate profits
    income-spending model 97–9
        dynamics 106–14
        real-world model for profits,
            building 99–106
        theory and policy 114–16
    see also profits
Amariglio, J.L. 39
Arestis, P. 154, 183, 229
Aschauer, D. 195
Asimakopulos, A. 98
Atkinson, Tony 13, 169

Bank for International Settlements
    154
banking system
    analysis only basic, circuitist
        development limitation 70–72

equations, SFC model 82–5
experiments, SFC model 86–8
monetary theory of production and
    52–5
    see also ECB; Federal Reserve Bank
        of New York
Barro, R.J. 195
Belke, A. 237
Bernanke, B. 220
Bhaduri, A. 120, 123, 224
Bharadwaj, Krishna 20
Bibow, J. 236
Blake, Andrew 23
Blinder, A.S. 197, 198, 201
Bliss, C. 21
Bofinger, P. 158
Bowles, S. 122
Boyer, R. 122
Brown, Allan 18, 23
Bundesregierung 159, 160, 162
Burke, Edmund 13
business see cycle; firms

Caldwell, B.J. 41
Cambridge tradition
    capital theory critique 20–22
    DAE (Department of Applied
        Economics) directors 23–4
    defined 2, 11
    economic history 22
    Keynes 13–16
    Malthus 11–12
    Marshall 12–13
    postwar developments 18–20
    Robinson 16–18
    today 24
capacity, individuals' learning,
    neoclassical institutional analysis
    and 145
capacity utilization 177, 191
capital theory 19, 20–22, 171–2
    see also theory

capitalist economy
  banking system and 53, 55
  credit and 51–2
  economic policy limits and 62, 63, 64
  employment and, neoclassical
    approach 58
  money and 50
  post-classical growth model and 179
  price level and 58–9
  production and 56
  trend and cycle and 60
  see also economy
cartels, Japan, neoclassical welfare
  economics and 193
  see also competition; monopoly
causality
  'feedback' weak exogeneity and,
    income-spending model
    dynamics 109
  'impact', impulse–response functions
    and, income-spending model
    dynamics 112–14
  'short-run', temporal, exogeneity
    and, income-spending model
    dynamics 106–8
  'variance', FEVD and, income-
    spending model dynamics
    109–12
Cecchetti, S.G. 220
central bank *see* banking system; ECB;
  government
Chick, Victoria 32, 53
Chortareas, G. 229
Christ, C.F. 197
Clarida, R. 229
Coase, R. 142
Cohen, A.J. 21
cointegration 105–6, 138
Colander, D. 32
competition 153–4, 161
  see also cartels; monopoly
consensus
  minimum, for alternative to
    neoclassical economics 3
  new, theory 1–2, 97–8, 114, 115
constructivism, heterodox and
  orthodox economics and 38–40
consumption
  aggregate demand and wages,
    France 124–6

expectations and institutions and
  149–50
  household, uncertainty and 51
  post-classical growth model and 174,
    175, 178
  structural reform and, Germany 163
'cooperative economy', Keynes and 47
  see also economy
Costa Storti, C. 237
costs
  labour, structural reform and,
    Germany 160, 161
  raw materials, price level and 59
  transaction, property rights theory
    and 144
  user, SFC model and 89
  see also expenditure; ULC
credit
  circuitists and 68
  income-spending model for profits
    and 115–16
  monetary theory of production 51–2
crowding out, fiscal/monetary policy
  link and 197, 198–204
currency reserves, minimum
  requirements, banking system and
  54
  see also money
cycle
  monetary/macroeconomic policy
    mix and, Euro area 226–7
  trend and, monetary theory of
    production 60–61

DAE (Department of Applied
  Economics) (Cambridge) 23–4
data
  definitions, aggregate demand and
    wages, France 136–7
  income-spending model 99–102
Davidson, Paul 147, 154, 170
Davies, R.O. 176
Davis, J.B. 31
De Bernis, G. 153
De Grauwe, P. 237
Deane, Phyllis 22
decisions
  investment, money and 50–51
  market, of agents, information for
    141, 142, 146

definitions
  Cambridge tradition 2, 11
  closed system 32–3
  data, aggregate demand and wages,
    France 136–7
  equilibrium 149
  open system 33
  structural reform 158
  uncertainty 147
deflation, monetary/macroeconomic
    policy mix and, Euro area 226,
    239
degree of monopoly theory of income
    distribution (Kalecki) 182
demand
  aggregate *see* aggregate demand
  private, model 201–4
  structural reform and, Germany 160,
    162, 163, 165, 167
  supply and, heterodox and
    neoclassical views 56
deposits, banking system and 53, 54
depreciation
  structural reforms and
      macroeconomics and 161
  rate, post-classical growth model
      and 178
distribution, of profits, income and
    expenditure relationship 4
  see also income distribution
DNRU (distribution-neutral rate of
    unemployment) 182
  see also NAIRU
Dobb, Maurice 22
Dornbusch, R. 198
Dos Santos, C.H. 85
Dostaler, G. 67
Dow, Sheila C.
  banks' liquidity preference and 53
  heterodox economics and 2, 3, 32,
    25, 44
  historical/logical time link and 150
Ducros, B. 67
Duong, M.H. 163
Düthmann, A. 160
dynamics, income-spending model
  exogeneity and 'short-run' temporal
      causality 106–8
  'feedback causality' and weak
      exogeneity 109

FEVD (forecast error variance
    decomposition) and 'variance
    causality' 109–12
impulse–response functions and
    'impact causality' 112–14

ECB (European Central Bank)
  fiscal/monetary policy link and 186,
    187–8, 206, 209
  inflation target 2001–2005, Euro
    area and 218
  monetary policy and 6
  monetary/macroeconomic policy
    mix and, Euro area 219
    2001–2005 monetary, fiscal and
      wage policies 221, 222, 223–4,
      225
    expanded Taylor Rule 233–4
    naïve Taylor Rule 229, 230
    policies since 1999 234–8
    unfriendliness to growth 228–34
  see also banking system; EU
ECM (error correction model) 124,
    125, 126, 127, 128, 131
  see also models; VECMs
economic history, Cambridge tradition
    and 22
economic performance *see* monetary
    policy, Euro area macroeconomic
    policy mix and economic
    performance and
economic policy
  institutional design and 4–5
  limits, monetary theory of
      production and 61–4
  new consensus view and 1
  new institutions for 141, 155–6
    economic policy and institutions
      nowadays 153–5
    expectations and institutions
      149–51
    historical time, importance of
      147–9
    neoclassical approach to
      institutions, new institutional
      economy 142–6
    social relationships, conflicting
      nature of 151–3
  structural reforms and 5
  see also macroeconomic policy

economics *see* Cambridge tradition;
    heterodox economics; neoclassical
    economics; orthodox economics;
    welfare economics
The Economist 189
economy
    'cooperative', Keynes and 47
    monetary, of production, circuitist
      propositions and 3, 67
    monetary flows and functions of,
      circuitist development
      limitations 69
    new institutional 142–6
    see also capitalist economy
Ederer, Stefan 4
efficiency
    neoclassical welfare economics and
      191
    social, conflicting nature of social
      relationships and 153
employment
    capitalist economy and, neoclassical
      view 58
    economic policy limits and 62, 63
    full, economic policy and
      institutions and 153
    growth relationship 56–7
    heterodox approach 57
    monetary/macroeconomic policy
      mix and, Euro area 218
    neoclassical approach 57–8
    prices and, neoclassical view 57
    production and, monetary theory of
      production 55–8
    structural reform and, Germany
      164–5
    wages and, heterodox and
      neoclassical views 57
    see also labour
EMU (European Monetary Union) *see*
    fiscal policy, EMU and theory of
    see also EU; Euro area
endogeneity, monetary/macroeconomic
    policy mix and, Euro area 233
endogenous growth models 172
    see also growth; models
endogenous money, finance motive
    and, circuitist propositions
      67–8
    see also money

Engle, R. 103
equations
    modified quantity, monetary/fiscal
      policy link and 200–201
    SFC model 73, 75–85
    standard quantity, monetary/fiscal
      policy link and 198–9
EU (European Union)
    aggregate demand and wages and
      119, 123, 134–5
    growth and employment and 57
    pension reform 159
    post-classical fiscal policy and 183
    productivity 189
    structural reform and 162
    see also ECB; Germany; Maastricht
      Treaty; SGP; UK
Euro area
    monetary/macroeconomic policy
      mix *see* monetary policy, Euro
      area macroeconomic policy mix
      and economic performance and
    structural reform and, Germany 162,
      163
Evans, Trevor 3
exchange rate
    price level and 59
    structural reform and, Germany 161,
      162
exogeneity
    'short-run' temporal causality and,
      income-spending model
      dynamics 106–8
    weak, 'feedback causality' and,
      income-spending model
      dynamics 109
expectations, institutions and, new
    institutions for economic policy
    149–51
expenditure
    distribution, income and profits
      relationship 4
    government *see* public expenditure
    see also costs
experiments, SFC model 85–8
exports
    aggregate demand and wages,
      France 121, 122, 128–31
    monetary/macroeconomic policy
      mix and, Euro area 226

structural reform and, Germany 161, 162, 163–4 , 167

Federal Reserve Bank of New York
heterodox economics and 54
income-spending model for profits and 98
monetary/macroeconomic policy mix and, Euro area
2001–2005 monetary, fiscal and wages policies 220, 221
ECB and 228, 236, 237
expanded Taylor Rule 231
naïve Taylor Rule 229
see also banking system; USA
Feinstein, C.H. 21
Felipe, J. 169, 171, 172
Ferguson, T. 97
Ferreiro, Jesus 4–5, 154
FEVD (forecast error variance decomposition) 109–12
finance motive 67–8
firms
equations, SFC model 76–9
loans and deposits and 53
post-classical growth model and 175, 176, 178
structural reform and, Germany 161, 164
fiscal policy
2001–2005, Euro area macroeconomic policy mix and economic performance and 219–28
economic policy and institutions and 153
EMU and theory of 5, 169–70, 182–4
new paradigm, need for 171–2
post-classical 179–82
post-classical growth model, foundations of 174–9
where to go 173–4
monetary policy decision making and 6
monetary policy link, lessons for Germany from Japan 186–7, 194–6, 209–10
ECB view 187–8
fiscal policy ineffectiveness,

explanations in literature 196–7
German government view 187
interest-rate based crowding out 197
policy implications for Germany 204, 206–9
policy implications for Japan 204–6
quantity-based crowding out, link to monetary policy and 198–204
Ricardian equivalence 197–8
supply-side argument, brief empirical evaluation 188–94
structural reform and, Germany 162, 163, 166
see also taxation
Fischer, S. 198
Fisher, F.M. 169, 171, 172
Fontana, G. 1
formalism, lack of, circuitist development limitation 69–70
France, aggregate demand and wages
see aggregate demand
see also EU
Friedman, Milton 154
functions
aggregate production, neoclassical economics and 171
economy, of, monetary flows and, circuitist development limitations 69
government, banking system basic analysis and, circuitist development limitations 70
impulse–response, 'impact' causality and, income-spending model dynamics 112–14
money, of (Keynes) 67

Gali, J. 229
Garegnani, 20
Garnett, R. 40
GDP (gross domestic product)
aggregate demand and wages theory and 121, 122
consumption and, aggregate demand and wages 126

exports and, aggregate demand and
wages 128, 130–31, 133, 134
fiscal/monetary policy link and,
Germany 187
fiscal policy ineffectiveness
explanations 196–7
Japanese government expenditure
195–6
neoclassical growth theory 188
neoclassical welfare economics
192
policy implications for Germany
208
quantity equations 198–9,
200–201
investment and, aggregate demand
and wages 127
imports and, aggregate demand and
wages 132 133, 134
monetary/macroeconomic policy
mix and, Euro area 216, 218,
219
2001–2005 fiscal policy 227
2001–2005 monetary policy 220,
221, 222, 223
2001–2005 wage policy 224, 226
ECB policies since 1999 235–6
expanded Taylor Rule 233, 234
structural reform and, Germany 163,
164
Gemmell, N. 172
Germany
aggregate demand and wages and
123
fiscal/monetary policy link, lessons
from Japan for *see* fiscal policy,
monetary policy link
monetary/macroeconomic policy
mix and, Euro area 222–3,
225–6
structural reform and
macroeconomic policy *see*
structural reform
see also EU
Gertler, M. 220, 229
Giovannoni, Olivier 4
Godley, Wynne
Cambridge tradition and 3, 23
SFC model and
development 66

equations 76, 77, 78, 81, 85
matrices 72, 73
'Golden Age' analysis 18–19, 20
Goldfeld, S.M. 199
Gomulka, S. 176
Goodhart, C.A.E. 199
Goodwin, C. 32
Goodwin, Richard M. 13, 18, 21
Gordon, D. 122
government
conflicting nature of social
relationships and 152
equations, SFC model 75–6
expenditure, post-classical growth
model and 175, 176, 178, 179
experiments, SFC model 86, 87
function, banking system basic
analysis and, circuitist
development limitations 70
Germany, fiscal/monetary policy
link and 187
SFC model matrices and 73
see also policy
Granger, C. 103, 106–8
Graziani, A. 68
Greenwald, B. 53
Gros, D. 237
growth
ECB unfriendliness to, Euro area
monetary/macroeconomic
policy mix and economic
performance 228–34
economic policy and institutions and
153
employment relationship 56–7
fiscal policy theory and 172
neoclassical theory, fiscal/monetary
policy link and 188–91
post-classical model, foundations of,
fiscal policy theory and EMU
174–9
trend and cycle and 60–61

Hahn, Frank 24
Hamburger Appell 119
Hamouda, Omar 16
Handa, J. 198
Hansen, B. 197
Harberger, A.C. 171
Harcourt, G.C. 2, 21, 23

Harrod, Roy 18, 19, 21
Hawtrey, Ralph 14
Hayek, F.A. von 18
Hein, Eckhard 6, 123, 216, 224
Heine, Michael 3, 57, 236
Herr, Hansjörg 3, 57, 236
heterodox economics
    money and 49–50
    orthodox economics duality 31
    schools of thought, thinking in
        terms of 2–3, 31–2, 43–4
        'new' views 37–42
        'old' views 33–7
        open and closed systems 32–3
    see also orthodox economics
historical time
    importance of, new institutions for
        economic policy and 147–9
    institutional change analysis and
        146
    logical time link, expectations and
        institutions and 150
    see also time
Hodgson, G. 145
Holtz-Eakin, D. 195
Horn, Gustav A. 5, 158, 163, 166
households
    consumer spending, uncertainty and
        51
    equations, SFC model 80–82
    experiments, SFC model 86
    loans and deposits and 53
    structural reform and, Germany
        161
Howell, D. 134
hypothesis *see* theory

IMF (International Monetary Fund)
    158, 194
imports
    aggregate demand and wages,
        France 121–2, 131–2
    price level and 59
income
    fiscal policy theory and 172
    post-classical growth model and 175,
        179
    structural reform and, Germany 160,
        161, 163
    see also wages

income distribution
    degree of monopoly theory of
        (Kalecki) 182
    marginal productivity theory of,
        neoclassical/post-Keynesian
        debate and 171
    post-classical growth model and 176
    price level and, monetary theory of
        production 58–60
    profits and expenditure relationship
        4
income-spending model
    aggregate profits and 97–9
    dynamics 106–14
    real-world model for profits,
        building 99–106
    theory and policy 114–16
    see also models
income tax, structural reform and,
    Germany 163, 165
    see also taxation
individuals 144, 145–6, 151–2
    see also agents
inflation
    economic policy and institutions and
        153, 154
    economic policy limits and 63
    monetary/macroeconomic policy
        mix and, Euro area 219, 225,
        234–5, 238
information
    asymmetric, institutions for new
        economic policy and 141, 143,
        144–5
    market decisions by agents, for 141,
        142, 146
    monopoly of agents, 144
    perfect, institutions for new
        economic policy and 142, 146
information paradigm, neoclassical
    paradigm compared, institutions
    for new economic policy and
    142–3
institutions
    design, economic policy and 4–5
    new, for economic policy 141, 155–6
        economic policy and institutions
        nowadays 153–5
        expectations and institutions
        149–51

historical time, importance of
    147–9
neoclassical approach to
    institutions, new institutional
    economy 142–6
social relationships, conflicting
    nature of 151–3
see also structural reform
interest rate
    aggregate demand and wages,
        France 121
    banking system and 54
    credit and 52
    crowding-out based on,
        fiscal/monetary policy link and
        197
    economic policy and institutions and
        154
    monetary/macroeconomic policy
        mix and, Euro area 228–30, 232
    structural reform and, Germany 162
investment
    aggregate demand and wages,
        France 121, 122, 127–8
    decisions, money and 50–51
    economic policy limits and 62–3
    expectations and institutions and
        149–50
    neoclassical view 56
    new consensus theory and 97, 114,
        115
    post-classical growth model and,
        Kalecki's theory compared
        176–8
    public, structural reform and,
        Germany 163
    saving and, circuitists and 68
    structural reform and, Germany 164,
        165
    trend and cycle and 61
IRFs (impulse–response functions)
    112–14
    see also functions
IW (Institut der deutschen Wirtschaft
    Köln) 160
IWK (Institut für Wachstum und
    Konjunktur) 119

Japan
    fiscal/monetary policy link, lessons

for Germany from *see* fiscal
    policy, monetary policy link
real wages and 57
Jevons, William Stanley 13
Johansen, S. 103, 104, 105, 106, 109
Joskow, P. 142
Junankar, P.N. 174
Juselius, K. 103, 109

Kahn, Richard 14, 16, 17, 18, 19
Kaiser, C. 57
Kaldor, Nicholas
    Cambridge tradition and 17, 18, 19,
        20
    capital theory critique and 21, 22
    heterodox economics and 58
Kalecki, M.
    aggregate demand and wages and
        134
    Cambridge tradition and 13, 18, 19
    capital theory critique and 21
    fiscal policy theory and 170, 173,
        176, 180, 181
    heterodox economics and 58
    investment theory, post-classical
        growth model compared
        176–8
Keynes and 173
Keynes, John Maynard
    aggregate demand and wages and
        134
    Cambridge tradition and 13–16, 17,
        18, 23
    'cooperative economy' and 47
    fiscal policy theory and 170, 173
    income-spending model for profits
        and 99
    institutions and expectations and
        149–50
    Kalecki and 173
    Malthus, on 11–12
    Marshall and 13
    monetary circuit approach and 66,
        67, 69, 89
    monetary theory of production and
        48
    money and 49, 50, 55
    price level and 58
    wages and 57, 119
Kitano, Y. 196

Kitson, Michael 23
Kneller, R. 172
Korea, neoclassical welfare economics
    and 192
Kotlikoff, L. 169
Krämer, H. 123
Kregel, J. 149, 150
Krugman, P. 197
Kuhn, Thomas 35, 37, 38

labour
    costs, structural reform and,
        Germany 160
    market reform, economic policy and
        institutions and 154
    see also employment; structural
        reform; ULC
lag structure, income-spending model
    105
Laramie, Anthony J. 5, 174, 177, 179,
    181, 182
Lavoie, Marc
    Cambridge tradition and 3, 23
    'circuitist school' and 67
    fiscal policy theory and 169, 170
    SFC model and
        banking system equations 83, 84,
            85
        development 66
        firms equations 76, 77, 78
        households equations 81
        matrices 72, 73
Lawson, Tony 24, 40
Lerner, A.P. 201, 204
Levine, R. 195
Leybourne, S. 102
loans
    banking system and 53, 54
    circuitists and 68
logical time, historical time link,
    expectations and institutions and
    150
    see also time
Lütkepohl, H. 105

Maastricht Treaty 187, 188, 206, 218,
    219, 239
    see also EU
macroeconomic laws, circuitist
    propositions and 68

macroeconomic policy
    Euro area monetary policy and
        economic performance and *see*
        monetary policy, Euro area
    macroeconomic policy mix and
        economic performance and
    structural reform and, Germany
        158–9, 166–7
    German example – a simulation
        162–6
    macroeconomics and structural
        reforms 159–62
    see also economic policy
Mair, Douglas 5, 174, 177, 179, 181,
    182
Malthus, Thomas Robert 11–12
Marchal, J. 70
marginal productivity theory of
    income distribution 171
Marglin, S. 120, 123, 224
mark-up
    determination of, price level and
        59
    post-classical growth model and 175,
        178, 179
markets
    decisions of agents and, information
        for 141, 142, 146
    economic stability and, economic
        policy and institutions 154
    labour *see* labour market
Marshall, Alfred 12–13, 15, 18, 21,
    23
Marx, Karl 48, 49, 50, 55
Mathieu, C. 183
matrices, SFC model 72–3, 74, 75
Matthews, R. 143
McCloskey, D.N. 39–40
McWilliams Tullberg, Rita 12
Meade. James E. 13, 16, 17, 23
Meinhardt, V. 163, 166
Mieszkowski, P.M. 171
Minsky, H.P. 52
models
    endogenous growth, fiscal policy
        theory and 172
    error correction (ECM) 124, 125,
        126, 127, 128, 131
    open, closed system, as 33
    post-classical growth, foundations

of, fiscal policy theory and
EMU 174–9
private demand, monetary/fiscal
policy link and 201–4
vector autoregressions (VARs) 103,
105, 106, 109–10, 123
vector error-correction (VECM)
103–4, 109–10, 112
see also income-spending model;
SFC model
monetary circuit approach
circuit school presentation and
criticisms 66–7, 88–90
circuitist developments,
limitations of 69–72
circuitist propositions 3, 67–8
SFC model 66, 72
equations 73, 75–85
experiments 85–8
matrices 72–3, 74, 75
monetary economy of production,
circuitist propositions and 3, 67
see also economy
monetary policy
decision making, fiscal policy and 6
ECB and 6
economic policy and institutions and
153, 154
Euro area macroeconomic policy
mix and economic performance
and 216–19, 238–9
ECB policies since 1999,
estimation results and course
of 234–8
ECB unfriendliness to growth
228–34
monetary, fiscal and wage policies
2001–2005 219–28
fiscal policy link *see* fiscal policy,
monetary policy link
new consensus view and 1
structural reform and, Germany
161
monetary theory of production
neoclassical economics and 47–8
credit and banking 51–5
economic policy limits 61–4
money 48–51
price level and income distribution
58–60

production and employment 55–8
trend and cycle 60–61
see also theory
money
endogenous, finance motive and,
circuitist propositions 67–8
monetary theory of production and
48–51
quantity theory of, banking system
and 54–5
see also currency reserves; exchange
rate
money supply, banking system and
52–3, 54
see also supply
monopoly
degree of, theory of income
distribution (Kalecki) 182
information, of, agents' 144
see also cartels; competition
Moore, G.E. 13
Mouakil, Tarik 3
Mouratidis, K. 154
Munnell, A.H. 195
Myrdal, G. 35

Naastepad, R. 123
NAIRU (non accelerating inflation rate
of unemployment) 1–2, 181, 182
see also DNRU
NAK (new anti-Keynesian) approach,
post-classical fiscal policy and
EMU and 183
Ndikumana, L. 76, 77
Nelson, C. 102
Nelson, R.R. 146
neoclassical economics
alternative to, minimum consensus
for 3
growth theory, fiscal/monetary
policy link and 188–91
institutions and, new institutional
economy 142–6
monetary theory of production and
47–8
credit and banking 51–5
economic policy limits 61–4
money 48–51
price level and income distribution
58–60

production and employment 55–8
trend and cycle 60–61
welfare, fiscal/monetary policy link
and 191–3
neoclassical institutional analysis
143–4
new consensus theory 1–2, 97 – 8, 114,
115
see also theory
Newbold, P. 102
NIE (new institutional economy),
neoclassical approach to
institutions 142–6
see also economy; institutions
Niechoj, T. 216
nihilism, heterodox economics and
38–9, 40
NIPAs (National Income and Product
Accounts) 98, 99–100
North, D. 143

Ochsen, C. 123
OECD (Organization for Economic
Co-operation and Development)
123, 159, 167, 189, 228
Olson, M. 181
Onaran, Ö, 123
open model, as closed system 33
see also models
orthodox economics
heterodox economic duality 31
'new' views on schools of thought
and 37–8
'old' views on schools of thought
and 33–5
see also heterodox economics
Ostaszewski, A. 176
output gap, monetary/macroeconomic
policy mix and, Euro area
227

Palacio-Vera, A. 1
parameters, income-spending model,
limitations and choice of 104–5
Parguez, Alain 4, 67, 98
Pasinetti, Luigi 18, 20
Pencavel, J. 32, 35
pensions, structural reform and 159
performance, economic *see* monetary
policy, Euro area macroeconomic

policy mix and economic
performance and
Pesaran, M. 112
Phelps, E.S. 33–4
Pigou, A.C. 13
Plosser, C. 102
pluralism
pure, schools of thought and
heterodox economics and 38–40
structured, schools of thought and
heterodox economics and 40–42
policy
competition, economic policy and
institutions and 153–4
theory and, income-spending model
and aggregate profits 114–16
see also economic policy; fiscal
policy; government;
macroeconomic policy;
monetary policy
positive economics *see* orthodox
economics
post-classical growth model 174–9
see also models
Poulon, F. 68, 69, 70, 89, 90
price level, income distribution and,
monetary theory of production
58–60
prices
economic policy limits and 62, 63
employment and, neoclassical view
57
post-classical growth model and 175
structural reform and, Germany 161
private demand model 201–4
see also demand; models
production
employment and, monetary theory
of production 55–8
monetary economy of, circuitist
propositions and 3, 67
see also monetary theory of
production
productivity, fiscal/monetary policy
link and, Germany 189–90
profits
aggregate *see* aggregate profits
banking system and 53–4
distribution, income and
expenditure relationship 4

economic policy limits and 62, 63
new consensus theory and 97–8, 114,
    115
post-classical growth model and 174,
    175, 176, 178, 179
price level and 60
'profit paradox' theory and 98, 115
property rights 144, 146
PSBR (public sector borrowing
    requirement), fiscal/monetary
    policy link and, Germany 196–7,
    207–8
public expenditure 175, 176, 178, 179,
    194–6
    see also expenditure; government
public investment, structural reform
    and, Germany 163
    see also investment

quantity, crowding out based on, link
    to monetary policy and 198–204
quantity equations, monetary/fiscal
    policy link and 198–9, 200–201
    see also equations
quantity theory of money, banking
    system and 54–5
    see also theory

Ramsey, Frank 22
rational expectation hypothesis 141
    see also theory
raw materials costs, price level and 59
    see also costs
Recktenwald, H.C. 169
Reddaway, Brian 23
reform, institutional, economic policy
    and institutions and 154
    see also structural reform
regulation, property rights, static
    analysis of institutions and 146
Renelt, D. 195
Reynolds, P.J. 182
Ricardian equivalence, fiscal/monetary
    policy link and 197–8
Ricardo, David 18
rights, property 144, 146
Robertson, Dennis 14, 17
Robinson, Austin, 17, 21
Robinson, Joan
    Cambridge tradition and 16–18

capital theory critique and 21
conflicting nature of social
    relationships and 151
'generalization of *The General
    Theory* to the long period' and
    18
'Golden Age' analysis and 18–19, 20
institutions and historical time and
    147, 148
Marshall, on 12
monetary theory of production and
    48, 61
Rochon, L.-P. 67, 71–2
Rossi, S. 67, 71–2
Rutherford, M. 143, 145

Salanti, A. 41
sales taxes, price level and 59
    see also taxation
Sattar, Z. 194
savings
    aggregate demand and wages and
        121, 122
    circuitists and 68
    neoclassical view 56
    new consensus theory and 97
    post-classical growth model and 174,
        178, 179
Sawyer, M.C. 154, 173, 174, 183
Say's law, production and employment
    and 56
Schabert, A. 204
schools of thought
    heterodox economics in terms of
        2–3, 31–2, 43–4
    'new' views 37–42
    'old' views 33–7
    open and closed systems 32–3
Schulten, T. 224
Schumpeter, J.A. 21
Scott, W.R. 150
Screpanti, E. 41
Seccarecia, M. 67
Sen, Amartya 13
Serrano, Felipe 4–5, 154
SFC (stock-flow consistent) model
    monetary circuit approach and 66,
        72
    equations 73, 75–85
    experiments 85–8

matrices 72–3, 74, 75
see also models
SGP (Stability and Growth Pact) 219,
227, 228
see also EU
Shin, Y. 112
Sichel, D.E. 199
Simon, H.A. 144–5
Sims, C. 99, 103, 105, 110, 112
Sinn, H.W. 158
Skidlesky, Robert 16
Smith, Adam 47
social relationships, conflicting nature
of, new institutions for economic
policy 151–3
Solow, R.M. 21, 197, 198, 201
Sraffa, Piero 17–18, 19, 20, 61
Sterdyniak, H. 183
Stiglitz, J.E. 53, 142, 143, 169
Stockhammer, Engelbert 4, 123, 134
stocks, omission of, circuitist
development limitation 72
see also SFC model
Stone, Richard 18, 23
structural reform
economic policy and 5
fiscal/monetary policy link and,
Germany 188–94
macroeconomic policy and,
Germany 158–9, 166–7
German example – a simulation
162–6
macroeconomics and structural
reforms 159–62
see also institutions
Summers, L. 169
supply
demand and, heterodox and
neoclassical views 56
money, banking system and 52–3, 54
structural reform and, Germany 158,
160, 162, 163
supply-side, fiscal/monetary policy link
and 188–94
SVR 158
Swan, 21

Tanaka, H. 196
taxation 59, 63, 64, 163, 165
see also fiscal policy

Taylor, J.B. 219, 228, 229
Taylor rules 228–34
theory
aggregate demand and wages,
France 120–23
capital 19, 20–22, 171–2
fiscal policy, EMU and 5, 169–70,
182–4
new paradigm, need for 171–2
post-classical EMU 179–82
post-classical growth model,
foundations of 174–9
where to go 173–4
investment (Kalecki) 176–8
marginal productivity, of income
distribution 171
monetary, of production *see*
monetary theory of production
neoclassical growth 188–91
new consensus 1–2, 97–8, 114, 115
perfect information 142, 146
policy and, income-spending model
and aggregate profits 114–16
'profit paradox' 98, 115
property rights, 144
quantity, of money 54–5
rational expectation hypothesis
141
time, SFC model and 90
see also historical time
Tobin, J. 81
Tobin's *q* ratio 76, 77
transaction costs, property rights
theory and 144
see also costs
trend, cycle and, monetary theory of
production 60–61
Truger, Achim 6, 224

UK (United Kingdom)
aggregate demand and wages and
123
neoclassical welfare economics and
191–2
post-classical fiscal policy and EMU
and 182
profits and *see* income-spending
model, aggregate profits and
PSBR funding and 207–8
see also EU

ULC (unit labour costs)
  aggregate demand and wages and
      121, 128, 129
  monetary/macroeconomic policy
      mix and, Euro area 225–6, 231,
      238
  structural reform and, Germany
      163–4
  see also costs; labour
uncertainty
  agents and 146
  consumer spending and 51
  credit and 52
  institutions for new economic policy
      and 141
  money and 50–51
unemployment *see* DNRU;
      employment; NAIRU
USA (United States of America)
  aggregate demand and wages and
      122–3
  monetary/macroeconomic policy
      mix and, Euro area 216, 217,
      218, 221, 224–5, 227
  neoclassical welfare economics and
      191–2
  productivity 189
  see also Federal Reserve Bank of
      New York
user costs
  SFC model and 89
  see also costs

Van de Velde, F. 72
VAR (vector autoregressions) model
      103, 105, 106, 109–10, 123
  see also models
VECMs (vector error-correction
      models) 103–4, 109–10, 112
  see also ECM; models
Vines, David 16, 23

wages
  aggregate demand and, France 4,
      119–20, 134–5

consumption 124–6
  data definitions 136–7
  econometric tests 137–8
  exports 128–31
  imports 131–2
  investment 127–8
  method 123–4
  theoretical background 120–23
  total results 132–4
economic policy limits and 62, 63
employment and 57
monetary/macroeconomic policy
      mix and, Euro area 219–28,
      238
post-classical growth model and 174,
      175, 178, 179
price level and 58, 59, 60
real, Japan and 57
structural reform and, Germany 160,
      161, 164–5
  see also income
Weale, Martin 24
Weintraub, E.R. 38
Weiss, A. 103
welfare economics
  classical view 142, 143
  neoclassical view, fiscal/monetary
      policy link and 191–3
Werner, Richard A.
  fiscal and monetary policy link 6,
      193, 200, 210
  German fiscal policy and 206,
      208
Western Europe *see* EU
Williamson, O. 143, 150,
      151
Winslow, Ted 15
Winter, S.G. 146
Wohar, M. 102
Wray, R. 204

Young, Allyn 20

Zezza, G. 85
Zwiener, R. 163, 166

NEW DIRECTIONS IN MODERN ECONOMICS

Post-Keynesian Monetary Economics
New Approaches to Financial Modelling
Edited by Philip Arestis

Keynes's Principle of Effective Demand
Edward J. Amadeo

New Directions in Post-Keynesian Economics
Edited by John Pheby

Theory and Policy in Political Economy
Essays in Pricing, Distribution and Growth
Edited by Philip Arestis and Yiannis Kitromilides

Keynes's Third Alternative?
The Neo-Ricardian Keynesians and the Post Keynesians
Amitava Krishna Dutt and Edward J. Amadeo

Wages and Profits in the Capitalist Economy
The Impact of Monopolistic Power on Macroeconomic Performance in the
USA and UK
Andrew Henley

Prices, Profits and Financial Structures
A Post-Keynesian Approach to Competition
Gokhan Capoglu

International Perspective on Profitability and Accumulation
Edited by Fred Moseley and Edward N. Wolff

Mr Keynes and the Post Keynesians
Principles of Macroeconomics for a Monetary Production Economy
Fernando J. Cardim de Carvalho

The Economic Surplus in Advanced Economies
Edited by John B. Davis

Foundations of Post-Keynesian Economic Analysis
Marc Lavoie

The Post-Keynesian Approach to Economics
An Alternative Analysis of Economic Theory and Policy
Philip Arestis

Income Distribution in a Corporate Economy
Russell Rimmer

The Economics of the Profit Rate
Competition, Crises and Historical Tendencies in Capitalism
Gérard Duménil and Dominique Lévy

Corporatism and Economic Performance
A Comparative Analysis of Market Economies
Andrew Henley and Euclid Tsakalotos

Competition, Technology and Money
Classical and Post-Keynesian Perspectives
Edited by Mark A. Glick

Investment Cycles in Capitalist Economies
A Kaleckian Behavioural Contribution
Jerry Courvisanos

Does Financial Deregulation Work?
A Critique of Free Market Approaches
Bruce Coggins

Pricing Theory in Post Keynesian Economics
A Realist Approach
Paul Downward

The Economics of Intangible Investment
Elizabeth Webster

Globalization and the Erosion of National Financial Systems
Is Declining Autonomy Inevitable?
Marc Schaberg

Explaining Prices in the Global Economy
A Post-Keynesian Model
Henk-Jan Brinkman

Capitalism, Socialism, and Radical Political Economy
Essays in Honor of Howard J. Sherman
Edited by Robert Pollin

Financial Liberalisation and Intervention
A New Analysis of Credit Rationing
Santonu Basu

Why the Bubble Burst
US Stock Market Performance since 1982
Lawrance Lee Evans, Jr.

Sustainable Fiscal Policy and Economic Stability
Theory and Practice
Philippe Burger

The Rise of Unemployment in Europe
A Keynesian Approach
Engelbert Stockhammer

General Equilibrium, Capital, and Macroeconomics
A Key to Recent Controversies in Equilibrium Theory
Fabio Petri

Post-Keynesian Principles of Economic Policy
Claude Gnos and Louis-Philippe Rochon

Innovation, Evolution and Economic Change
New Ideas in the Tradition of Galbraith
Blandine Laperche, James K. Galbraith and Dimitri Uzunidis

The Economics of Keynes
A New Guide to *The General Theory*
Mark Hayes

Money, Distribution and Economic Policy
Alternatives to Orthodox Macroeconomics
Edited by Eckhard Hein and Achim Truger